GUBERNATORIAL TRANSITIONS

The 1983 and 1984 Elections

Edited by Thad L. Beyle

)))))

Duke Press Policy Studies
Durham and London 1989

© 1989 Duke University Press
All rights reserved
Printed in the United States of America
on acid-free paper ∞
Library of Congress Cataloging-in-Publication Data
Gubernatorial transitions : the 1983–1984 elections / edited by Thad
L. Beyle.
p. cm.—(Duke Press policy studies)
Includes bibliographies and index.
ISBN 0-8223-0858-4
1. Governors—United States—Transition periods. 2. Governors—
United States—Election. I. Beyle, Thad L., 1934– .
II. Series.
JK2447.G82 1989
353.9'134—dc 19 88-14711

Contents

Two Special Case Studies

Foreword

)))))

Barry Van Lare

It is an American tradition that newly elected governors must move quickly to make their own marks on the governments of their states. Historical practice and legislative and constitutional calendars also demand that the governor-elect be prepared to act on a variety of issues instantly upon inauguration or very shortly thereafter. For most newly elected governors, election brings not a respite, but heightened demands on their time and the need for immediate direction and decisions. Constituency groups and campaign personnel press for early staff and cabinet decisions. The budget process, already well under way during the outgoing administration, requires direct attention. The new administration's program and policy themes need to be fine-tuned and woven into the inaugural address and developed in the first legislative package. Finally, the governor must think through issues related to management style and office structure and effect a personal transition from candidate to governor.

While some governors-elect have had the luxury of addressing these issues during the campaign, most have not. As a result the relatively brief period between election and inauguration is an extremely critical time for the governors-elect and can have a strong impact on their ability to effectively lead and manage state government. While an increasing number of states recognize the demands placed on the governor-elect and provide at least some assistance during the transition process, such assistance is limited at best and often confined to the provision of office space and support staff. Hence the transition into office is one of the most challenging, stressful, and dangerous times of any new administration. New policy initiatives and unforeseen crises may test the administration in the future, but never again will the governor be expected to do so much in such a short time with so few resources. As a result it is imperative that those limited resources that are available be carefully managed and devoted to activities of the highest priority.

In general, experienced governors agree that a successful transition depends on three factors: the appointment of competent personnel, control of the executive budget, and the clear articulation of program and policy objectives. For most new governors the most immediate lesson is that they cannot do everything. It is not surprising, therefore, that the first advice offered for transition is to establish firm priorities. Priorities will help drive the decisions to delegate both authority and responsibility. For example, there is little need for the governor-elect and key staff of the emerging administration to become enmeshed in the details of the campaign wind-down or with detailed plans for the inaugural. Setting priorities will also help focus the governor-elect's personal time and staff resources on the most critical issues. Constituency and political advice to the contrary, not all gubernatorial appointments need to be made during the transition period. The cautious use of "holdover" appointments can allow a transition to focus attention on those agencies that have serious management problems or where the governor expects to develop major new program or policy initiatives. Once these key appointments have been made, additional time will be available during the first months in office for other important but less critical selections. Holding over staff and appointees from the outgoing administration can, therefore, buy valuable time and allow the governor-elect to focus on campaign and policy themes to set the tone for his or her term of office.

Similarly, not all budget decisions carry equal weight. A new governor will want to pay close attention to revenue forecasts and broad fiscal policy. Careful consideration must be given to make certain that adequate resources are available for program and policy priorities; however, there is little to be gained from a line-by-line review of the budget, unless the new governor is prepared to make decisions at that level of detail. Experienced governors will also recommend that new governors limit their personal program and policy agenda to a few initiatives so that they can develop the necessary support from the public and the legislature. An overly broad policy agenda is often difficult to sell and provides little focus for the public to form a clear perception of the new administration.

Discussion of the transition is a major part of the curriculum of the seminar for new governors that is sponsored by the National Governors' Association, and general guides for the transition period are an important part of the publications and training material directed at new governors.

These crosscutting materials, however, tell only a part of the story. In the end the nature of a transition will vary not only from state to state, but from governor to governor. Transition is a very personal process, and one that is influenced strongly by the institutional and political environment in individual states at specific points in time. In some states the incoming and outgoing governors maintain regular contact, while in others there is virtually no formal or informal communication between the two. In some states the governor-elect is provided with state funds for offices and staff, while in others, all transition activities must be financed from remaining campaign funds or conducted on a volunteer basis. In some states the governor-elect will be given early and regular access to the budgetmaking process, while in others the outgoing governor may propose a final budget with no input from the governor-elect. Finally, in some states the transition will have received considerable attention during the campaign, while in others there is little thought given to the organization of the new government until after the election.

The complete story of the transition process must combine the general theory with specific examples. Transitions are real events, with real people. To fully understand what works and what does not, both participants and interested observers must perceive the general theory in the context of actual events.

This book tells the story of the transition process in eight states. It is based on close observation of the participants during the transition period itself. It takes a hard look at personalities and politics. It highlights opportunities and obstacles. In total, it provides a unique insight into how governors responded to the challenges of their transition periods and the ways in which their transitions influenced their first few critical months in office.

Increasingly the transition determines the structure and success of the government that will follow. It is an important prelude and, like the processes of government, it will be improved by a more complete understanding of the transitions that have gone before. The state-by-state analysis in this book represents a valuable addition to our overall knowledge of the transition process and deserves careful attention.

Acknowledgments

)))))

This book is made possible through the efforts of many individuals in the several states studied—the state analysts, those they watched and interviewed, and those who provided the news coverage to read and assimilate; and the earlier state analysts who studied and analyzed the 1982–83 gubernatorial transitions which Duke University Press published in 1985, *Gubernatorial Transitions: The 1982 Elections.* These state analysts' untiring efforts give this and the earlier book the depth of understanding needed when studying such changes as a gubernatorial transition.

Thanks also to Robert Huefner for his assistance in bringing his interest, experience, understanding, and analysis to these events, and to Dan Garry and Barry Van Lare of the Office of State Services of the National Governors' Association for their interest and support. Grants from the National Governors' Association and the University Research Council of the University of North Carolina at Chapel Hill helped underwrite the cost of publication.

Reynolds Smith and the various editors and staff at Duke University Press have capped this effort with their usual fine production of the manuscript.

To all, thanks.

Thad L. Beyle
April 1988

Introduction

)))))

Gubernatorial Transitions: Lessons from the 1982, 1983, and 1984 Elections

)))))

Thad L. Beyle

Transitions between gubernatorial administrations are major political and governmental events occurring routinely in the states. In fact, they are important indicators of just how seriously we as a people believe in the concept of representative democracy. Those leaders we elect are able to take office without the force of arms or a coup d'état and those leaving the governor's office do so rather easily, with but a few minor exceptions. Certainly there are tensions involved, and occasionally bitter and/or strategic politics poison the atmosphere, but to many observers the significant story is that these transitions do occur. As former Tennessee governor Lamar Alexander (R, 1979–87) observes, "In America the torch is always passed peacefully and with grace."[1] Well, almost always, as we will see.

However, Alexander's own first entry into office in January 1979 had what he felt were the aspects of a coup d'état as he was sworn in three days ahead of schedule because U.S. attorney Hal Hardin felt his predecessor, Ray Blanton (D, 1975–79), was "about to release some state prisoners who we believe have bought their way out of prison." (One of the prisoners allegedly involved was James Earl Ray, the convicted assassin of Martin Luther King, Jr.) Hardin asked Alexander if he would "take office as soon as you can, to stop him?" Alexander did and Blanton later was convicted of selling pardons and served time in prison.[2]

Beginning in the late 1960s, attention began to focus on the transition period in the governorship, when the retiring governor leaves office and the newly elected governor assumes office. The reason for this concern was the newer, more aggressive individuals being attracted to state service as governors found that period in their governorships to be one of the most critical and uncharted times they faced. There were few guidelines, many horror stories of finding evidence of out-going governors' "scorched earth" policies where little was left behind, and their own appearance of incompetence was often tied to their lack of knowledge or understanding of what they were getting into due to a poor transition. The need to have a new team in place and working be-fore the legislature arrived in town was understood; how to accomplish it was not.

Earlier Studies of Gubernatorial Transitions

The study of gubernatorial transitions is relatively new, beginning in the late 1950s and early 1960s. This timing is most interesting as our form of democracy, with its regularly scheduled changes in executive leadership, would appear to be of great interest to scholars. How do these transfers of power occur, especially when the outgoing governor has just been defeated at the polls by the newly elected governor?[3]

Because politics and transition provisions and practices vary so much from state to state, much of the research on gubernatorial transitions is based on case studies. A good portion of this literature, both academic and practitioner-based, was written by people who had "endured" the phenomenon.

There have been studies of New York in 1958,[4] Illinois in 1960,[5] Indiana in 1962,[6] Kansas and North Carolina in 1964,[7] California in 1966,[8] West Virginia in 1968,[9] Tennessee in 1970,[10] Virginia in 1977,[11] and Arkansas in 1978.[12] There has been at least one comparative study of gubernatorial transitions,[13] one on transition planning,[14] and two in which practitioners discussed their experiences,[15] and several state agencies conducted studies for use within their own state.[16]

Their generalized findings tended to suggest several basic political and governmental factors: (1) The magnitude of the transition task is considerable with few guidelines to help the new governor.[17] (2) The transition process is a political process that requires knowing how to share power and when to exert influence.[18] (3) Controlling the budget process is most important; however, it is difficult to induce major budgetary change.[19] (4) Though prescriptions abound, many of them seem to center on the extent to which the new governor can use the transition period to "define the situation."[20] (5) Although transition by definition denotes change, in reality there may be less change than meets the eye.[21]

In a comparative study of the 1982 gubernatorial elections and subsequent transitions, two further findings were presented: (6) There are at least three levels of transition: the logistical transition in which a working governor-elect's office is established; the administrative transition in which the personnel selection and decisionmaking processes are fit to the new governor's personal and preferred style; and the policy transition in which the goals, principles and programs the new governor wishes to pursue are brought into play. (7) Despite the commonalities in the transition process, gubernatorial transitions do vary from state to state based on personal, political, structural, and process factors.[22]

Recently, former Utah governor Scott Matheson (D, 1977–85) wrote of his experiences in office and observed that "the gubernatorial transition and the first few months in office are critical for any new administration. Early mistakes can plague a governor throughout an entire term, and a successful start can lead to a honeymoon with the press and public. A good start provides important momentum to accomplish objectives."[23] It is all the more critical in his view because "rarely does one prepare to be a governor. There is no pre-governors' training school. You bring whatever skill and experience you have to that responsibility, and in your first year or so in office, you get on-the-job training."[24]

There also were studies of transitions at the presidential level that provided not only a model but a message to the states.[25] Lauren Henry's study, *Presidential Transitions*, has been regarded as "the leading authority and only general work on the subject [of presidential transitions] a quarter of a century later."[26]

The most recent study by Mosher, Clinton, and Lang reviews the five post–World War II presidential transitions from Truman–Eisenhower in 1952–53 through Carter–Reagan in 1980–81 with a special focus on foreign affairs. They and others view the easiest transitions to have been when Eisenhower, Kennedy, and Nixon assumed office; the most difficult when Carter and Reagan did.[27] The authors believe that while there were several reasons for these differences, a good portion of the differences could be attributed to the "nature and backgrounds of the successful candidates themselves": the first three incoming presidents were somewhat "old hands in government," while the latter two were outsiders who ran against government in their campaigns.[28] It also should be noted that the first three men were entering an open office with the incumbent not seeking to retain the presidency, the latter two beat an incumbent en route to the office.

These authors also marveled at how our democracy, at the federal level in this instance, handles a change in leadership of such magnitude. "The turnover of power, especially in the modern era, requires more than the mutual toleration of incoming and outgoing officials; it demands their active collaboration in an extended task of immense complexity and delicacy."[29] These authors conclude a successful presidential transition is more likely:

) to follow a political campaign that has not "been bitter, ideological, and personal."

) if the "members of the new administration have given serious, early thought to problems they will face."

) if the newcomers realize it is most often dependent on their own spirit, experience, and wisdom.

) if the newcomers do not give the sense that everything attached to the outgoing administration "is bad and must be corrected . . . [and] that their predecessors [and the career staff] are incompetent."

) if the newcomers do not believe "that change in government can be easy and quick."

) if the newcomers do not believe "that government agencies should be run as nearly as possible like closed corporations, protected from congressional and public scrutiny."

) if the newcomers learn that government "is different and is difficult . . . [and] that they too will be leaving in a few years, and that in the meantime they are operating as trustees in the people's interest."[30]

The Scope of Gubernatorial Transition: 1977–1986

Why so many gubernatorial transitions? Three state constitutions allow only a single four-year term, twenty-four others have a two-term limit, which means that frequent gubernatorial transitions are virtually mandated in these twenty-seven states. The vagaries of politics and life ensure that there are more.

As indicated in table 1 this norm of gubernatorial turnover and transition has increased in the mid-1980s compared to the earlier elections covered in the period due in good part to constitutional restrictions and the expiration of individual governors eligibility to serve another term. Over the last full bank of gubernatorial elections, 1983 through 1986, there were fifty-four separate elections for governor, in which thirty-four new governors were selected (63 percent). This is more turnover than in any other four-year bank of elections during the 1977–86 period.

In 1986 alone there were eighteen open seats in the thirty-six elections (50 percent), and three other races in which an incumbent seeking re-election lost, leading to a turnover in twenty-one of the thirty-six states (58 percent). Therefore, newly elected governors continue to be a norm in the American states, and transitions to and from the governorship are a common event.

For the 146 elections involved over the ten-year period from 1977 to 1986, incumbent governors were eligible to seek reelection in 110, or 75 percent, of them, and eighty-eight (80 percent) did. Sixty-three of those eighty-eight won their quest for another term (72 percent), while twenty-five lost their attempt in their own party's nomination process (five, or 20 percent, of those seeking reelection), and twenty (80 percent) lost in the general election. Up through the 1983 elections Democratic candidates were considerably more successful than their Republican counterparts, winning sixty-one of ninety-five elections (64 percent). Beginning with the 1984 elections Republican candidates have been more successful, winning twenty-six of the fifty-one elections (51 percent).

The National Governors' Association (NGA) has attempted to assist these newly elected governors by bringing those elected in the even-numbered years together in a "New Governors' Seminar" shortly after election, with incumbent governors serving as the faculty. The NGA also provides written materials on the governorship that can be used in setting up the various necessary processes, organizations, and positions and has provided on-site advice as a new gubernatorial administration begins its planning and activities.[31] All of this advice and assistance is based on the experience of practitioners—incumbent and former governors and their staffs—and brings a real hands-on sense to the advice given: the insider's view of the process.

In an attempt to obtain another perspective on gubernatorial transitions, a network of state analysts was set up to observe and analyze the gubernatorial transition in their states. The analysts were academicians

Table I Gubernatorial Elections, 1977–86

Year	Races	Democratic winner		Incumbent governor[a]			
				Elig.		Ran	
		Number	Percent	Number	Percent	Number	Percent
1977	2	1	50	1	50	1	100
1978	36	21	58	29	81	24	83
1979	3	2	67	0	0	—	—
1980	13	6	46	12	92	12	100
1981	2	1	50	0	0	—	—
1982	36	27	75	33	92	25	76
1983	3	3	100	1	33	1	100
1984	13	5	38	9	69	6	67
1985	2	1	50	1	50	1	100
1986	36	19	53	24	67	18	75
Total	146	86	59	110	75	88	80

a. Incumbent governor status: eligible to run, did run, won, or lost.
b. Dukakis (D, Mass.).
c. Bennett (R, Kans.), Perpich (D, Minn.), Thompson (R, N.H.), Straub (D, Ore.), Wollman (D, S.D.), Briscoe (D, Tex.), Schreiber (D, Wisc.).
d. Judge (D, Mont.), Ray (D, Wash.).
e. Clinton (D, Ark.), Teasdale (D, Mo.), Link (D, N.D.).

—usually in departments of political science, public administration, or public policy—all with a professional interest in the subject. With few exceptions, they were members of the faculty of their state's major public university or a branch in the state's system.

The 1983 and 1984 Gubernatorial Elections and Transitions

Twelve of the sixteen states with gubernatorial elections in 1983 and 1984 selected new governors (75 percent), seven states because of constitutional restrictions; in two other states the incumbent was defeated in the general election; and in three other states the incumbent governor decided against seeking reelection although eligible. The Democrats and Republicans each won six of these elections with the winning margin over 5 percent in all the states except Vermont, which selected its first woman governor. There was a shift in partisan control of the governorship in eight of these twelve states, but in the other four states, where the winner continued his or her party's control of the gover-

| Incumbent governor | | | | Where incumbent lost | |
| Won | | Lost | | Party | General |
Number	Percent	Number	Percent	primary	election
1	100	—	—	—	—
16	67	8	33	1 [b]	7 [c]
—	—	—	—	—	—
7	58	5	42	2 [d]	3 [e]
—	—	—	—	—	—
19	76	6	24	1 [f]	5 [g]
—	—	1	100	—	1 [h]
4	67	2	33	—	2 [i]
1	100	—	—	—	—
15	83	3	20	1 [j]	2 [k]
63	72	25	28	5 20%	20 80%

f. King (D, Mass.).
g. White (R, Ark.), Thone (R, Nebr.), List (R, Nev.), Gallen (D, N.H.), Clements (R, Tex.).
h. Treen (R, La.).
i. Olson (R, N.D.), Spellman (R, Wash.).
j. Sheffield (D, Ark.).
k. White (D, Tex.), Earl (D, Wisc.).

norship, there was no decisive intraparty factional shift in the change between governors.

In table 2 the importance of having previously run for statewide office is clear as the twelve winners included three lieutenant governors, two attorneys general, and two former governors. The other four winners were a congressman, a speaker of the house, and two local officials. However, two governors, two attorneys general, and one lieutenant governor did not win in their attempts.

The monetary cost of these elections, in constant 1985 dollars, was less than the same elections had been four years earlier. For those three states holding their elections in 1983, their 1979 elections cost $48.5 million, with Louisiana's "Great Spendathon" leading the way;[32] in 1983 these elections cost $43.1 million, or a decrease of 11 percent. For those thirteen states holding their elections in 1984, the 1980 elections cost $46.4 million; in 1984 these elections cost $48.5 million, a slight increase of 5 percent. Of course, these dollar figures are only those officially reported and do not include monies spent on a candidate's behalf by other organizations and individuals.

Table 2 Politics of the 1983–1984 and 1984–1985
Gubernatorial Transitions

	Candidates	
	Democratic	Republican
1983–1984		
Ky.	* Martha Layne Collins, Lt. Governor	Jim Bunning, State Representative
La.	* Edwin Edwards, Former Governor	David Treen, Governor
Miss.	* William Allain, Atty. General	Leon Bramlett, Farmer/businessman
1984–1985		
Del.	Michael Quillen, Former Supreme Court Justice	* Michael Castle, Lt. Governor
Mo.	Ken Rothman, Lt. Governor	* John Ashcroft, Atty. General
N.C.	Rufus Edmisten, Atty. General	* James Martin, Congressman
N.D.	* George Sinner, State Representative	Allan Olson, Governor
R.I.	Anthony Solomon, State Treasurer	* Edward DiPrete, Mayor, Cranston
Utah	Wayne Owens, Former Congressman	* Norman Bangerter, Speaker of House
Vt.	* Madeleine Kunin, Lt. Governor	John Easton, Atty. General
Wash.	* Booth Gardner, County Executive	John Spellman, Governor
W.Va.	Clyde See, Speaker of House	* Arch Moore, Former Governor

* Winner
P = Primary
GE = General election

Of interest in these figures is the great differential between the average costs in those states holding their elections in the off-years ($16.2 million in 1979 and $14.4 million in 1983) compared to those holding their elections in the even presidential election years ($3.6 million in 1980 and $3.7 million in 1984). The size of the states does not seem to be a factor in these contests, but the intensity of electoral politics for the governorship in the three southern states of Kentucky, Louisiana,

Victory margin (in percent)	Political shift		Incumbent	
	Party	Faction	Party	Who governor supported
10	No	Yes	D	Loser, P
26	Yes	—	R	Loser
16	No	No	D	Winner
12	No	No	R	Winner
14	No	No	R	Winner
9	Yes	—	D	No one
10	Yes	—	R	Loser
20	Yes	—	D	Loser, GE
12	Yes	—	D	No one
2	Yes	—	R	No one
6	Yes	—	R	Loser
6	Yes	—	D	No one

and Mississippi most certainly is. Table 3 and table 4 present the data on the total costs of the 1983–84 elections.

Table 5 indicates the forty-three big spenders in the 1983–84 gubernatorial campaigns in constant 1985 dollars. Of the seven candidates who spent more than $3 million on their campaigns, five won, and the two who lost, incumbent governor David Treen of Lousiana and incumbent attorney general Rufus Edmisten in North Carolina, lost to one of the other five. Of those sixteen candidates spending between $1

Table 3 Dollars and Elections for Governor: The 1983 and 1984 Bank

Cost of Gubernatorial Elections: 1979, 1980, 1983, 1984

Year	Number of races	Total campaign costs (actual dollars, in thousands)	Total campaign costs[a] (constant 1985 dollars, in thousands)	Average cost per election (constant 1985 dollars, in thousands)
1979	3	32,744	48,531	16,177
1980	13	35,551	46,411	3,570
1983	3	39,954	43,142	14,381
1984	13	46,830	48,501	3,731

Changes in the Costs of Gubernatorial Elections, 1979–1983, 1980–1984 (constant 1985 dollars, in thousands)

Years	First year	Second year	Change (in dollars)	Change (in percent)
1979–1983	48,531	43,142	− 5,389	− 11
1980–1984	46,411	48,501	+ 2,090	+ 05

Sources: Thad L. Beyle, "The Cost of Becoming Governor," *State Government* 56:2 (1983), 74–84; *The Book of the States, 1986–87* (Lexington, Ky.: Council of State Governments, 1986), 25; Public Affairs Research Council of Louisiana, "Financing the 1983 Gubernatorial Campaign in Louisiana," *PAR Analysis* No. 171 (Baton Rouge: PARC, Mar. 1984).

a. Comparative campaign costs in constant 1985 dollars were determined by dividing the actual campaign expenditures by the value of those dollars in equivalent 1985 dollars (1983: .9261; 1984: .9655). Based on the Consumer Price Index for All Urban Consumers, U.S. Department of Labor, Bureau of Labor Statistics.

million and $3 million only three won, with six losing in the general election and seven losing in their party's primary; however, ten of these thirteen lost to candidates who spent more than they did.

The Transition of Power between Governors

After the election all attention turns to how the new governor will prepare for the next administration. Who will be the actors appointed to the key positions? What policies will be pursued? Will the new governor and the legislature be able to work together? Will the successful candidate become a successful governor?

This book contains the second in a series of studies of that critical period in a gubernatorial administration: the transfer of power from

Table 4 Costs of Individual State Gubernatorial Campaigns: 1983–1984

State	Year	Winner	All candidates	Winner's percentage
Arkansas [d]	1984	D	1,944,113	45[*]
Delaware [e]	1984	D	1,057,759	62
Indiana [d]	1984	R	4,199,264	64
Kentucky [e]	1983	D	16,516,598	28[*]
Louisiana [f,g]	1983	D	18,638,793	67
Mississippi [e]	1983	D	4,798,659	19
Missouri [e]	1984	R	7,014,292	42
Montana [d,h]	1984	D	482,113	77
New Hampshire [d]	1984	R	1,097,918	59
North Carolina [e]	1984	R	13,727,628	21
North Dakota [f,i]	1984	D	630,000	48
Rhode Island [e]	1984	R	3,475,483	40
Utah [e,j]	1984	R	2,621,289	34
Vermont [e]	1984	D	1,609,917	36
Washington [f]	1984	D	5,388,163	54
West Virginia [e,g]	1984	R	3,582,150	49

Total expenditures[a]

Sources: Public Affairs Research Council, "Financing the 1983 Gubernatorial Campaign in Louisiana," PAR *Analysis* no. 171 (Mar. 1984); Council of State Governments, phone survey of campaign filing offices in the states, Feb. 1986; Diane Blair of the University of Arkansas, Randy Patterson of the Mississippi secretary of state's office, Theodore Pedeliski of the University of North Dakota and John Patrick Hagan of the University of West Virginia.
D = Democratic candidate won.
R = Republican candidate won.
* = Winning candidate spent most money.
a. Includes primaries and general elections.
b. Determined by dividing total campaign expenditures by total general election votes.
c. Comparative campaign costs, constant 1985 dollars, was determined by dividing the actual campaign expenditures by the value of those dollars in equivalent 1985 dollars

one administration to another. The analyses of the thirty-six gubernatorial elections and seventeen transitions of 1982–83 were published in two separate volumes: *Gubernatorial Transitions: The 1982 Election* and *Re-electing the Governor: The 1982 Elections.*[33]

In this volume are the studies of eight of the twelve 1983 and 1984 gubernatorial transitions in addition to two other interesting analyses of a transition effort within a reelection context in Indiana and the special problems of the transition of lieutenant governors into office with

Table 4 Continued

Winner's vote percentage	Cost per total vote[b]	Comparative campaign costs (Constant 1985 dollars)[c]
63	2.19	2,011,394
56	4.34	1,095,556
52	1.92	4,349,315
57	8.30	17,834,572
62	12.29	20,126,112
55	6.46	5,181,578
57	3.33	7,264,932
70	1.31	499,340
67	2.86	1,137,150
54	6.19	14,218,154
55	2.00	652,512
60	8.51	3,599,672
56	4.18	2,714,955
50	6.99	1,667,444
53	2.85	5,580,697
53	4.83	3,710,150

(1983: .9261; 1984: .9655). Based on the Consumer Price Index for All Urban Consumers, U.S. Department of Labor, Bureau of Labor Statistics.
d. Incumbent ran and won.
e. Open seat.
f. Incumbent ran and lost.
g. Former governor ran and won.
h. Includes expenditures for lieutenant governor's campaign as there is a joint nomination and election of the governor and lieutenant governor.
i. Expenditure reports not required by law.
j. August gubernatorial primaries for both the Democratic and Republican parties were held as a result of inconclusive state party conventions. Includes three candidates who spent $179,283 in the preconvention period but did not run in the primaries.

Missouri as a case in point. These chapters chronicle and analyze what happened in each state as power was sought and then transferred from the incumbent governor to the new governor. Robert Huefner provides us with an overview of gubernatorial transition from his unique vantage point of having participated in the NGA New Governors' Seminar as an evaluator, having matched the experiences of the 1982–83 transitions with the NGA materials and advice, and having served as the transition coordinator to the outgoing governor of Utah in 1984–85.

As noted, the state analysts for this volume and the earlier volumes

Table 5 Most Expensive Individual Gubernatorial Campaigns:
1983–1984 (in constant 1985 dollars)

Candidate (party)	State	Year	Outcome	Actual dollars (in thousands)	1985 dollars (in thousands)
Over $5,000,000 (2)					
Edwin Edwards (D)[a,b]	La.	1983	Won	12,363	13,350
David Treen (R)[c]	La.	1983	Lost, G	6,276	6,777
$3,000,000 to $4,999,999 (5)					
Rufus Edmisten (D)	N.C.	1984	Lost, G	4,453	4,612
Martha Collins (D)	Ky.	1983	Won	4,029	4,351
John Ashcroft (R)	Mo.	1984	Won	2,941	3,046
James Martin (R)	N.C.	1984	Won	2,935	3,040
Booth Gardner (D)[a]	Wash.	1984	Won	2,926	3,031
$2,000,000 to $2,999,999 (6)					
Harvey Sloan (D)	Ky.	1983	Lost P	2,669	2,882
Robert Orr (R)[c]	Ind.	1984	Won	2,702	2,799
Edward Knox (D)	N.C.	1984	Lost, P	2,577	2,669
Lauch Faircloth (D)	N.C.	1984	Lost, P	2,123	2,199
John Spellman (R)[c]	Wash.	1984	Lost, G	1,999	2,070
Kenneth Rothman (D)	Mo.	1984	Lost, G	1,957	2,027
$1,000,000 to $1,999,999 (10)					
Arch Moore (R)[b]	W.Va.	1984	Won	1,752	1,815
Mike Sturdivant (D)	Mich.	1983	Lost, P	1,613	1,742
Jim Bunning (R)	Ky.	1983	Lost, G	1,557	1,681
Gene McNary (R)	Mo.	1984	Lost, P	1,555	1,611
Wayne Townsend (D)[d]	Ind.	1984	Lost, G	1,415	1,466
Edward DiPrete (R)	R.I.	1984	Won	1,401	1,451
Anthony Solomon (D)	R.I.	1984	Lost, G	1,318	1,365
Leon Bramlitt (R)	Miss.	1983	Lost, G	1,213	1,310
Grady Stumbo (D)	Ky.	1983	Lost, P	1,187	1,282
Evelyn Gandy (D)	Miss.	1983	Lost, P	983	1,061
$500,000 to $999,999 (10)					
Bill Allain (D)	Miss.	1983	Won	900	972
Norman Bangerter (R)	Utah	1984	Won	895	927
John Easton (R)	Vt.	1984	Lost, G	791	819
Joseph Welsh (D)	R.I.	1984	Lost, P	757	784

Table 5 Continued

Candidate (party)	State	Year	Outcome	Actual dollars (in thousands)	1985 dollars (in thousands)
James Green (D)	N.C.	1984	Lost, P	742	769
Michael Castle (R)	Del.	1984	Won	656	680
John Sununu (R)[c]	N.H.	1984	Won	646	669
Madeleine Kunin (D)	Vt.	1984	Won	581	602
Dan Marriott (R)	Utah	1984	Lost, P	548	568
Wayne Owens (D)	Utah	1984	Lost, G	544	563
$250,000 to $499,999 (10)					
Kem Gardner (D)	Utah	1984	Lost, P	455	471
Tom Gilmore (D)	N.C.	1984	Lost, P	453	469
James McDermott (D)	Wash.	1984	Lost, P	441	457
John Ingram (D)	N.C.	1984	Lost, P	410	425
William Quillan (D)	Del.	1984	Lost, G	401	415
Ted Schwinden (D)[c]	Mont.	1984	Won	371	384
Norman Merrell (D)	Mo.	1984	Lost, P	344	356
Allan Olson (R)[c]	N.D.	1984	Lost, G	340 est.	352
Chris Spirou (D)[d]	N.H.	1984	Lost, G	328	340
George Sinner (D)[a]	N.D.	1984	Won	300 est.	311

Sources: "Financing the 1983 Gubernatorial Campaign in Louisiana," PAR *Analysis*, no. 171 (Mar. 1984); Randy Patterson, secretary of state's office, State of Mississippi; a survey by the Council of State Governments; and reports from individual states.
G = general election.
P = primary election.
Comparative campaign costs in constant 1985 dollars were determined by dividing the actual campaign expenditures by the value of those dollars in equivalent 1985 dollars (1983: .9261; 1984: .9655). Based on the Consumer Price Index for All Urban Consumers, U.S. Department of Labor, Bureau of Labor Statistics.
a. Defeated incumbent governor.
b. Former governor.
c. Incumbent governor.
d. Lost to an incumbent governor.

call academe their professional home and were not involved in the transitions except as observers. None was called upon to paint a rosy picture of the process to benefit any of the participants. These analysts knew their states, the literature on gubernatorial transitions, and especially what NGA and other participants were suggesting as the way to assure a smooth transition and a steady start for a new administration. They were especially informed by the results of the studies of the

1982–83 transitions because the guidelines and process of the project were the same. The general outline of subjects to cover provided to the state analysts is contained in the appendix, "Outline for the State Analysts." There were no obvious biases in their observations and analyses, although it is clear that some analysts were closer to the key actors than were others.[34]

In all, there were twenty-four state analyses of gubernatorial transitions in the two volumes, plus the two other special state studies. The insights and suggestions of these state analysts are the basis for the analysis that follows.

Suggestions on Gubernatorial Transition from the State Analyses

What we can now do is take a broader view of the gubernatorial transition process in the states.[35] In doing so we will focus on three specific areas in which these individual state analyses provide an additional insight for the participants now and in the future: what the incumbent, outgoing governor can do or not do to ensure a smoother transition; what a gubernatorial candidate and governor-elect should do or not do to enhance the transition into office; and how the new governor's policy agenda is established and the ramifications of the process involved.

In this section of the presentation there is a prescriptive bias: how do results of these studies of past transitions inform us so that future transitions in the states might be made more smoothly and effectively for all parties? Some observations and suggestions parallel NGA and other participants' suggestions; some do not. But as noted, all aim at the same goal: to ensure smoother and more effective transitions based on a better understanding of what has happened before.

Rather than presenting an overview of what the analysts reported or a series of case studies, the first two sections on what the two principals —the outgoing and the incoming governors—should be thinking about are presented in the form of checklists of actions and concerns for them to consider as the general election approaches and the transition begins.

The third section takes direct aim at what appears to be a weak link in the gubernatorial transition process for the incoming governor: how these new governors of 1982, 1983, and 1984 put their initial policy agendas together. The initial policy agenda is especially important because it sets the tone and perspective of the new governor and his or her administration. Further, this agenda will guide what the governor's first legislature will consider as the new governor's priorities, thereby guiding at least the first year of the administration, if not the second year and even the entire term.

The Transition Out of Office: Trials of the Outgoing Governor and Staff

When focusing on gubernatorial transitions, states have generally developed policies, processes, laws, budgetary considerations, and other preparations that aim to assist the new governor assume office. Mention of the incumbent or outgoing governor and his role is usually coupled with the responsibilities he and his staff have toward the new governor. So outgoing governors often have to fend for themselves and seek private help and financial assistance as they leave office and sort through the details and loose ends of their administration.

Most evidence shows that there is often very little preparation for the transition out of office—especially as regards the outgoing governor. Some characterize the planning that may occur as ad hoc, letting everyone fend for themselves during the process. There are even examples of a "scorched earth" policy, in which there are no survivors left in the office—people, records, previous correspondence, or notations of impending responsibilities. In this case, preparations for leaving are simple: take everything or destroy it. As George Weeks described it, these are the "governors who have left in a huff and taken all the stuff." [36]

However, some outgoing governors see their leave-taking as an important part of their record and try to make it as smooth and positive a situation as is possible. In effect, it is a priority of action for them.

Often, there is confusion, political in nature, between what an outgoing governor is mandated to do in helping the governor-elect and is seeking to do to leave a record or legacy. Information on policies, programs, agencies, initiatives, and budgets is presented to the new governor by the outgoing administration on an informative basis; but this "information" can be seen as being political propaganda—the old administration's attempt to sell (or hide) the outgoing governor's record, priorities, or agenda. Or it is seen as individual departments and agencies seeking to lobby the new governor and staff for their own self-interest. This perceived or actual bias can effectively block the use of materials and briefings because they are perceived as being tainted.

Much of what an outgoing governor can do to prepare for the transition falls heir to the politics of the transition and the principals involved.
If the incumbent and new governor are not compatible either personally
or politically, such preparations probably will not work or will have
minimal effect. If the two principals are compatible, some or most of
the preparation may work. Politics—both in general and personal—is
the bottom line.

At a minimum, the logistical transition can be prepared for and, even
in a bad political situation, can still help in smoothing the transition
between administrations. The logistical transition concerns providing
office space, budgeting for new staff and consultants, and providing
supplies and other support needs, security, and housing needs (i.e., the
governor's mansion or residence). But even here politics and/or the
desire of the new administration to be seen as completely separate from
the old administration as is possible can negate the basic logistical
preparations to the detriment of a smooth transition both to and from
office.

Some of the logistical aspects of the transition are tied to enabling
legislation and the budget. Generally the time to effect legislation regarding transitions is early in an administration when the problems of
the transition are most clearly in mind. Unfortunately, the problems
addressed tend to be those of the incumbent governor who just went
through them and the rigors of assuming office. The former governor has little clout or access to press the issue of the problems of an
outgoing governor and how they might be addressed for future transitions. Further, few newly installed governors are thinking of their future
leave-taking at all. Still, there are actions that the outgoing governor
can take without the need of enabling legislation.

The Incumbent Governor's Checklist for
a Smooth Transition

) See the transition as part of your record and a legacy to be left to
the state.
) Keep meetings and communications between your staff and the staff
of the incoming governor private. Do not play the transition out
before the media and the public eye.
) Try to adopt a norm of standing aside in which your administration
will attempt to stay out of the way of the new. You reduce the
demands on the agencies and departments of state government,

thereby allowing the new governor to work with them without causing confusion in the state's bureaucracy.

) Develop briefing books and reports on the individual departments and agencies as to their responsibilities, budgetary considerations, issues, and pending problems. Provide a definition of the various functions of the offices, how they operate, who is responsible, and how they are funded.

) Establish a coordinated process by which the transition will take place. This process seems to work best when a single individual is responsible rather than a team. Most governors stay within the administration in selecting this person, but the right person from the outside can work well also.

) Involve the potential governors (candidates) in the budgetary process as early as possible so that they can have an opportunity to shape the first year's budget.

) Designate, and even detach, certain key personnel to work with the incoming administration, for example, a budget director.

) Hold positions open so that when your own staff leaves for new jobs, the new governor's people can be placed on the payroll early. Provide office space, telephones and other equipment, and supplies for the new governor and his staff to use.

) Do not fill positions in the judiciary, boards and commissions, and the bureaucracy with your supporters; leave these open for the new governor to make the appointments unless it is absolutely necessary to fill the positions.

) Seek funds for the transition from the legislature, and if that doesn't work use the emergency or contingency funds available to the governor. Or do both. Seek to have a "Transition Assistance Act" adopted by the legislature so transition processes can be institutionalized.

) If you were defeated in a bid for reelection, be gracious in defeat, saving your political recriminations and ambitions for another day.

) Set a tone of cooperation and noncontroversy for the process, even to the point of issuing memos to that effect. Where this may be personally difficult, instruct the staff to do so and stay out of the way. Even think of mentioning the new governor in positive and respectful terms in such speeches as the final state of the state address.

) When major problems occur, such as a budget shortfall, either address them yourself as part of your remaining responsibilities and/or involve the incoming governor in the policy decisions. He or she will have to live with the impact of the decision or action taken.

) Have someone selected as governor whom you like and trust. Then turn everything over to him, or as much as he wants to have.

The Incumbent Governor's Checklist
when a Smooth Transition Is Not the Goal

) Make no plans for transition when running for reelection because defeat is not expected or for fear that to be seen making such plans would indicate a sense of insecurity about your chances in the race. When defeat occurs, this is added to the rancor of the campaign; the operating mode of your administration is of everyone suddenly seeking to find new jobs and leaving as soon as possible, acting more in the private than the public interest.

) Adopt a scorched-earth policy and leave no or few survivors in the office: people, records, correspondence, or a checklist of important dates or impending problems for the new administration. Even equipment and furniture can be fair game here.

) Allow the staff in your office to work until the end of your term and then permit them to use their accumulated annual leave time as a cushion in their shift from their current position to their next. The fact that this accumulated leave time is paid from the new governor's office budget is the new governor's problem and not yours.

) In developing briefing materials and the budget try to insure that your administration and various departments' pet programs and projects are protected—but do so in a surreptitious manner so that this won't be found out immediately, only suspected.

) Try to fill as many appointive positions as possible in the judiciary, on boards and commissions, and in key bureaucratic slots in the remaining time available to you. After all, these people helped you and now is the time to reward them.

) Hold the last budget close to the vest because it is your last one for the state and contains the priorities of your outgoing administration. If there are revenue shortfall problems, duck them and let the incoming governor grapple with them. In fact, in administering the budget of the administration or the governor's office, do not worry about the full twelve months—the last six are the next governor's problem—so what if there is an overrun?

) Open your meetings with the new governor to the media so the citizens will know what is happening. This leads to a very formal and generalized discussion between you—leading nowhere.

) Get into a dispute with the newly elected governor that must be adjudicated by the state's supreme court; topics for the debate might include when is the day one leaves office or who has the responsibility to make a certain appointment.

) Die and leave a rudderless ship at the very time it is most vulnerable because of the fears raised by the impending unknowns of a new administration.

The Transition into Office: Preparing to Become Governor

This section focuses on the preparations that the winning gubernatorial candidates made as they approached becoming governor. Observers and governmental participants know these transitions must occur and adjust their planning and activities to fit this reality. What is so surprising to those close to the activities of the governors is how little planning and forethought are given to the potential transition by those running for governor: the politics of winning an election seems to drive out any such efforts in too many cases. The following is a checklist of actions a gubernatorial candidate and then a governor-elect should consider in preparing to become governor.

Checklist for a Potential Incoming Governor

) Have someone you trust do the preplanning for the transition period so that there is a blueprint of action ready. It can be modified, expanded, or reduced according to the circumstances after the election; but it is a starting point and should set out the priorities of action over the first 110 days after the election.

) Be sure that the person working on the transition plan is not in the campaign; keep these efforts separated as they are two different activities with different goals, and the campaign will swamp any other activities. Do not be afraid to let an academic do the necessary research and drafting of the initial blueprint—academics often have a professional interest in such an endeavor.

) Be sure that such a blueprint is kept under lock and key, with few people—maybe just the candidate and the author—knowing of its existence. If it leaks to the press, the document becomes part of the politics of the campaign with no end to the mischief that can be made with a poor turn of a phrase, a light-hearted suggestion, or even good, hard-headed advice.

) Go out of your way to ease the transition out of office for the incumbent governor, even if you won by beating him in a tough or even nasty political campaign. Poor winners are worse than sore losers. Praise, respect, cooperation, and coordination of both governors' actions and staffs set a most positive tone as the change in leadership occurs.

) Remember you are only the newly elected governor, not the governor, even though all the attention is now focused on you in the media, in state government, and among those with an interest in state government. The incumbent governor still has the responsibility for governing the state until you are inaugurated. Second-guessing the incumbent governor's actions publicly not only stirs up unnecessary controversy but undermines the incumbent's already fragile hold on the reigns of state government. You will have plenty of time to be the leader soon.

) Do not go to the department heads serving under the incumbent and ask them to help in seeking budget cuts. They just finished putting the budget of the incumbent together and this only calls on them to divide their loyalties, frustrating both them and the incumbent governor.

) Try not to get into a fight with the outgoing governor and staff over issues of the transition. Meet face-to-face with the incumbent governor and indicate those areas in which you have a concern (last minute appointments to the bench, the budget) and those in which you do not. If necessary, bargain or "cut a deal" on touchy appointment situations so that each of you wins a bit and each loses a bit, or seek joint responsibility for all or portions of the budget. But do it face-to-face and not in newsprint or on the six o'clock television news. This can even be put into writing as a memo of understanding between the two administrations to reduce the areas of potential conflict.

〉 Name a transition coordinator immediately after being elected in order to give the transition a focus. This can also help to remove you from the day-to-day, nitty-gritty work that must take place; and, most importantly, it can reduce the amount of press questioning for hints of what you plan to do as governor (before you really know what you will be doing in any detail) and for comments on whether you agree or disagree with what the incumbent governor is doing. The latter could spark an unnecessary fight—as noted above, you will have plenty of time in the limelight and to get into fights once in office.

〉 Although naming a transition coordinator focuses the transition on that person and his or her staff, you must lead the transition effort through this coordinator. Basic policy decisions and directions must be made by you; the coordinator sees that decisions are carried out. But do not get lost in the transition details. Remember to keep your focus on the larger picture, the key issues to address, the first steps of the administration and, above all, the budget.

〉 Be sure that, if you have not had experience in state government, you have an insider or someone with tactical state government experience located at a high position on your transition team. This person can provide guidance and try to ensure that the transition coordinator and staff do not make unnecessary errors that might lead observers to pin an amateur label on the new administration.

〉 Select a transition headquarters in the capital city as near to the governor's office and administrative buildings as is possible. This eases communication between you and the outgoing governor and between both staffs, allows you and your staff to get a feel of the turf on which you will be running, and cuts down on unnecessary traveling time and expense.

〉 Do not fear to utilize key campaign staff during the transition—go with the ones who got you there. Some of them can be part of the transition staff and process; some can be used to wind down the campaign; and others who will not be in the new administration— either by your choice or theirs—can be used to plan and carry out the inauguration festivities.

〉 But be ready to drop campaign staff and move them out of the transition and new administration. It is best for all involved, although it may be painful at the time, for you to let them know early that they will not be in the new administration. They then can make plans for the future rather than staying around waiting for the appointment that never materializes.

) Assign someone to compile all the campaign promises made, so that you will be ready to implement or answer questions about them.

) Do not hesitate to use committees and task forces to help in certain necessary activities and processes—such as personnel screening and developing policy options—during the transition period. This is a good way to involve a broad range of individuals and interests in the formation of your administration. However, be sure it is understood at the outset that serving on any such committee or task force is a public service and not a private way of obtaining a position in the new administration. You may find potential administrative staff on these committees or task forces, but that decision should be made separately.

) If you use committees and task forces to help in the transition process, they must act under your control, usually through the transition coordinator and staff. The last thing you want is a runaway committee or task force saying and doing things with which you do not agree in your name. Remember they should be advisory only, so do not let them be in a position of voting on what you should do—that is for you to decide.

) When looking for assistance in your initial efforts do not overlook university personnel. Many scholars have a professional interest in administration, certain processes such as the budget and personnel, and various policy areas. They often are more than willing to help and have some experience that can be very helpful to the new administration.

) Do not overlook former governors of your party when seeking assistance in the transition and the new administration. They have been there, know the turf, and often are very willing to help you. They should know what errors to avoid from their previous experience, and they also, with the symbolism and presence of a former governor, add a sense of continuity.

) Get input on government policy, programs, and issues from government agencies themselves. They probably developed briefing papers or books for the new administration anyway; but be aware that these are usually quite positive in tone and sometimes self-serving. Gain control of this process by asking the agencies to respond to specific questions you have: for example, prepare a 90- or 120-day calendar listing all important due dates, such as legislative deadlines, grant applications, policy guidelines, appointments, and administrative regulations. Also you may wish to request a list of the five most important issues facing the agency or program right now and five years from now.

) Be careful in your relations with the media. Off-the-cuff remarks can return to haunt you and constrain the options available to you. Remember that the media needs you and you need them; establish some working rules early so both sides understand what to expect. Such rules can be: once-a-week press conferences; no press conferences until being sworn in as governor; no background interviews; a series of rotating background interviews showing no favoritism for any particular media outlet. Then stick by the rules.

) Prioritize the appointments that you must make and remember that everyone, whether media, state employee, state legislator, interest group, or the public, is looking for clues and signals on what you will be doing in the next administration. But also remember, it is very important that certain key positions be filled by people you know and trust: the budget director, director of administration, and certain departments of importance in your state.

) Do not fear to seek the best people available in the country for some of the critical positions in your administration. But be certain to temper this desire with the real need to have "natives" as the basis of your administration rather than a group of "out-of-staters."

) The timing of your appointments is crucial both for the strategy you plan to use in becoming governor and the signals that any appointment or set of appointments sends out to those with an interest in state government. Above all, such announcements as the early appointment of the new budget director or head of the department of administration can be used to give a sense of your ability to govern and your readiness to take over the reigns of state government. Waiting deep into the transition period or into the new administration can create considerable uncertainty.

) Do not be afraid to use holdover appointments: holdover staff know what is going on and what the problems are and are often pleased to have the chance to work in state government for another governor's term of service. They can provide stability during the initial period of your administration when you face your first legis-

lative session. You can then evaluate them based on their performance in your administration. Wholesale demands for resignations
only create more transition problems and unnecessary animosity in
many quarters.

) Get on top of the state budget that will be presented to the legislature in the first few months of your tenure. This will be your guiding
star for the next fiscal period—well into your administration. It
not only provides the lifeblood of money to state government, but
it contains many policy decisions that you must understand and
change if you are trying to shift priorities. Try to attach someone,
even yourself, to the budget process as soon as possible so that what
finally appears is not a surprise or unrealistic in terms of projected
revenues. And make sure that the revenue projections fit the current
reality, not some hoped-for future.

) Move carefully in establishing legislative relations. Do not pick a
fight with the legislature or legislative leaders; you will be needing
their support to achieve your goals. There is a range of steps you
can take in working with the legislature, from involving some key
legislators in the transition process to selecting a respected former
legislator as your legislative liaison; to caressing individual legislators; to stepping into the legislative leadership selection process.
If you choose the latter strategy, be sure you can win before you
enter, because you will lose from then on if you are not successful.

) To give the impression of hitting the ground running, develop two
or three key legislative ideas to introduce and push.

) In setting up your office and determining how you will operate as
governor, remember that the main person to satisfy as to structure,
processes, and procedures is you, the new governor. Certain parts
of the office should run by rote, others should not. Attention will
have to be paid to those squeak points so that glitches do not occur
(unanswered job applications, conflicts over the scheduling of your
time). Save time for yourself to think about being governor.

) Be wary of salesmen with sophisticated computers and programs,
even if their products are free. Without the proper trained personnel
and the correct programming such equipment can get you deeper
in trouble if you and your staff are not able to use it in an effective
and timely manner.

) If you feel most comfortable at the center of everything and have
operated this way in the past with ease, do not attempt to follow

the chief-of-staff model just because someone advises you that it is best for your office, or your state, or because it works best in other states. Conversely, do not experiment with an open system if you are and have been more comfortable with a chief-of-staff system of management. Too many new governors find themselves frustrated with the basic system they initially established and have to reorganize the system and staff later—sometimes uncomfortably for both the governor and the staff.

The Newly Elected Governor's Initial Policy Agenda

Reading the studies of the gubernatorial transitions in the 1982–83/1983–84 period leaves one with a feeling that there is one area in particular that needs to be thought through more carefully: setting the initial policy agenda that the governor will use in the first months of his or her administration.

The NGA publication *Transition and the New Governor: A Critical Overview* clearly provides considerable guidance to a new administration in terms of the mechanics of transition, setting up the office and the various procedures used, personnel selection, establishment of a management style and related procedures, budget, and policy agenda over the long term. But in the real life of the transition and the opening of a new administration, budget and policy agenda—especially policy agenda in the very short term—need attention in order to be of more assistance to the new governor.

Did these newly elected governors studied bring a policy agenda to the new administration, and what was the process by which they did? There appear to be at least six different approaches the governors used, and for each approach different results can and sometimes did follow. They are presented from the least policy-agenda-oriented approach to the most.

They Didn't. The newly elected governors were surprised to have won the election, and each had spent the few months prior to the election attacking the opponent on his or her liabilities and character, or lack thereof. There were few if any real policy issues or differences in the campaign except the desire to win and become governor.

Result. The momentum of the outgoing administration's policies and decisions carries forward; departments, agencies, and other units of government have the freedom to "freelance"; appointments to positions may provide some sense of control, but this is somewhat vitiated by the lack of a guiding star from the governor's office; and, the legislature sets its own agenda.

They Can't. The state faced such a fiscal (or other) crisis that there was no time or flexibility for anything except to address the crisis. Other governors-elect found the lack of time between the election and the inauguration and/or when the legislature convened to be so tight that little time was available other than to set up the governor's office and the administration; some were not even able to do that completely. The mode of action was coping.

Result. Even the momentum from the past is disrupted, especially in a crisis situation; the governor reacts to the situation in the same way as do the departments and agencies: taxes are raised or cutbacks are imposed to stem a fiscal hemorrhage and legislative leadership is on-the-fly. Some overcome the crisis and make it, others do not.

Someone Else Does. The former governor's shadow extends forward because he was so strong and well regarded that to change things would not be politically savvy. As a variation, the development of the agency-by-agency and department-by-department briefings and briefing books lays out the agenda already on hand, from the outgoing governor and bureaucracy's points of view.

Result. The new administration reacts to others' policy agendas often without a clear handle or goal in mind, or without the ability to impose a new perspective to the agenda. The former governor, the agencies, and the legislature set and control the agenda. In one case, the new governor not only inherited the policy agenda but the gubernatorial staff of the previous administration.

How Did I Get Here? Look back at the campaign and attempt to understand which policy aspects tied to your platform were critical to your win. This will allow you to use the campaign momentum and the electoral mandate to set the policy agenda of the administration. At a more crass level, count the campaign promises made—one newly elected governor found he or she had made 160 or so campaign promises, which had to be delivered—was this the agenda?

Result. Who sets the agenda of a political campaign—the candidate or the polls? If the latter, the polls may or may not have told the candidate what was really needed for the state, but certainly helped the candidate to be elected. (No need to go into the problems of polling here, but poor question wording or leading questions can skew what the candidate learns from a poll; and the canned campaign-management approaches that out-of-state consultants bring with them can raise difficulties.) Further, most campaigns are loaded with broad platitudes such as bringing "a new era," "ousting arrogant" Democrats or Republicans, "change," "get jobs here," or "improve the business climate," which do not easily translate into a specific policy agenda. The specifics are still with the bureaucracy and the legislature. Finally, such an approach can be unduly restrictive because the new administration is stuck with what it used to win a political campaign and possibly may not have what it needs to be a successful administration.

Do Something. The new governor calls for the departments and agencies to let him or her know their status and any problems they may have. Their activities are triggered by the governor's queries, often built around a series of policy themes. Task forces of governor's appointees and state employees may be established to follow the queries, analyze the results, and make policy recommendations. Quite often these policy themes are a variation on seeking more economy and efficiency in state government and a commission consisting of private sector leaders and other citizens is established (à la the Grace Commission under President Reagan) to undertake an intensive study of state government operations and finances, which issues a set of recommendations to the governor to achieve the goals he or she is seeking.

Result. The new governor is the initiator of the action, yet the activity is still tied to the responses of the agencies and departments. The hit-and-run nature of state-level "little Grace Commissions" is a problem: they tend to stir up a lot of dust and controversy in their probing; provide a set of recommendations that often uses the economy and efficiency theme as the only goal—often overlooking other needed goals of state government; hold a well-publicized press conference deploring the waste and inefficiencies they have found in state government; and retire from the fray. It is then up to the governor and staff to sort the real from the unreal in the report—and to mend all the walking wounded. If the queries for such task forces and commissions are policy-specific enough, they may work to help the governor in the agenda-setting process, but many observers suspect that when such a "*do something*" approach is undertaken, it is more sound and fury than substance—more symbolic than real in establishing a policy agenda.

The Planned Approach. The new governor arrives ready to undertake the necessary policy planning and evaluation to bear on the creation of the new administration's agenda. There is an orientation toward the future of seeking to achieve goals, rather than to just fight the fires of yesterday and today. Prior to the political campaign there began a long and serious review of the state, its situation and problems, the hoped-for future, and what the new administration could and should do. The actual campaign may have been used to prepare the state and state government for the agenda. The first steps taken are to fill the critical policy positions and to use all gubernatorial vehicles, such as press conferences, the inaugural address, the state of the state message, the legislative address, to continue the process of establishing and selling the administration's agenda for the future.

Result. This approach brings a view and understanding of future problems to the current situation. The particular situation can be lodged within a larger context, so decisions are more informed and have the possibility of even being correct. Leadership is provided from a policy viewpoint rather than a political or day-to-day reactive perspective. However, too few candidates take this approach for a variety of reasons—including the fact that it requires time and effort well before running for and becoming governor, a luxury few potential governors have. And for those that try it, the needs of a close political campaign can drain away staff who might undertake these activities, for after all, what good is all that policy planning if the candidate loses the election? To the campaign manager, such activity is only wasted manpower and money. Finally, these attempts can run afoul of the day-to-day problems and needs of the new administration as it moves through the transition period and the early days in office. Nuts and bolts too often drive out vision.

These are only six of what are probably many ways to approach the short-term agenda problems as evidenced by the state analysts and their view of what occurred in those critical early post-election days in the gubernatorial transitions of 1982, 1983, and 1984. What is presented here could be much more elegant in style, or it could be much more specific with examples for the situations described. But I opted to make the observations more generic in nature so that in thinking them through I was not clouded by personal feelings toward any particular individual governor or administration.

These approaches may seem to be too stereotypical, and indeed no one administration fits neatly into any one approach. In fact, any particular administration may have used two or more approaches as it addressed the policy concerns of the state. But it would seem to be important to identify the approaches used and what they purport to do, along with the possible results, which are very often unanticipated.

Clearly the optimal goal would be to seek to approach the problem of the first policy agenda by the most rational means possible, though events and circumstances may militate against this as the newly elected governor is thrown directly into a problem-solving mode. But in too many of the cases the analysts reported that the establishment of a policy agenda followed politics, appointments, establishing processes, and procedures as a priority. Creating the initial policy agenda wasn't necessarily an afterthought, but too often it was driven out by the other seeming necessities of the transition. The message conveyed here should be read: make the establishment of the initial policy agenda a top priority; it is a crucial aspect of any gubernatorial transition and administration. You may have the right people in the right positions and the best procedures in place, but without the substance and clear direction of the governor's goals the administration can falter at the worst possible time.

Conclusion

In sum, after observing, participating in, and analyzing the gubernatorial transition process over two decades, I would suggest there are two major overarching components to a successful gubernatorial transition: planning and communication.

The first component, planning, must be initiated even before either party to the actual transition is comfortable in doing so. For the incumbent, planning for a gubernatorial transition means admitting too early the truth of the calendar and that the governor and administration constitute a lame duck. Or it could mean preparing for an exit while fighting a reelection battle and thereby sending the wrong message to the governor's own supporters about the prospects for reelection. For the candidate seeking the office, planning for the transition could betoken an arrogance or certainty of victory that is off-putting to those involved in and observent of the state's politics. Further, to those in the campaign it could seem to be a misuse of scarce resources in a very competitive political contest. Yet the success of the outgoing administration and of the first year of the new administration must rely on such planning, as is evidenced by what so often happens when planning is missing.

The second component, communication, must occur even when there are considerable personal, political, and logistical roadblocks mitigating against free and open relations between the major actors. Nevertheless, a successful gubernatorial transition requires that avenues of communication be developed to overcome these roadblocks in order to assure that the longer-range goal of successful gubernatorial transition is achieved.

Both of these components of a successful gubernatorial transition, planning and communication, translate into a state government and governorship that can serve the citizens of the state better. Without them, the citizens are ill served by the short-term roadblocks involved.

Perspectives on Transition
)))))

Protecting Options

))))〉

Robert Huefner

When should governors postpone, and when should they make, commitments? Patience builds understanding of circumstances and options, but decisiveness builds achievement and reputation. New governors come inclined toward action. Empowered by the energy and mandate of the most invigorating political victories of their lives, urged on by spectators, and committed to improving what are now more than ever *their* states, they are eager actors.[1] But the experience of others, and frequently their own instincts, counsel that options be protected by building, not burning, bridges ahead.

Gubernatorial transitions reveal the importance of democratic processes—and how little we know about improving them. Recent decades do show progress: transitions go more smoothly and give governors quicker starts, partly because of such studies as this volume and the assistance provided by the National Governors' Association (NGA). But experience with transitions, as participant and observer, prompts a confession that more is uncertain than certain: transitions plead for further understanding. A crucial uncertainty is when will decisions help the governor and the state, and when will they hurt?

The following discussion focuses upon three types of choices related to this uncertainty: selecting staff, setting the policy agenda, and delegating responsibility. The suggestions are tentative judgments, not final conclusions; references in the notes do not prove these views, but should help readers explore them.

A Conflict in Expectations?

The transition from one governor to the next marks the beginning of an extraordinary period. Beginning with the campaign, the new governor and the governor's associates embark upon an incomparable learning experience about management, human behavior, leadership, politics, and American democracy.[2] The governor becomes the state's focus of political communication. The governor draws technical understanding and advice from one of the most elaborate and skilled bureaucracies in modern society. Because even all this cannot make the governor omniscient, the state's most visible manager and leader is daily instructed and corrected—by the press, interest groups, and individuals. Except for the presidency and parenting, there is no more complete and rigorous educational opportunity.

The transition from one governor to the next sets the form of the new administration. It usually does more to determine the success of a governor's tenure than any other period of the governor's term. The campaign, followed within three months by the governor's first budget, inaugural address, and state of the state message, announces the governor's policy agenda. The appointments of personal staff, agency officials, and members of boards and commissions largely determine the energy, competence, and perspective of the executive branch. With these actions and the first legislative session, the governor establishes relationships with the legislature, the press, the bureaucracy, and the public. Thus the transition shapes the governor's program and capability.

Can both these descriptions be true? Can it be that we expect governors to set the agenda for the most influential roles of their lifetime at the point that just begins the most extraordinary learning experience of their lives? Might the descriptions exaggerate?[3] Not by much—and their irony is compounded by the time pressures and confusion of the transition. Is it fair? No. Is it sensible? No. Is it inevitable? Mostly. Can the irony be managed? We should try.

What Guides Are Possible?

Guides must be general, yet still useful. They must be general because our knowledge is so limited and because of the differences in circumstances and the need to give room for creative leadership. But even general guides can help new governors understand and deal with the conflict between patience and action. Just having that conflict aired and discussed explains the ambivalence governors face in anticipating and outlining their tenure. It may then provide an understanding that can be consciously used in balancing or scheduling learning versus action. More specific help comes when the understanding of the tension between action and patience is reflected in guidelines offered to governors, such as those suggesting the setting of priorities in making appointments. It may be possible to suggest means to combine action and learning or to describe ways in which action may be reasonably limited in order to better accommodate future learning, or to outline criteria and circumstances important in considering tradeoffs between action and patience.[4]

Guides, of course, must not be carried too far. A good transition works because it fits the unique situation (the state's economy, politics, public worries, and public enthusiasms, and the governor's personal style, hopes, and capabilities). Therefore the approaches discussed below are offered not as universals but as a menu from which to choose or formulate procedures useful for a particular transition.

Selecting Staff

Quick appointments help, but quality appointments help more. Focus early attention on personal staff and directors of high priority programs. The governor, who must work through others, naturally seeks early appointments to communicate direction and give energy to the new administration. Delays cut the governor's effective time in office, and may cause him to appear uncertain and lethargic. However, haste closes an option with each appointment and may box in the governor with future personnel problems while missing the able people who identify and enhance future options. New governors should resist haste. Poor appointments, though early, remain poor. So effort should focus upon appointments for the governor's staff and programs at the top of the governor's agenda. Appoint board members and directors of other programs as time and law allow.[5]

Seek associates who are able to communicate and who have contacts, understanding, and trust that are broadly based. Learning must link the governor, as well as other decision makers whom the governor hopes to influence, to broadly distributed sources of facts and judgments. (Communications with the legislature deserve special and early attention.)[6] Governor Bill Clinton's apology to the people of Arkansas for his having to learn that he could not "lead without listening," and the success of his subsequent tenure, constitute a poignant and powerful lesson.[7] Associates who have diverse perspectives and are trusted by influential people across the state facilitate communication.[8] But multiple viewpoints also may increase internal conflict and confusion.[9]

Trust is especially important within the governor's personal staff, while technical understanding is more important for program directors. Learning within the governor's own office particularly depends upon openness of communications—usually, but not necessarily, building upon past association (which may bring charges of cronyism).[10] All communications "filter", effective communications screen out insignificant information and pass on what is crucial. Communication with the governor, like that with others, should go two ways: it should deliver the important information to the governor and facilitate learning from and using the governor's conclusions. Trust is essential both to "warn and give confidence,"[11] in other words to deliver the truth when it hurts but also to give assurance when that is needed.

Learning from (and with) state departments, on the other hand, depends more upon the governor's confidence in the technical and administrative skills of program directors. The skills sought depend upon the role envisioned; program expertise and management skills may best serve for a stable program, where efficient and effective delivery of existing services is the primary concern, while public leadership and political skills might be sought if major program changes are envisioned.[12]

Campaign staff can be valuable in the new administration, if carried over for the right reasons. The NGA raises appropriate concerns about appointing campaign staff to the new state administration: they may be too narrowly partisan and not able to connect with the whole state. In Utah the election of each new governor brings a contest between party and governor over who runs the state; the governor always wins, and victory often is accomplished and announced by appointing a governor's staff that has distance from the campaign and the party.[13] Yet Rhode Island's new administration, well aware of the NGA's advice, carried the campaign manager through as transition director and then chief of staff. In fact this is common, perhaps because campaign leaders provide the communications links that the governor needs for constructive learning.[14] But even when campaign staff do not meet the needs of the administration, the new governor may feel considerable obligation to provide them appointments. The NGA's warnings help protect governors in this position. Special care to not raise unrealistic expectations during the campaign may help avoid pressures.[15]

Contacts can be expanded through a kitchen cabinet, where membership is more easily changed. Trusted advisors broaden the sources of learning and, like the personal staff, warn and give confidence. Communication with other influential people also helps implement policy.[16] Options can be enhanced by informality, which anticipates flexibility in those who participate.

Board appointments offer helpful options. Board appointments offer alternative roles for party and campaign people: to recommend and evaluate candidates. Board appointments provide options for political, geographic, ethnic, and sex balance, and to broaden communications.[17] Note that the time of the first appointments to each board may be the time when options are most open to reconsider statutory qualifications and roles and even the necessity of the board.

Existing administrators may be carried over to allow some future flexibility. But again it must be for the right reason. Retaining respected administrators from previous administrations is more common than a reading of the NGA guide might suggest. By providing such persons with general guidance and delegating to them the responsibilities for administration, the governor can postpone major policy shifts and reduce the disruptions of the transition period, while gaining credit for openness or bipartisanship and being in a position to more easily shed problems that might arise.[18] This presumes the appointees serve at the governor's pleasure and hence the carry-overs do not require a long-term commitment; it presumes that the governor is alert to the NGA warning against being pressured to maintain persons because of their own political power base.[19]

Seek agency directors who understand the process and value of democratic leadership. Political processes and interests frequently frustrate agency directors intent upon accomplishing programs according to professional standards. A natural and appropriate tension arises between professional standards and political interests. But agency heads who see this simply as a moral contest between professional good and political evil aggravate the conflict and close options. Better administrators respect both the political process and their own integrity; they seek options that reconcile legitimate professional and political values and join their capabilities.[20]

Seek personal staff who appreciate professional expertise. This attitude reciprocates and facilitates the appreciation of political processes by the agency directors. It enables a professional/political linkage that helps to spot and pursue effective policy options.

Find persons who listen to facts and to people, not just to the governor. If learning is central to success, then what one knows or who one knows may not be as important as how one knows. Traditional measures of qualification (the most easily measured skills, enshrined by a century of merit systems) need to give more space to the "softer," commonly suspect, measures of attitude. Given the limits of present understanding, this is a speculative conclusion. But it enjoys a deductive logic. If governors learn from the gubernatorial term, staff and administrators must share the commitment and capacity to learn. Governors gain from subordinates who seek new understanding, presume that understanding cannot be complete, and can act in the face of uncertainty (i.e., they are not disabled by uncertainty but manage it by avoiding the worst risks, keeping options open, monitoring developments, and making timely reactions to new information).

To summarize several of the above suggestions: the capacity to learn depends upon a staff that quickly develops effective communication links with important sources of information. The effectiveness of these links depends upon trust and openness, upon skills to incisively and articulately share information, and upon commitments to a two-way flow of learning to establish understanding and consensus for effective action.[21]

Setting the Agenda

The NGA's *advice to focus on no more than three policy initiatives protects options.* The value derived from learning, during the governor's term, depends upon having future opportunities to use this learning. Limiting initial commitments leaves room for new initiatives after some experience is gained.[22] It also allows concentration of effort, to help ensure successes that open new options and bring quicker support for future initiatives.

The campaign makes this advice hard to follow because it builds commitment to too many initiatives: commissioned papers on policy positions build commitment, campaign encounters between candidates develop commitment, and commitments are made in seeking the support of particular interests.[23] Some governors avoid this if campaigns are not issue oriented (Kentucky), though the campaign still may test and adjust an agenda already set (Indiana), or if the public campaign issues may be no more than the voters' rationales for how they intend to vote (Utah). However, a confident candidate may use the campaign to exercise leadership, building support that allows more ambitious programs (Arkansas in 1982).[24]

The chapters in this book and in the 1982 edition show the value of limiting commitments, in the campaign and after, by recognizing that capacity is constrained by:

) state financial resources (Kentucky and Washington).
) the size and skill of the governor's staff (Alaska, Kentucky, and North Dakota).
) the extent of influence with the legislature (Kentucky); effective influence increases future flexibility (Utah).
) political limits upon the legislature itself (Kentucky).
) the strength of the public mandate (North Carolina and Utah).
) understanding of uncertain circumstances (Utah).
) particular weaknesses in the governor's political position. Clinton (Arkansas) could not be immediately generous with pardons and commutations; particular strengths open up options and capacity: Joe Frank Harris dominated the Georgia budget.
) particular environmental circumstances. Nearly every new governor in 1982–83 needed room on the agenda for the financial crisis, and so did Kentucky and North Dakota in the transitions reported in this book.

Give priorities to initiatives that can pay off, both in terms of success and in terms of opening up the right new options. Agenda setting is a strategy of investment: close some choices now in order to build more and better future choices. The governor becomes a pool player, lining up a shot with such confidence that concern shifts to what the next shot will be. But don't put all the eggs in one basket.[25] Be careful that initiatives are feasible.[26] Don't raise false hopes: only so much can be done by strong management and the elimination of waste, and the promise to raise no new taxes can hobble a new administration.

Make the commitment to the basic purpose; leave flexibility in detail and implementation. An effective governor, who learns in office, exercises vigorous leadership but still learns during the negotiations necessary to accomplish the initiatives of that leadership. This leadership/learning mode of decision making means that the governor expects to make yet-undetermined adjustments in the final form of the policy or program and in the means to accomplish it.[27] The policy of limiting the agenda appears to have been violated by the experienced West Virginia governor Arch Moore and his sixteen policy initiatives. But his focus was the single broader policy of economic development, so that his sixteen initiatives allowed considerable flexibility in dropping or changing individual proposals as he found better ways to pursue the basic policy.

Special committees can be appointed after the election to generate options. The Washington study describes such an approach. This may delay action or pressure for action, as the committee report is awaited, though it may build pressure for action after the report and may reduce options by sanctioning specific approaches.[28] Washington governor Booth Gardner controlled this last problem by making clear that the report only provided options, in order to help the governor identify workable approaches. In North Dakota the governor's control probably was enhanced because there was just one committee, it was made up of persons close to the governor, and it looked only at the governor's three issues. Still, it took some actions that inhibited the governor's flexibility.

Use actions that have symbolic impact, but keep policy choices open. Governor Gardner gained an image of businesslike professionalism, which built confidence in him and in the state's fiscal soundness, by appointing professionals rather than leaders of causes, thereby making the appointments less of a commitment to particular policies. By gaining favorable exposure for his style of management he established a positive reputation without making program commitments. North Dakota governor George Sinner symbolized action without reducing options by moving his transition office to the capitol.

Take some early heat for a bland administration, if it provides time to build later effectiveness. West Virginia governor Moore, an experienced politician and governor, dropped out of public view after the election and then hit the ground running after inauguration.[29] California governor George Deukmejian did the same, gaining time to prepare and intensifying the press' curiosity.[30] Missouri governor John Ashcroft bought time when he told the press not to expect announcements until late December and then directed the transition from an "undisclosed downtown location." [31] But the Washington transition shows too slow a start, which killed influence in the first legislative session.

Delegating Responsibility

Delegate responsibility for lower priority programs in ways that allow it to be recaptured. The initiatives included in the governor's basic program should be the governor's major leadership efforts. But actions will be required in every state activity. To allow a focus on the leadership initiatives, and to help preserve future options for the rest of government, other decisions might be approached in a different way, in which key gubernatorial actions are to select competent managers and then delegate administrative responsibility to them. In this management/adjustment mode the governor exercises only general guidance and an oversight and coordinating role, while managers focus upon management and minor rather than major policy issues. The governor remains flexible in regard to an ultimate purpose, allowing that to develop with experience. The governor also maintains flexibility through distance, thus limiting personal commitment and facilitating adjustments in personnel and program as time proves them desirable. [32]

The delegation proposed by the management/adjustment approach presumes that delegation can be recalled. This becomes questionable if the delegation is to a person or body with an independent political base. For example, what roles should be delegated to the lieutenant governor? Former governor William Guy in North Dakota counseled that this delegation should proceed slowly; once power is delegated it can rarely be retrieved. [33]

Good Transitions Build Bridges and then Pale

Are transitions the beginning or the end? Former governor Guy offers thoughtful counsel to new governors feeling the pressure to get things going: take power as soon as possible, but then know that it's all right to take one's time in effecting a transition; not every problem needs to be immediately solved nor every appointment immediately made; the time frame for taking power allows the deferral of many problems. [34]

Good transitions open up the journey, they don't constitute it, nor should they even set a definite course. They help new administrations learn how to learn from the gubernatorial experience, and they make major contributions to that learning.[35] They are and should be busy times, but with a focusing of energy upon actions that enhance future opportunities to learn and enlarge future options to apply what's learned. The best transitions pale in comparison with the progress they enable during the governor's term.

Individual State Studies
of the 1983 and 1984
Elections and Transitions

))))

The Gubernatorial Transition in Kentucky, 1983–1984

)))))

Malcolm E. Jewell and
Philip Roeder

The Political Setting

Kentucky normally has a gubernatorial transition every four years, because it is one of the four states where the constitution prohibits a governor from being elected for a second successive term. Usually the transition is from one Democrat to another. The last Republican governor in Kentucky, Louie Nunn, served from 1967 to 1971. Some Kentucky Democratic governors have tried to pick a successor, or at least to influence the voters' choice in the primary, but their rate of success has not been very high.

John Y. Brown, Jr., who was elected in 1979, entered a crowded Democratic primary relatively late and used his own financial resources to wage a skillful television campaign. He won the primary with 29 percent of the vote, defeating five opponents, including the candidate endorsed by outgoing governor Julian Carroll. He then easily defeated former governor Louie Nunn in the general election.

Brown ran his campaign independently, with little reliance on traditional political organizations, and he governed the state in the same way. He took little interest in political party matters and was relatively inaccessible to local politicians and officials. In making appointments he paid little attention to the norms of patronage. Instead he filled many of the major positions of government with businessmen, including some who had been his business associates, and as he repeatedly promised he would do, he tried to run Kentucky government like a business. In the process he antagonized many Democratic political leaders. The most important characteristic of his administration was unplanned, however. The national recession hit Kentucky hard, and during Brown's years in office a series of revenue shortfalls forced him to make numerous cuts in his budget. Throughout his four years, however, he held the line against tax increases proposed to make up for the shortage of funds.

During Brown's term the legislature was dominated by the Democratic Party; its 3 to 1 margin of control has been typical of the party balance in recent years. In other respects, however, the legislature was not a typical one. Traditionally the Kentucky governor has dominated the legislature by dictating selection of the leadership and committee chairmen, developing a legislative program, taking a stand on most major bills, and working effectively to win the support of legislators for his position on bills.

The strong governor has been matched by a weak legislature with short biennial sessions, limited staffing, and a high turnover of membership. But in recent years the legislature has developed more independence and a higher level of professionalism. More of the members serve longer, staffing has been improved, a strong interim committee system has developed, and the members have devoted more time and resources to scrutinizing the executive and reviewing the budget.

During Brown's term the legislature was also in a period of transition to a new schedule of elections and sessions, based on a constitutional amendment adopted in 1979 that was intended to strengthen the legislature during both the regular sessions and the interim period. The biennial session of the legislature had been limited to the first sixty days of the year (excluding Sundays and holidays). The amendment retained the limit of sixty meeting days for the legislative houses but permitted these sessions to be scheduled at any time until mid-April, adding about a month to the time the legislature could meet and making it possible to reconvene at the end of the session to override vetoes. Legislative elections were shifted from odd-numbered to even-numbered years (with the gubernatorial election remaining in odd-numbered years). This made it possible for the legislature to hold interim committee meetings for a full year after the election before the regular session. During the transition, house members elected in 1981 served a three-year term and senators a five-year term. This meant all house members would face reelection after the 1984 legislative session.

Governor John Y. Brown followed a strategy in dealing with the legislature that reduced his influence compared to that of his predecessors. First, he decided not to play any role in the selection of legislative leaders, a move that was welcomed by most members. Second, he largely avoided personal involvement in legislative matters and the face-to-face meetings with members that had been the norm. While he made demands on the legislature, he was unwilling to devote time to building support for his programs and was unwilling to wheel and deal with the members. Legislators were puzzled and often frustrated by this behavior. Finally, when revenue shortfalls occurred, he assumed full responsibility for deciding on the cutbacks that should be made, rather than calling special sessions either to make budget cuts or to increase taxes. Some legislators felt that these tactics eroded legislative authority over the budget; however, some were also relieved that they were spared the responsibility of making these politically unpopular decisions.

The 1983 Election

There were three major candidates in the 1983 Democratic gubernatorial primary: Martha Layne Collins, who had been elected lieutenant governor in 1979 after serving four years in the elected position of clerk of the court of appeals; Harvey Sloane, who was serving a second nonconsecutive term as mayor of Louisville and who had run second to Brown in the 1979 gubernatorial primary; and Grady Stumbo, who had served as secretary of Human Resources during most of Brown's administration. Collins won the primary with 34 percent of the vote, only 4,500 votes ahead of Sloane, who received 33 percent of the vote, while Stumbo was a close third with 30 percent of the vote.

There were two major elements to Collins's campaign. She followed the traditional pattern of Kentucky politics, building a strong personal organization at the county level and expanding the organization she had developed in her two previous statewide campaigns. She was particularly able to attract support from local leaders who were frustrated by Governor Brown's policy of benign neglect of the party organization and local leaders. Collins made it clear that she preferred to return to more traditional ways of governing the state. The second element in the Collins campaign was a skillful and expensive media campaign. She proved to be an effective performer in television ads, and they were used extensively throughout the state. This large-scale advertising campaign was possible because the Collins organization raised and spent $2.6 million for the primary campaign. This was an unusually high level of spending for a statewide race in Kentucky and was about a half-million more than Harvey Sloane spent in his race. Collins's husband Bill, a dentist, played a major role in the fund raising.

Collins's campaign was not heavily issue oriented. In her speeches and advertisements she emphasized her experience in government and her role as a kind of ombudsman in the lieutenant governor's office. She repeatedly told the voters that she had been to all 120 counties, knew their people, and understood their problems. She advocated improvements in education and programs to raise the standards of teaching and learning, but she carefully avoided any commitments to large-scale increases in spending for education. Although most observers and some legislative leaders believed that very few new programs for education or anything else could be adopted in the state without tax increases, she insisted that new taxes were unnecessary and undesirable. All of the gubernatorial candidates agreed that tax increases should be avoided.

In his first campaign for governor, Harvey Sloane was generally perceived to be a liberal and a reformer. His close second-place finish to John Y. Brown in 1979 and his election to a new term as mayor of Louisville made him the apparent front runner in the 1983 primary. In addition, he picked up considerable support from established political and business leaders. However, Sloane made two decisions on issue positions during the primary campaign that probably cost him the nomination by alienating two of his natural constituencies. First, he refused to take a stand against a right-to-work bill in Kentucky, and as a consequence most of the unions shifted their support to Grady Stumbo. Second, he fully endorsed the position of antiabortionists, upsetting some of the women most active in state politics. He was also handicapped by a speaking style, in commercials and personal appearances, which many thought was less than dynamic. Many observers also felt that he was never able to weaken or eliminate the widespread perception that he was a "Louisville candidate" rather than a "statewide candidate."

Grady Stumbo started the primary race far behind Collins and Sloane, but ended up with 30 percent of the vote. Stumbo, like Sloane, was a physician by profession; however, unlike Sloane he had never run for political office. He was running a health clinic in eastern Kentucky when Governor Brown brought him into the administration as secretary of Human Resources. He was an articulate and effective public speaker and did well in debates with the other candidates. After a slow start, he spent over $1.1 million, nearly all of it in the last few weeks of the campaign. As expected, he won support from eastern Kentucky and from most unions.

Grady Stumbo also won support from Governor Brown; however, it may have become overt too late to win him the nomination. Although Brown's preference for Stumbo was generally known, it was only eight days before the primary that the governor publicly announced his strong support for Stumbo and started a whirlwind campaign for him across the state, while his associates helped to raise money for the campaign. Brown's support presumably helped Stumbo gain ground late in the campaign, but there is no way of knowing whether earlier support from Brown could have given Stumbo a victory.

The general election, as is often the case in Kentucky, was an anticlimax. The Republican Party carried on an extensive search for a candidate and was rejected by several prominent members of the party before state senator Jim Bunning, after first turning down the offer, agreed to run. Bunning, who was best known as a major league pitcher with a perfect game to his credit, lost to Collins by more than 100,000 votes. He was handicapped by a late start, a shortage of funds, a conservative legislative record, a perception as being a cold and distant figure from northern Kentucky, and as holding an ambivalent attitude toward the Brown administration. (He alternated between attacking Brown's administration and claiming that Collins would undermine the reforms accomplished by Brown.)

The themes and techniques of Martha Layne Collins's fall campaign were similar to those used in the primary. She emphasized personal style and qualifications and deemphasized issues. Once again she ran an extensive television campaign. The campaign organization raised another $2.25 million for the general election and ended the campaign with a surplus of more than a quarter-million dollars, which was later donated to the state party to pay off the debt on its state headquarters building. Collins was helped by the fact that she had the support of the defeated candidates and all elements of the Democratic Party—a situation that Democratic candidates have not always enjoyed.

The New Governor

Martha Layne Collins was the first woman governor elected in Kentucky and only the third in the nation to be elected without having succeeded her husband in office. She was forty-seven years old at the time of her inauguration, December 13. A former school teacher, Collins was the mother of two grown children. She got her start in politics as a campaign worker, and after years of work on behalf of other candidates, especially U.S. senator Wendell Ford, she decided to campaign for herself. In her first race in 1975 she was elected clerk of the court of appeals. Though the office is relatively unimportant and almost invisible (and is no longer elective), her statewide campaign enabled her to build an organization and develop some name familiarity with the voters.

In 1979 she defeated three opponents in the Democratic primary for the nomination for lieutenant governor, getting 31 percent of the vote and winning by a margin of 3,300 votes, and then easily won the general election. As is usually the pattern, Governor Brown gave her no significant role to play in his administration, so she spent most of her term serving as an ombudsman in Frankfort, making speeches and establishing personal contacts around the state. She had an unusually large number of opportunities for such activities because Governor Brown showed little interest in local visits and speeches and spent considerable time outside the state.

As lieutenant governor Collins presided over the senate competently but generally kept a low profile in legislative matters. She did not try to use her position to influence the selection of committees or the outcome of legislation, and only rarely did she cast a tie-breaking vote. She wisely avoided taking actions that might embarrass Governor Brown when he was out of the state and she was acting governor. In short, she was as cautious and low-profile in governmental matters as she was active and visible in public relations and politics. Her experience as lieutenant governor had prepared her well to run a successful campaign for governor; it was less obvious that it had given her the experience needed to serve in that office.

The Administrative Transition

After the election Governor-elect Collins set up a transition team based on existing cabinets (e.g., a Finance Group, a Transportation Group, a Natural Resources Group, etc.).[1] The groups varied in their tasks and their levels of activity. All of the groups included members of the campaign team while some groups included a few members of the Brown administration and members of previous administrations. Although the groups varied in activity level, all were primarily involved in issues of organizational structure and the philosophy and priorities for the new administration. The groups were not involved in budgetary issues, and discussions about personnel involved only types of persons and qualifications needed for particular positions. Task force reports to the governor-elect did not include names of individuals to be considered. Names could be submitted using other means, and the "nominations" were considered by Collins and a small number of close advisers.

Collins moved quickly in naming a transition team and on November 11 announced the appointment of six key cabinet secretaries. Most of the rest of her major appointments were not announced until December 9, just before the inauguration.

Of Collins's first six cabinet-level appointments, one was a holdover from the Brown administration (the only black cabinet secretary in either administration); one was a cousin of Bill Collins, her husband; a third was a leading campaign adviser and strategist; and the remaining three were major fund raisers in the Collins campaign. The four remaining cabinet secretaries included two women, and the man who had been treasurer of the Collins political campaign.

The sensitive post of secretary of Natural Resources and Environmental Protection appeared to be the most difficult to fill and involved the most visible appointment decision. Collins first offered the post to a state senator, who refused it but agreed to head the search committee. This position was one of the few that caused a great deal of public speculation and interest and for which there was spirited competition among a number of applicants. One of these was the incumbent, Jackie Swigert, who had held the job for almost four years. Shortly before the choice was announced, a newspaper story listed eleven major candidates for the job, and described the campaigns being mounted by various groups for and against particular candidates.[2] Among those not on the list of eleven was the eventual nominee: Charlotte Baldwin, the mayor of a small town in western Kentucky, a state co-chairwoman of the Collins campaign, and a member of the transition task force for Natural Resources and Environmental Protection.

Questions were raised about Baldwin's knowledge and experience in environmental affairs, but Larry Hayes, the secretary of the cabinet-designate, stated that her lack of technical expertise would be made up for by her experience in management as mayor of Madisonville. Since this cabinet deals with coal mining and regulation of the environment, it is one of the more visible and controversial agencies in the state. One person involved in the search was quoted by the *Courier-Journal* as saying, "I don't believe the Natural Resources and Environmental Protection Cabinet is a place to enhance your popularity." [3]

Not surprisingly, Governor Collins was criticized because so many of her major appointments were drawn from persons who had been active in her campaign, particularly as fund raisers, and/or because they had little apparent experience in the areas of their employment. Even those with previous experience in Frankfort were criticized as having been part of the traditional patronage system. Some of Collins's statements during the campaign had suggested that she intended to restore at least some features of the traditional patronage system, and her critics perceived many of her appointments as a return to a system of patronage and cronyism.

By contrast, Governor Brown had campaigned against old-style politics and the patronage system, arguing that government should be "run like a business." Few of Governor Brown's appointees were traditional politicians, and many of them were businessmen, including some very able individuals who were personal friends of the governor. Brown's success at holding the line on government spending, cutting state employment, and placing businessmen in government all helped to solidify the image of a nonpolitical, businesslike administration.

With a few exceptions, such as the Natural Resources position, it appears that Governor-elect Collins and the transition team did not conduct extensive searches for persons to fill key administrative positions. These jobs were filled by persons in a close circle of supporters, some of whom were personal friends of the new governor or her husband and most of whom had held positions in the election campaign; many of these persons were identified publicly before the election as being in line for major positions.

The transition to a new administration was relatively smooth. One reason may be the fact that many of the key appointees had worked closely together and with the new governor during the campaign; another reason is that a number of them had had previous experience in Frankfort. As soon as they were named key officials, they found desks and moved into offices to begin preparing for the new administration before the inauguration. There was relative stability in the Brown administration during its closing months, and leading members of that administration worked closely with their successors to make the transition successful.

The Collins administration (unlike its predecessor) had no goals requiring fundamental changes in the way government was run. There were no major, open disputes between the outgoing and incoming administrations, and there appeared to be a high degree of cooperation between them. This was particularly true in the budgetary process.

Development of the 1984–1986 Budget

As in the past, the budgetary transition process began well before the inauguration of a new governor in December 1983. Prior to the fall election, two events occurred that made the 1984–86 process quite different from previous budget cycles. For the first time, a new governor would be faced with having to submit a biennial budget in mid-to-late January, a little over one month after being inaugurated. This change was a result of HB 649 passed in the 1982 General Assembly, which, among other things, revised the statutory basis for the state budget process and was part of an evolving effort to increase the role of the legislature vis-à-vis the executive in the budgetary process. The specific part of HB 649 relating to the timing of the budgetary process was a requirement that the newly elected governor's first biennial budget must be submitted to the General Assembly on the fifteenth legislative day of the first legislative session.

The other major factor influencing the budgetary process was a case before the Kentucky Supreme Court: *Legislative Research Commission* vs. *Brown*. This "friendly suit," which raised major issues of separation of powers between the executive and legislative branches, was the result of the numerous pieces of legislation passed by the 1982 General Assembly that enhanced the power of the Legislative Research Commission (LRC, in effect, the interim legislature) and thereby reduced the power and prerogatives of the executive branch. Because the separation of powers case had not been decided (and was not decided until January 19, 1984), the budget office and the LRC were operating under unusual conditions of uncertainty and ambiguity.[4]

Although numerous issues regarding control of the budgetary process remained unresolved, in June 1983 the state budget office—the Office for Policy and Management (OPM)—issued executive budget instructions to state agencies. These budget instructions in draft form had been sent to the LRC (actually a subcommittee of the Appropriations and Revenue Committee) in late April–early May, and a series of meetings were held between legislative and executive officials to discuss these draft instructions. After these meetings, the legislative representatives sent their version of the budget instructions to OPM. The two sets of instructions differed in only minimal respects, but OPM issued one set of executive budget instructions to state agencies in June. These instructions incorporated certain ideas and suggestions from the legislature, but were executive rather than legislative budget instructions. In effect, the two parties to the dispute agreed to disagree. Because of the bleak financial picture (discussed below), the instructions to the agencies were very conservative and assumed there would be no tax increases, no new programs or expansion of existing services, and limited increases for salaries and certain other cost items.

Finally, the 1984–86 budgetary process was influenced significantly by the existing revenue or fiscal environment of the state. In fiscal year 1984, for the seventh year since fiscal year 1976, the state faced a revenue shortfall. To make a complicated story somewhat simple: General Fund expenditures had exceeded General Fund receipts almost every year since 1976. The state had managed to maintain a balanced budget under these conditions by spending existing surpluses; transferring special, agency-specific funds into the General Fund; imposing a series of job freezes; and making severe cuts in the work force and operating budgets of state agencies. It is also important to note that during this period Kentucky was experiencing large reductions in federal funding, which also had a serious impact on a number of state agencies. The severe revenue problems continued throughout the latter part of 1983 and into 1984.

Against this backdrop of revenue problems and disputes over the roles of the executive and legislative branches in the budgetary process, executive agencies conducted planning and analysis of program needs and then submitted budget requests to the OPM in September. The OPM began conducting preliminary reviews of these agency requests at about the same time that preliminary General Fund revenue estimates were issued by the Revenue Cabinet (October 15, 1984).

The OPM schedule called for an executive budget to be prepared by December 1. A communication from the state budget director to outgoing governor Brown in early December indicated that, after extensive review and analysis, a "comprehensive budget information data-base" was now available to the incoming administration. The communication spelled out the many assumptions underlying the fiscal year 84 budget and the actions that had been taken to balance it, highlighted the fiscal problems of the past and potential problems in the future, and indicated that the budget analysis and preliminary budget options were based on the October 15 preliminary revenue estimates, which could be further revised by January 1984 revenue estimates.

The Collins administration chose as its budget director Gordon Duke, who had previously held that position during the administration of Julian Carroll (who immediately preceded Brown) and therefore had the experience and knowledge to help effect a smooth transition from a Brown budget to a Collins budget. There was no shortage of budgetary experience or information confronting the Collins administration; however, there was a shortage of revenue.

The new administration began its work on the budget the day after Thanksgiving, when Governor-elect Collins held her first meeting with the OPM staff. She made it clear that her strategy was to produce a balanced budget without any tax increases. Collins took office on December 13, and during the next few weeks she and her aides struggled with the problems of determining budgetary priorities. They sought to find ways of rearranging priorities in order to provide at least a modest increase in funding for education. By mid-January work had been completed on a no-tax budget for the next biennium.

Then the revenue roof fell in. On January 13 Collins was informed by the revenue secretary that the new revenue projections for the biennium were $132 million less than had been predicted in mid-October. The reduction in the anticipated revenue growth, combined with the need to repay agency funds that had been borrowed during the ongoing biennium, meant that the Collins administration would have very little new revenue during the following two years to pay for salary increases, meet the inevitable growth in fixed costs, or do anything for education.

On January 15 Collins met with her top advisers to review the new revenue projections and discuss alternatives for revising the budget. By the end of the day she had decided to scrap the budget that had already been completed and to develop a package of tax increases. Moreover, Collins decided that if tax increases were necessary, they should be large enough to make possible some significant improvements in education, not just the minimum necessary for balancing the budget.

In evaluating the budgetary process during the transition, we can conclude that it operated smoothly in a bureaucratic sense. The legislative-executive conflict over sharing power, which was about to be settled in court, created no significant problems for the new administration. The legislative requirement that the governor submit a budget early in the legislative session did put significant pressure on the governor to make decisions quickly. But the major difficulties faced by the Collins administration resulted from the prolonged, severe shortage of revenue and the disclosure in mid-January that the fiscal recovery during the next biennium would be slower than had been anticipated.[5]

The Governor and the Legislature

During her campaign for office, Martha Layne Collins did not propose any extensive legislative agenda, although she suggested a number of reforms that were necessary in the field of education. In the short period of time between her election and the start of the 1984 legislative session, she did not develop a legislative program. She was preoccupied, first, with making appointments to office and, second, with the budgetary crisis. Governor Brown had asked the executive agencies to prepare proposals to be submitted to the 1984 legislature, but no systematic effort was made by the Collins administration to put together a package of such proposals.

Governor Collins's state of the commonwealth address on January 5 contained two major themes: there was a statewide consensus on the need for reform in education, and "we must find ways of improving our schools that don't take vast sums of money." The governor painted a discouraging picture of the state's financial situation: "No legislature or governor since the Depression has had so little money available to pursue the policies needed to make life better for all Kentuckians."[6] She said that "no windfall of money will be available to solve our problems in education." She suggested a number of steps that could be taken to raise educational standards without large increases in spending and promised to make specific legislative proposals shortly.

The pressures for educational reform in Kentucky had been building for some time. A series of national studies over the previous year had documented shortcomings in elementary and secondary education, and several of these studies had provided evidence that the problems were worse in Kentucky than in most states. On the day that Collins delivered her pessimistic state of the commonwealth address, the U.S. Department of Education released data on the rankings of the fifty states. Under a front-page headline, "State schools near bottom in U.S. ranking," the *Lexington Herald-Leader* reported that Kentucky was tied for forty-sixth place in pupil expenditures and was forty-fourth in pupil-teacher ratios and in the proportion of ninth graders graduating from high school.[7]

At the beginning of the legislative session, the House and Senate Education Committees sponsored a forum for legislators on educational reform that emphasized the progress being made in other border and southern states. At the meeting and in talks around the state, the new Kentucky superintendent of public instruction urged the legislature to give priority to education reform. Later in the month a statewide "Excellence in Education Task Force" issued a report that proposed a broad range of reforms and urged tax increases to pay for them. A statewide public opinion poll released in mid-January by the University of Kentucky Survey Research Center showed that the proportion of citizens ranking education as one of the state's most important issues had doubled in two years (up to one-third) and that a very narrow majority of those with an opinion on the issue would support a tax increase to help education.

In mid-January, once Collins had decided to seek a tax increase and channel much of the new funding into education, she began to construct the full-scale program of educational reform that she was to propose on January 26 along with her budget message. Although little time was available to develop such a proposal, there was no shortage of specific suggestions available. She relied heavily on specific proposals already developed by the Interim Education Committee of the legislature, the superintendent of public instruction, and the Excellence in Education Task Force.

In her budget message to the General Assembly on January 25 Governor Collins proposed tax increases that would total $324 million in the biennium, in order to make possible $298 million in new spending for primary and secondary education. Most of the increases would come in the second year. Her education proposals included increased funding for remedial instruction in the first three grades; mandatory kindergartens; more funding for poorer school districts; a 5 percent pay increase for teachers in each year; and a career ladder program for teachers, to begin in 1985, designed to reward the best teachers with higher salaries. She also proposed a number of steps to make the education system more accountable, such as testing the competency of teachers and reviewing the performance of school administrators.

The governor's tax program was changed several times during the session as she reacted to criticisms of specific proposals and tried to find a combination of increases that could command support and produce the necessary revenue. The administration's final tax package was introduced late in the session. The chairman of the House Appropriations and Revenue Committee made it clear that he would not try to gain approval for the administration's tax program unless it could pass the house. On March 19 the house Democratic caucus discussed the tax program and then took a secret ballot on it; the results showed only thirty-two votes for the plan and thirty-three against, with the remainder undecided or not voting. The house Republicans had already announced opposition to the plan.

Two days later Governor Collins conceded that she did not have the necessary votes and withdrew her tax program from the legislature. The House and Senate Appropriations and Revenue Committees each drafted "no-tax" budgets, which were approved by the two chambers. The final budget that emerged from the conference committee and was enacted into law largely followed the house version. It is somewhat ironic that, after years of criticisms of the executive budget process being so dominated by the governor and rarely impacted by the legislature, the 1984–86 state budget was developed by ten legislators behind closed doors.

The legislature made cuts in a number of areas and juggled revenue from a variety of funds in order to make possible some new funding for education. The budget provided limited amounts of new funding for mandatory kindergartens, remedial education, school operating funds, and assistance to poorer school districts—with most of the increases postponed to the second year of the biennium. To make some of this funding possible, however, the legislature authorized pay increases for teachers and other employees of only 2 percent for the first year and 3 percent for the second, which were the smallest increases in years. No funding was allocated for a teachers' career ladder, but a committee was established to study and develop such a plan.

The legislature also adopted some important educational reforms that would cost little or nothing. Some were part of the governor's program, and others were strictly legislative initiatives. The legislature required new teachers to pass competency tests and serve a one-year internship, authorized training and evaluation for administrators, required school board members to have a high school education, sought to encourage local funding by permitting local school districts to impose a wider variety of taxes and requiring them to have a minimum property tax, and authorized the Department of Education to take over academically deficient school districts that failed to make improvements.

When the session ended, Governor Collins could claim credit for helping to focus public attention on educational needs, prodding the legislature to adopt some important but inexpensive reforms, and bringing about some small and delayed increases in educational spending (achieved by making cuts in other areas). But she had failed in her efforts to get new taxes that would make possible major new financial support for educational reforms as well as funding for other urgent programs such as prison reform. Why had the governor's tax program failed so completely? What could she have done to gain legislative support for all or a part of it?

There are many answers to these questions. The governor's first liability was that during her primary and general election campaign she had firmly committed herself to oppose tax increases, and consequently she was unable to assert that she had any mandate from the voters to raise taxes. Legislators, who were being asked by Collins to demonstrate political courage by voting for new taxes a few months before their election, resented the fact that she had consistently opposed tax increases in her campaign.

Once she was elected Collins moved too slowly and uncertainly to seek tax increases. The Kentucky legislative session is a relatively brief one; members adjourn at the beginning of April, returning for a couple of days for a veto session before the April 15 constitutional deadline. When the governor was inaugurated in mid-December, only 3½ months remained before the end of the session; when she announced her commitment to new taxes in the budget message, only about nine weeks remained. During this period she changed her specific tax proposals several times in response to objections from legislators and interest groups. When her tax package was finally introduced in the legislature on February 28, only about four and a half weeks remained.

In recent years several southern governors have attracted attention because of their ability to win legislative approval for large-scale increases in educational funding and, in some cases, for their success in gaining adoption of other reforms, such as the career ladder. In none of these states was the legislative victory accomplished in a few months. In every state the governor found it necessary to engage in a long-term, extensive, even exhaustive campaign to win public support. In contrast, Governor Collins took her case to the public in a brief campaign. She sent letters to state newspapers and public service announcements to radio stations. In mid-March she made a speech on public television. She spoke at several forums around the state that were sponsored by education and teachers' groups and attended largely by persons already supporting her program. She rejected proposals for a much larger public-relations campaign, and it could be argued that she simply did not have time to carry out the kind of grassroots, county-by-county speaking campaign that might have been successful.

Collins gained considerable support from the press, but she received surprisingly little specific support from the organized groups that had been urging her to propose a bold tax and education package. As a consequence, legislators received relatively little mail, organized or unorganized, in support of her tax and education programs. In particular, the Kentucky Education Association did not appear to be in the forefront of efforts to win votes for her program. Collins had made two decisions that affected support from teachers. She decided that the priority for spending in education should go to programs rather than to pay salary increases for teachers; and in addition to a 5-percent annual pay increase (no more than in recent years), she advocated a career ladder plan that would not be funded until the second year and that aroused considerable doubts and fears among many teachers. Because of the highly political atmosphere that pervades many of Kentucky's local school systems, particularly in rural areas, teachers had questions about whether criteria for rewarding the "best" teachers would really be based on merit and accomplishment.

Traditionally Kentucky governors have used with great success a variety of techniques to win legislative support for their major programs.

Many of these techniques were not available to Collins, and others she failed to utilize effectively. Unlike the governors who preceded John Y. Brown, she was unable to select her own leaders or committee chairmen; under the new legislative schedule they had been in office for a year before the session. Because the budget was so tight, it would have been difficult for her to promise legislators projects in their districts in return for their votes. Because she did not have full control of the legislature, she was also unable to hold up the passage of bills authored by particular members until those legislators had agreed to support her budget and tax program.

While recognizing that Collins lacked some of the resources employed by her predecessors, many legislators privately criticized her for ineffectiveness in dealing with the legislature. The criticisms extended beyond her handling of the budget and tax program to other legislation. The most frequent complaint was that no one on her staff or among her top administrators understood the legislative process or had firsthand familiarity with members of the legislature, although she had close working relationships with several senate leaders, particularly President Pro Tem Joe Prather. This lack of experienced aides was considered a particularly serious problem because Collins did not have personal experience as a legislator. During her term as lieutenant governor she had not played a very active role in the legislative process. Members complained that the administration often failed to take a clear, unified position on issues, and that legislators often had to alert the governor's office to bills that would create problems for it. On several occasions her office seemed to be unable or unwilling to control agency heads who were working for or against particular pieces of legislation without coordinating their strategy with the governor. (Later in the session her office made efforts to develop better coordination and legislative planning.)

Members also complained about the governor's inaccessibility; individual legislators often found it difficult to get appointments with her. She rarely called them or asked them to visit the office. During the final stages of her campaign for the tax program, Governor Collins called most Democrats to her office for one-on-one meetings, but it appears that she was not very effective in either bargaining with or persuading the members.

The governor used public pressure tactics on only a few occasions in an effort to generate support for her tax plan. She announced a series of cutbacks that would be necessary if the tax increase failed, including the elimination of all pay increases for teachers and faculty members, wage freezes and substantial layoffs for public employees, and the elimination of a number of projects promised in various parts of the state. These tactics seemed to arouse more resentment than support, particularly among legislators in Jefferson County, where she threatened to eliminate several programs including the long-promised renovation of Freedom Hall, about to begin. In the last analysis these threats turned out to be hollow because it was the legislature rather than the governor that determined what programs would actually be included in a "no-tax" budget.

Collins could not be expected to have working relations as close to the leaders as some of her predecessors had enjoyed after having the opportunity to select leaders. She met with them no more than once a week during the session, primarily to discuss her tax and education programs. The governor's relationships with legislative leaders varied with the chamber. Senate President Pro Tem Joe Prather had been her campaign chairman, and she had also chosen him to be state party chairman. The majority leader, Joe Wright, and several of the other leaders had been close to her politically. Therefore, she had no problem in working with the senate, and it was expected that she could have won passage for her tax program in that senate had it gotten that far.

Speaker of the House Bobby Richardson served as campaign manager for one of Collins's opponents (Harvey Sloane) during the gubernatorial primary, and during the fall campaign he had irritated her by proposing a constitutional amendment to abolish the office of lieutenant governor. Nevertheless, he supported her tax program and worked for it in the house. At the same time, the house leadership was weakened by a factional split. The speaker pro tem, Donald Blandford, had spread the word that he might challenge Richardson for the position of speaker in the next session, and the other three leaders were divided between the two, with only floor leader Jim LeMaster clearly allied with Richardson. Legislators were divided in their opinion of whether this disunity helped to explain the lack of support for the governor in the house. But Blandford was opposed to the tax package, and some of the other opposition to it came from his allies. It is certainly safe to say that Richardson did not have the political power he would have needed to pressure his colleagues into supporting the tax program.

One other major obstacle to passage of the governor's tax package was the fact that, because of the constitutional amendment adopted in 1979 (mentioned above), members of the house faced elections in 1984, starting with a primary in late May. When the amendment was adopted by the legislature and voters, little consideration was given to the political vulnerability of members who might have to vote for unpopular measures, such as tax increases, a few months before an election. This was especially important for those sessions in which a newly elected governor would be seeking support for his or her program only to be faced by a legislature whose members were more concerned with their upcoming elections. The representatives' sensitivity to elections was shown in the 1982 session, when they voted to move the primary from May to August, and again in 1984, when they voted to move it back to May but to schedule the filing date early enough so that members would know what opposition they faced before voting on tough issues at the end of the session. Veteran legislators believed that the 1984 session was more dominated by political and electoral considerations than normally was the case.

Given all the obstacles to passage of the governor's tax package, it is not difficult to understand why it failed. It may be harder to see why the governor thought it could be passed. However, knowledgeable observers feel that the tax package was only a few votes short of passage in the house and had majority support in the senate. Some observers believed that Governor Collins was laying the groundwork for a longer-term effort that might produce results in a special session in 1985, when legislative elections were in the past and more support might be generated for the program.

The governor's attention was devoted almost entirely to the tax and education program, and she was not identified with any other major pieces of legislation that were taken up during the session. The most controversial of these bills was a multibanking bill to permit bank holding companies to own more than one bank and to operate across county lines. As lieutenant governor she had opposed it and cast a vote against it when the senate vote was tied. As governor she remained neutral and let it become law without her signature, though it was reported that some high officials in her administration were working for it.

Summary and Conclusions

In attempting to summarize the 1983–84 gubernatorial transition in Kentucky, it is useful to divide the period into two phases: the immediate phase from the election to the inauguration (November–December)

and the secondary phase from the inauguration to the end of the legislative session (December–April). These two phases differed in many
ways.

The period from the electoral victory to inauguration was relatively
quiet and uneventful. Friends of Governor-elect Collins and key members of the campaign team were designated relatively quickly as appointees to most cabinet positions in the new administration. Task
forces mirroring the cabinet structure of state government were set up
to develop priorities and organizational structure for the incoming administration, and meetings were held between the governor-elect, her
major advisers, and the staff of the state budget office, who had been
working for months on the 1984–86 budget.

In more mundane terms, work space and assistance were provided to
the transition team, and there were no reports of lost or shredded files
or records, no changed locks, or other surprises. There are a variety of
reasons why the first phase of the transition was problem free, but the
three most important factors were the stated desire of the outgoing governor to effect a smooth transition, the involvement of certain veteran
state officials in the Collins transition team, and the apparent desire by
the incoming administration not to seek major changes in the operation
of state government. The stage was set for an uneventful but productive
legislative session.

In contrast to the smoothness of the immediate transition, the period
from the inauguration through the end of Governor Collins's first legislative session was difficult and disappointing. The downward revision
of the official revenue estimates in mid-January was the event which
triggered the change from an uncomplicated, quiet transition to a difficult, problematic transition. After campaigning on a platform of no new
taxes and working on a continuation budget based on October revenue
estimates, the new governor was confronted with a newly projected
revenue shortfall that posed serious problems for the commonwealth.
From January through the end of the legislative session Collins and the
legislature struggled to develop a legislative program (primarily in education) and a tax package that would support an ambitious education
reform package.

Observers disagree in evaluating the accomplishments of the new
administration and the 1984 General Assembly. Although some needed
reforms in education were adopted, the governor was criticized by
some observers for her inability to achieve major educational reform

supported by needed revenue. However, Collins faced a number of problems in dealing with the legislature, most of which will confront her successors: severe revenue constraints, the requirement to present a budget early in the session and soon after the inauguration, the increased experience and professionalism of the General Assembly, and legislative independence from the governor. On the other hand, some veteran observers of state government marvel at how quietly and quickly the executive–legislative balance has changed. A legislature that used to approve a gubernatorial budget in a few days without so much as a change in punctuation has now forced a governor to withdraw her budget and tax package and has drafted and adopted its own budget.

The new political and fiscal realities in Kentucky will probably force future governors who seek major reforms to adopt new strategies and timetables. Instead of pursuing quick legislative victories in the first few months of an administration, they will need to lay the groundwork for reform more carefully, build a stronger base of public support for their programs (preferably starting during the election campaign), work closely with legislators, and perhaps make more use of special sessions of the legislature to cope with the more difficult issues.

The Norm of Standing Aside: Gubernatorial Transition in Missouri in 1984

)))))

Dean L. Yarwood and
Richard J. Hardy

> I left the "Tums." They may be of use to you. I doubt
> I'll need them anymore. Good luck.—A note left by a
> member of Governor Teasdale's senior staff for his
> successor in the Bond administration who, in turn, left
> it for his successor in the Ashcroft administration.

January 14, 1985, dawned chilly. A brisk northern wind cut through
the rolling hills of Jefferson City, biting sharply at those who braved the
elements. It was no day to be sitting idly in the open air attending political rites of passage, with the accompanying oaths, exhortations, and
promises; but that is what 5,000 Missourians, shivering under blankets
and extra garments, did. This was the day that John Ashcroft was to
become the forty-eighth governor of Missouri and the first Republican
to succeed a Republican in that office since 1928. If the weather was
any harbinger, it would be a difficult transition. In fact, the transition
had been, and would continue to be, exceptionally smooth.

The inauguration, along with the associated festivities, is a part
of gubernatorial transition, the ceremonial component—if you will—
marking the orderly transferal or renewal of public authority. The term
"gubernatorial transition" itself is much broader, encompassing the
period from the primaries through the end of the first legislative session,
and it applies to cases in which gubernatorial authority changes hands.
During this time, the new governor secures the endorsement of his or

her political party, wins a majority (usually) of the votes cast by the citizens of the state, and sets about trying to establish control over the instruments of state government. This essay focuses on the transition in Missouri in 1984.

The 1984 Gubernatorial Contest

Partisan Balance

Gubernatorial transition begins with the contest for public office. Missouri is a modified two-party state, with Democrats generally holding the electoral edge over Republicans in most local, statewide, and congressional races. In the Missouri General Assembly, for example, Democrats have held a majority in the house since 1952 and a majority in the senate since 1946. Historically, Democrats have also controlled those state offices that are contested statewide; besides the governor, these include the lieutenant governor, attorney general, secretary of state, treasurer, and auditor. In addition, Democrats have held a majority in Missouri's congressional delegation since 1946. A significant change on the Missouri electoral stage has been the emergence of a number of young Republican stars since the late 1960s. These attractive GOP candidates, who have been able to successfully challenge Democrats statewide, include John Danforth, Christopher Bond, James Antonio, and John Ashcroft, among others.

The historical migration patterns in Missouri are an important part of the political setting of gubernatorial politics. Traditionally, the regions of the state that have voted solidly Republican have been the western Ozarks, settled primarily by Scotch-Irish, who opposed slavery during the Civil War; the northwestern "cornbelt," comprised mainly of midwestern immigrants who favored the Republican party's post–Civil War agricultural policies; and the "Rhineland," or lower Missouri Valley, which was settled mostly by German immigrants. Democrats have garnered their strongest support from the "Bootheel," or southwest lowlands, settled primarily by southerners who were attracted to cotton-growing land along the Mississippi River; the eastern Ozarks, settled mainly by southerners farming small tracts of land; the west-central region, comprised of midwestern immigrants; "Little Dixie," in the upper Missouri Valley, settled by Virginians and Kentuckians whose sympathies were for the South in the Civil War; and large cities, namely

St. Louis and Kansas City, which contain large blocs of voters that traditionally support the Democratic Party—blacks, union members, Catholics, and Jews.[1]

The Candidates

The Missouri Constitution guaranteed that the 1984 election would be followed by the inauguration of a new governor. Christopher "Kit" Bond was completing his second term in the governor's mansion and was ineligible for another term. Though it was generally conceded that in the future he would run for another office, he was temporarily leaving public life.

The leading Democratic candidate was Lieutenant Governor Kenneth Rothman. A native of St. Louis, the 49-year-old Rothman had earned the reputation of being a fair, competent, and tough-minded politician. After graduating from Washington University Law School, he served as assistant prosecutor in St. Louis County. Rothman was first elected to the Missouri house in 1962, where he rose through the ranks to become house majority leader and speaker.[2]

Rothman earned the right to represent the Democratic Party as its gubernatorial candidate by soundly defeating six rivals in the August primary, including state treasurer Mel Carnahan and state senator Norman Merrell. In all, he won 56 percent of the vote and carried 82 of the state's 114 counties. As expected, Rothman did well in metropolitan counties, winning 78 percent of the vote in St. Louis City and County and 71 percent in Jackson County. In addition, he did surprisingly well in rural counties where he was not expected to win.[3] Rothman's greater name-recognition undoubtedly helped him defeat his primary opponents. Also important was the fact that his campaign was better organized and financed. Rothman spent about $816,000 in the primary, more than his two closest rivals combined.[4]

Unfortunately for Rothman, the Democratic primary was divisive. Much bitterness surfaced during the campaign, especially between Rothman on the one hand and Carnahan and Merrell on the other. Carnahan did offer to bury the hatchet on primary election night, but Merrell remained unplacated. Merrell's wife, for example, credited the St. Louis, Kansas City, and Columbia newspapers for Rothman's success. "The press wanted to nominate a Jewish Governor [Rothman]," she said, "and they did."[5]

John Ashcroft, the 42-year-old state attorney general, projected an image in stark contrast to Rothman's. Known as a straight arrow, this piano-playing, gospel-singing conservative often referred to his bedrock religious faith and traditional values. Although an honors graduate of Yale University and the University of Chicago Law School, he punctuated his conversation with "dad gum" and "shucks," a trait endearing to rural Missourians.

Upon completing his law degree, Ashcroft returned to Springfield, where he practiced law and was an associate professor on the business faculty of Southwest Missouri State University. In 1973 he was appointed state auditor. Defeated in his bid for election as auditor in his own right, in 1975 he was appointed assistant attorney general. In 1976 he was elected attorney general, where he served for eight years. Interestingly, Ashcroft won reelection in 1980 by winning 64.5 percent of the vote and carrying 96 percent of Missouri's counties.[6]

Ashcroft won the right to square off against Rothman by defeating Gene McNary, the St. Louis County executive, in a hard-fought August primary. Although McNary outspent Ashcroft by $1.6 million to $1.5 million, he netted only 32 percent of the vote. That was about $13.46 per vote![7] Ashcroft's campaign produced a controversial television ad that showed a court document filed in the St. Louis school desegregation case, which was utilized to depict McNary as supporting forced busing. On the evening of the primary, Tracy Mehan, McNary's campaign manager, complained that Ashcroft's "very effective, well-financed negative campaign (on busing) gave a reason to a lot of undecided voters to switch back to the Ashcroft side."[8] Unlike the Democrats, however, the Republicans for the most part united after the primary, a factor that worked to Ashcroft's advantage in the general election.

The Campaign

The general election campaign was in full swing by Labor Day. Ashcroft got out of the blocks quickly, establishing himself as the front runner. Statewide polls taken in September showed him with a six-percentage-point lead.[9] A great deal of the campaign centered on image. Rothman, portrayed as the tough, Jewish lawyer from St. Louis, was pitted against Ashcroft, the good-looking conservative from the Bible Belt of southwest Missouri. There was definitely a metropolitan versus outstate aspect to the campaign.

Battlelines were also drawn on several issues. On social issues, Rothman came out strongly in favor of the Equal Rights Amendment and comparable worth, but was "pro-life" on the abortion issue. Ashcroft emphatically opposed the Equal Rights Amendment and comparable worth, and said he would support a constitutional amendment to prohibit abortions. On economic issues, Rothman opposed the Hancock Amendment, which placed a lid on state spending, and supported the proposed state lottery that was to be voted on in the November ballot. Concerning Hancock, Ashcroft said "we can live with this amendment," and regarding the state lottery, he opposed it on moral grounds, but said he would comply with the will of the people. To the surprise of no one, neither candidate advocated increasing state taxes.[10]

The most important issues, however, centered on education. Both candidates pledged to make education their top priority by increasing school appropriations, improving test scores, and raising teachers' salaries to the national average. However, they differed on how to achieve these results. Rothman opposed career ladders for teachers and teacher competency examinations. In his words, "I want to test students, not teachers."[11] This position pleased Missouri's teachers' associations, especially the Missouri State Teacher's Association, the Missouri National Educational Association, and the American Federation of Teachers. Ashcroft, for his part, said he favored some form of teacher competency testing, and proposed establishing a Master Teacher Career Ladder Program. In addition, he advocated more discipline in the schools and greater interaction among schools, the business community, and volunteers, especially retired persons.[12]

Unfortunately, most of these issues were obscured by negative campaigning on both sides. One of Rothman's television ads criticized Ashcroft's role as attorney general in the wording of Proposition B, a November ballot issue designed to limit the rate increases Union Electric Company (UE) could charge its customers for costs incurred in building the controversial Callaway nuclear plant. It showed a *St. Louis Post-Dispatch* headline criticizing Ashcroft and saying that Proposition B looked as though it had been drafted "in the board room of UE." Though negative in its message, the ad appeared to be positive in results, as polls showed Rothman pulling even with Ashcroft.[13]

Not to be outdone, Ashcroft returned fire with two negative television ads of his own. The first charged that Rothman had neglected his duty as lieutenant governor by missing three out of four days as presiding officer of the senate; it also drew attention to the fact that Rothman was absent when a tie-breaking vote was needed to pass $11 million in education funds. The other ad attacked Rothman for sponsoring, as speaker of the house, the 1977 pay hike for legislators. It made it appear as though he had voted himself a pay raise. Again negative campaigning appeared effective, as Ashcroft regained a commanding lead of eleven points or more in statewide polls.[14]

Belligerence between Rothman and Ashcroft reached the boiling point during the second and last of their televised debates sponsored by the League of Women Voters. One reporter likened the debate to "two alley cats [scrapping] over truth in advertising."[15] Rothman began by criticizing the Bond administration for the loss of 80,000 Missouri jobs, then he associated Ashcroft with Bond. Said Rothman, "John [is] Kit Bond's protégé; everyone knows that."[16] Ashcroft countered, citing figures that showed a net increase of 129,000 jobs during the same period.

Attention turned to the negative campaign ads, with Rothman firing the first salvo. "The campaign of my opponent has dropped into the gutter of distortion, half-truths and untruths."[17] Concerning the charge that he had voted himself a pay raise, Rothman said, "The truth is, I supported salary recommendations made by Governor Bond's non-partisan citizen's commission which includes a $20,000 raise for the Attorney General—a raise which was larger than my entire salary!" "John," Rothman glared at Ashcroft, "you're a hypocrite."[18] He then refuted the second commercial that depicted him as ignoring his duties as lieutenant governor. Noted Rothman, "He [Ashcroft] doesn't mention that presiding over Senate is strictly a ceremonial part of my job."[19] Ashcroft responded by saying, "the facts in the ad are true. . . . When you have a responsibility of casting votes in tie situations on very important matters, I don't think you can call or characterize that responsibility as totally ceremonial."[20]

With one week remaining before the general election, Ashcroft held a comfortable lead in the polls. At a news conference on October 31, he confidently predicted his first week's schedule as governor-elect. "On Wednesday morning after the election I'll begin the process of transition government. I'll work through Saturday and then take a few days' rest."[21] Nonetheless, Halloween of 1984 had to conjure up the spectre of the "ghost of '76" for Ashcroft. In that year Governor Bond had a safe lead in the polls in the closing weeks of the campaign, only to lose in a political upset to "Walkin' Joe" Teasdale, a Kansas City lawyer. To make sure history did not repeat itself, Ashcroft mounted a vigorous, last-minute cross-state campaign. Stumping for Ashcroft in the final days were Representative Jack Kemp (R, N.Y.), U.S. senator John Danforth (R, Mo.), and outgoing governor Kit Bond.[22]

Election Results

Shortly before the November sixth election, John Ashcroft said he expected "to win in central Missouri, St. Louis County, in Southwest Missouri, north of the Missouri River, and south of the Missouri River."[23] Results far exceeded his expectations. Ashcroft won 57 percent of the vote and carried 107 counties, making it the largest Republican gubernatorial victory in the state's history.

All five Republican candidates for statewide offices hailed from southwest Missouri, while three of the Democratic hopefuls were from the St. Louis area. With one exception, Republicans swept all statewide offices. Counting the Republican state auditor who is elected in nonpresidential election years, this gave the GOP five of six statewide offices —the most since 1928. The lone Democrat elected statewide was state Senator Harriett Woods, who won the lieutenant governorship by defeating Springfield businessman Mel Hancock, author of the Hancock Amendment.

Although Republicans did unusually well in the statewide races, Democrats continued to control the state legislature. In the 1985 General Assembly, Democrats controlled 108 of 163 house seats and 21 of 34 senate seats (a net gain of two for the Republicans). That the Republicans failed to make any significant gains in the General Assembly was expected. In fact, Republicans fielded no candidates in seventy-seven house and six senate districts. Republican state chairman Hillard Selck told a *Columbia Daily Tribune* reporter, "We were not gunning for legislative races this time. We dumped our money and we dumped our efforts into the statewide candidates. I don't think we expected to do much more."[24] He vowed it would be different in 1986.

The election that John Ashcroft won was the most expensive gubernatorial election in Missouri's history. According to campaign finance reports filed with the secretary of state's office, total spending in both the primary and general election for governor came to $7.2 million. This amounted to 16.7 percent more than in 1980 and 312 percent more than was spent in 1976 in unadjusted dollars. The general election alone cost Ashcroft $1.5 million while Rothman spent $1.1 million.[25]

While the transition into office was just beginning, some members of the legislature speculated aloud about how effective Ashcroft would be with their branch. Senate president pro tem John Scott (D, St. Louis) wondered about fallout from the bitter campaign and negative ads. "I think John Ashcroft is going to have problems with the legislature. Just talking around, there's a lot of mistrust of John Ashcroft."[26] Others pointed to Ashcroft's lack of legislative experience and the fact that he was an outsider to the General Assembly. Columbia senator Roger Wilson (D) mused, "The historical pattern shows Joe Teasdale and Kit Bond, both [of whom] were out of the structure, had some trouble working with the legislature."[27] Clearly, as the transition moved into its next phase, the governor-elect had his work cut out for him.

Transitions Past

The 1976 Transition

The watershed gubernatorial transition in Missouri in recent decades took place in 1976. That autumn election had pitted incumbent governor Christopher Bond against Democrat Joseph Teasdale. As indicated above, Teasdale upset Bond, overtaking him in the final days of the election with a last-minute media blitz. The ensuing transition, characterized as it was by a lack of preparedness on the part of the governor-elect and a deficiency of cooperation by the outgoing administration, was almost the complete opposite of what a transition should be. Compounding the succession problem was the fact that Missouri had no statute mandating funds for office space and support facilities for the incoming transition team. The practice at the time was for the governor-elect to establish a not-for-profit corporation to raise money from private sources to fund the transition.

One might suppose that a candidate for governor would imagine himself sitting in the governor's chair and that while so daydreaming his thoughts would turn to the problems of setting up shop. Governor-elect Teasdale seemed to have given little forethought to the transition. He appointed four persons to his transition team, all lawyers, none of whom had had any prior experience of consequence in state government. Perhaps to compensate for their lack of experience, they contracted with three private management firms, Arthur Young & Company, Price Waterhouse & Company, and Cooper and Lybrand, to get aid with the transition. The process was probably made more difficult because Niel Nielsen, Bond's commissioner of administration, vacated his office shortly after the election. Teasdale appointed as acting commissioner of administration Bill Kimsey, an employee from the Arthur Young firm assigned to help the transition team.[28]

An almost total lack of cooperation and communication from Governor Bond's office was another characteristic of the 1976 gubernatorial transition. In the blunt words of Teasdale aide Gary Passmore, "Zero aid was provided by the Bond administration."[29] Thus members of the Teasdale team were allowed no access to the governor's office prior to the inaugural save but one time to assure themselves that there were sufficient office supplies on hand. They might as well not have bothered. When they moved into the governor's offices on inaugural day, they found the shelves barren of supplies and the offices without equipment. One aide complained that not even a paper clip was to be found.[30] The supplies had been given to Republican lieutenant governor William Phelps along with some of the office equipment; much of the equipment and furniture had been "surplused." The supplies problem was solved a few days later when Teasdale officials carried them back on flat carts while the unsuspecting lieutenant governor was at the General Assembly for an official presentation by the governor.[31]

But there were other problems as well. Telephone lines in the governor's office had been sabotaged and it took some time to restore an adequate phone system. Likewise there were problems in the governor's mansion. The Teasdales arrived there on inaugural day to find all but one room in the living quarters without furniture. Nobody had bothered to tell them that the mansion would be turned over unfurnished, nor had access to the living quarters prior to the inaugural been allowed.[32]

Another problem of the 1976 transition involved public records, and it, too, was exacerbated by lack of communication. Incoming Teasdale officials complained that records pertaining to ongoing public business had been sent by Bond officials to the state archives. The acting director of the archives at the time, Robert Nienhueser, explained that Bond was following state law by turning over records relating to current official business even though it might inconvenience the new administration.[33]

Another dispute surfaced in late summer of 1977. Long-time Democratic secretary of state James C. Kirkpatrick publicly charged that the Bond administration had violated state law by destroying all general correspondence during the governor's first term of office.[34] The general correspondence, which makes up the bulk of a governor's public papers, is comprised of letters from officials of federal, state, and local governments, as well as from citizens. Kirkpatrick pointed out that Bond had turned over a paltry 18 boxes of papers to the State Records Commission, whereas the previous five governors had sent anywhere from 122 to 602 boxes.[35] After much public comment, a meeting was held between Kirkpatrick and Republican attorney general John Ashcroft. They agreed that there was no impropriety in Bond's actions in destroying the correspondence. Though the 1965 State and Local Records Law was sweeping in what it included as a "record," the 1969 records retention schedule that applied that law to the governor's office allowed for the destruction of general correspondence. A Bond aide, Ralph Smith, had signed a new records retention schedule on October 8, 1976, which did call for the retention of general correspondence. However, the schedule was never formally ratified because the meeting of the State Records Commission at which it was to be implemented was canceled because of a severe snow storm. Both Kirkpatrick and Ashcroft agreed that steps would be taken to assure that future administrations would preserve all such general correspondence. However, an estimated 20,000 documents comprising the general correspondence of the first Bond administration had been destroyed—lost forever to Missouri state historians.[36]

Gubernatorial appointments were yet another sore point during the 1976 transition. Several Democratic senators charged that Governor Bond had violated an agreement not to make appointments after November 2, the date of his surprise defeat.[37] In one case, Perry Roberts, a member of Bond's staff, was appointed to a nonpaying position as trustee of the Missouri local government retirement system on the day Governor Teasdale was inaugurated.[38] Another appointments-related problem involved the uncertainty by the Teasdale transition team about the implications of the U.S. Supreme Court's decision in *Elrod* v. *Burns*.[39] Because the decision seemed to strike a blow against patronage, they replaced fewer of Bond's appointees than might otherwise have been the case.[40]

The 1980 Transition

The 1980 gubernatorial transition, which followed an election in which Christopher Bond defeated Joe Teasdale to regain control of the governor's mansion, was as smooth as the 1976 one had been turbulent. No doubt one major reason for the change was the passage in 1977 of a statute providing state funds for gubernatorial transitions. The law, passed largely as a result of the poor transition of 1976, provides that up to $100,000 be appropriated each year in which a nonincumbent is elected governor. The funds are to be used to provide office space for the governor-elect and his transition staff, as well as to pay for office equipment, supplies, and furniture.[41] The coordinator of Bond's 1980 transition, C. K. "Chip" Casteel, credited the transition statute as one reason why the 1980 transition had gone well.[42] Another reason he mentioned was that Bond and several members of his staff had had previous experience with transitions, both in the governor's office and in the state auditor's office.[43]

Credit for setting precedents leading to a harmonious transition also must go to the defeated incumbent. When the results of the often bitter campaign became apparent, Governor Teasdale phoned to congratulate Governor-elect Bond and promised his help in the transition.[44] To his aides he said, "I want to teach those people how they should have treated me."[45] A number of actions were taken to smooth the transition. For example, Teasdale designated Chief of Staff Carolyn Ashford and Executive Assistant Gary Passmore to act as contacts with the Bond team during the transition.[46] Cabinet officials in the Teasdale administration were asked to cooperate with incoming officials in the transition. The outgoing governor also passed up opportunities to make "midnight appointments."[47] In addition, the governor's offices were vacated on the Friday prior to the inaugural to give the new administration the weekend to move in.[48]

Governor Teasdale did one other thing, which some observers might think inappropriate and ill-advised—he left Jefferson City and let others tend to the transition.[49] As to why he did so, we can but speculate. It was not unusual for Teasdale as governor simply to disappear from the seat of government, and perhaps he, for personal reasons, was anxious to leave. The consequences for the transition undoubtedly cut both ways. On the one hand, it meant that he was not there personally to see that there was cooperation with those making the transition in, and he left his responsibilities to his advisers during the transition out to others. On the other hand, he was not on the scene where he could possibly have been baited by partisans to engage in obstructionist tactics or to drain the Office of Administration of time and resources in defending the record of his administration. He quite literally stood aside.

This is not to say that the 1980 gubernatorial transition was without its problems. It was not. A couple of large problems loomed in relation to the budget. When Governor-elect Bond met with commissioner of administration Stephen Bradford for the first time, the latter stated the problem with unusual clarity: "Governor, I'm sorry to tell you this but there is no money."[50] Those present saw Bond's face drop. For several reasons, including a nationwide recession, the liberal spending policies of the Teasdale administration, and sales tax exemptions, Bond was faced with a revenue shortfall of $29.4 million.[51] Moreover, the governor's office budget had been overspent. It was estimated at the time that Bond had four months' worth of budget when half the fiscal year remained.[52] Bond's legal and legislative counsel, Chip Casteel, noted that the governor's budget was short $50,000 because several outgoing Teasdale advisers took their accumulated annual vacation time as they left office.[53]

Accrued annual vacation time represents a significant transition problem. Gubernatorial advisers often delay taking their annual vacation time while in office because of the press of responsibilities. But if several of them take large chunks of it at once, as is the practice at the end of a governor's term, the incoming administration experiences a significant shortfall in its budget. This must be made up, either by absorbing the shortage through cuts or by paying the political costs of going to the legislature and requesting a supplemental appropriation during the early months of an administration. Governor Bond chose to absorb the shortage, which meant that several members of his staff had to take pay cuts of $2,000 during the first year of office. Casteel noted that he had hired one assistant for an agreed upon salary only to have to inform him that it would be reduced by $2,000 before the individual had even shown up for work.[54] Though the payout may vary from case to case, the matter of accrued annual vacation time is a recurring transition problem in Missouri.

The 1984 Transition

As with all gubernatorial transitions, in 1984 two administrations in Missouri were undergoing important political passages. The Bond administration was transiting out as the Ashcroft administration was transiting in. Though the media fixes attention on the incoming administration, the outgoing one is faced with some interesting tasks.[55]

The Transition Out

The outgoing governor has at least four significant responsibilities to which he *can* attend. These include: (1) working out a relationship with the incoming administration, (2) preparing messages and reports presenting and defending the record of his administration, (3) providing support and guidance to staff members as the administration winds down, and (4) providing for the preservation of documents generated during his or her term of office.

One aspect of working out a relationship with the new administration might be to provide briefings for gubernatorial candidates. In 1984 Governor Bond did not make such special arrangements. However, many of the candidates held high state offices and thus were well informed about state governmental affairs. In addition they served on various commissions that gave them opportunities to ask questions. It was the policy of the Bond administration to respond to all requests from the candidates for information.[56]

Another way an outgoing administration can assist an incoming one is by requesting that cabinet officials prepare briefing books about problems, present and imminent, in their departments. Again, no such formal instruction was given in 1984. Some cabinet officials, however, especially the directors of the Department of Social Services, the Department of Natural Resources, and the Department of Economic Development, did so on their own initiative.[57] In addition, the Division of Budget and Planning of the Office of Administration was active in preparing an end-of-the-term briefing booklet as well as several position papers.

After the November election there was much consultation and cooperation between the governor and the governor-elect. Governor Bond requested that his appointees cooperate with those of the incoming administration.[58] Governor-elect Ashcroft personally solicited Bond's advice as to who might be well suited to serve and in which positions.[59] They also decided who would serve as contacts between the two administrations during the transition. It would be the two "Chips": Bond's legal and legislative counsel Chip Casteel, and Edward "Chip" Robertson, the deputy attorney general under Ashcroft.[60] Moreover, Casteel sat in on many meetings with the Ashcroft transition team.

Far and away the most interesting and important principle guiding the relationship between the two administrations during transition periods in Missouri is the "norm of standing aside." This norm, first called to our attention by Casteel, was confirmed by almost all other officials we interviewed. As to its scope, it may include positive acts of cooperation by the outgoing governor to the incoming one, though that does not seem to be at its heart. Its most central meaning seems to be that the old administration will stay out of the way of the new. In the words of Teasdale official Passmore, "Almost everything of a policy nature comes to a stop."[61] There is the expectation that the outgoing governor will very substantially reduce his claim on the time and effort of the Office of Administration, which is released to work for the new administration in the early days of the transition.

The norm also means that the departing administration will not surprise the incoming one with midnight appointments. The lack of midnight appointments was one evidence cited by Casteel of Teasdale's standing aside.[62] The date on which the outgoing governor must cease making appointments is negotiated between the governor and prominent members of the senate, and the agreement is enforced by those senators. In 1984 Bond agreed not to make appointments after September 30.[63] It seems to be the case in Missouri that midnight appointments will not be confirmed. In 1976 the names of forty persons nominated by Bond to serve on commissions were returned by the senate to Teasdale for his action.[64] The senators claimed that Bond had broken his agreement with them not to make any appointments after his November 2 election defeat.

A caveat is in order in regard to the norm of standing aside, which incidentally relates to the outgoing administration's defense of its record. A couple of respondents thought it worked most completely when partisan control of the statehouse changed. In a partisan shift they felt that the outgoing governor would want little to do with the new administration and would stay out of its way. These respondents felt that the test of the norm would come when both the new and retiring governors were of the same political party. Indeed, Tony Moulton of the Division of Budget and Planning described 1984 as a dualism: "As the Bond administration tapered down, the Ashcroft administration picked up."[65] There was, he noted, still an active Bond presence in early January

1985. What concerned the outgoing governor the most was establishing the record of achievements of his administration, and much of this was done by the Division of Budget and Planning. Moulton expressed concern that potentially the workload demands placed on the division by the departing and incoming administrations could in some cases cause conflict between them.[66]

The third role of an outgoing governor might be to look after the needs of his staff members as they face the personal crises of transition. There was very little of this during the transition out in Missouri in 1984. There was, for example, no general meeting to discuss the options the individual staff members might follow. They were informed, however, that they could not involve themselves in the campaign on the state's time. What they did after hours was their own business. Governor Bond did offer to forward resumes of persons in his administration to Governor-elect Ashcroft. Moreover, the governor was personally concerned and offered to make inquiries on behalf of staff members where appropriate. The general assumption was, however, that members of the administration were able persons, and that they would decide when it was appropriate to seek other employment and where they might want to look.[67]

The transition out was a time of psychological stress for members of the staff. Casteel, for example, spoke of "after-election panic." He observed, "Holding public office pumps you up and the thought of losing it can be very emotionally threatening for some."[68] Regarding appointed professional staff in the agencies, Moulton spoke of "uncertainty" or "terror" during the transition because of anxiety about who would be replaced and who would be kept on.[69]

It should be noted that the governor fares no better than his staff during the out-transition in Missouri. For instance, the governor is not provided with funds, staff assistance, or office space to wind down the business of his administration after his successor has taken the oath of office. Nor is there any formal provision for consultation after the governor's term expires.

Missouri law provides for the preservation of public records.[70] The rather sweeping provisions of the statute are supplemented by a schedule or a set of guidelines promulgated by the state archivist with the approval of the members of the State Records Commission. These guidelines specify what records are to be kept and for how long. The

Division of Archives does not have any employees physically present at the governor's office to monitor the task of records preservation, so much discretion is left to the governor's staff. One can readily imagine that much interoffice communication would not make it to the archives even though point number 14 of the current guidelines calls for its preservation. Still, in 1984, Governor Bond sent 220 boxes of records to the archives.[71]

The Transition In

The transition in actually includes four transitions. They are the logistical transition (the establishment of a viable office and support facilities for the governor-elect and his transition team), the budgetary transition (the establishment of influence over the ongoing budgetary process), the administrative transition (the selection of key personnel and the establishment of decisionmaking structures and procedures consistent with the governor-elect's style), and the policy transition (ranking and selecting the policies and programs that the governor-elect will pursue and the order in which they will be pursued).[72]

The Logistical Transition

Serious thought about the transition into office seems to come about after the election or during the last week of the campaign, when the final polls inspire confidence. This late attention on the logistics of transiting-in did not create any special problems for the Ashcroft administration. Transitions into state public office were not new to Ashcroft because he had been Missouri attorney general. Moreover, he and his staff had a conception of what they wanted to accomplish in office, which they had developed during the campaign. Missouri's transition law is also a very important factor shaping the logistical transition. In addition to providing funds for the governor-elect's transition expenses, it stipulates that the transition shall commence November 15 and will end with the swearing-in of the new governor.[73] Further, relations between Bond and Ashcroft, both Republicans, were cordial. Bond shared his thoughts about transition with Ashcroft and his staff on the day following the election. Another source giving shape to transition planning was *Transition and the New Governor*, a publication of the National Governors'

Association. When asked about sources of ideas, Ashcroft's transition coordinator, Carl Koupal, took this publication from his bookshelf and cited its checklist as being important.[74]

The assignments given to members of Ashcroft's transition team yield insights as to how the task of transition was conceptualized. Carl Koupal, Ashcroft's campaign manager, was named as the transition coordinator; Chip Robertson, Ashcroft's deputy attorney general, was asked to coordinate budget preparations; Duncan Kincheloe, the associate attorney general under Ashcroft, was assigned to act on executive appointments; Thomas Deuschle, deputy campaign manager, was to deal with personnel and appointments; and Randy Sissel, press secretary while Ashcroft was attorney general and during the campaign, served in that capacity during the transition.[75] Planning for the inauguration was the task of Mary Beth Cook (not mentioned in press releases as a member of the transition team) and Janet Ashcroft, working in association with the state adjutant general's office.[76]

Though the transition is likely to seem pell-mell to insiders, it must be made to appear orderly—and the new administration worthy of confidence—to the public. The task of managing the image of the transition falls to the press secretary. An important aspect of working out a relationship with the media during the transition is "setting the stage." According to Sissel, "We set the stage by letting them know how we were going to do it."[77] In regard to gubernatorial nominees to major positions, this meant informing reporters early on that there would be no announcements until late December, and that then they should not expect a large news conference to announce the entire cabinet. When names of potential appointees were leaked by senators, the leaks were not confirmed until the governor-elect was ready to make an announcement. To allay fears of legislators about whether Governor-elect Ashcroft would be able to work effectively with their branch, it was announced in an early press release that an individual with legislative experience would be appointed to work on the 1985 legislative program.[78] Relations with the media were also structured by a decision to treat all members as equals. Thus callbacks were made with consideration of who called first or with an eye to deadlines, rather than the size of the newspaper or station making the inquiry. Having set the stage in this way, the transition team bought some time to do its work in an undisclosed downtown location. The media did not expect any news from it until late December, and members of the media felt comfortable that they would not be scooped.[79]

The Budgetary Transition

An incoming governor in Missouri faces three compelling truths about the budget: (1) the budget process is ongoing and he has only a limited ability to influence it; (2) the budget deadline is imminent so there is little time for the governor-elect to put his imprint on it; and (3) the Office of Administration plays a central role in the budgetary process and the transition generally.

The earliest stages of the budget cycle occur in midsummer. This is before the primaries have been held to determine the candidates of the major political parties. While the candidates are hotly contesting the election, the various departments and agencies are submitting their budget requests for the coming fiscal year. By the time the election is held, the budget process is in its advanced stages—the new governor has only a limited ability to influence it.

When the governor-elect focuses on the transition, he will find that time is short. "You have to make initial budget recommendations in 45 days, then there are appeals, then the budget goes to the printers."[80] In all, the new administration has about sixty days in which to present its budget.

With this deadline fast approaching, and with the budget already in its advanced stages, the governor-elect finds that he is dependent on the Office of Administration to an uncomfortable degree in gaining any control over the budget. We found general agreement with the assertion that "the Office of Administration is the glue that holds the administrations together."[81] Casteel went so far as to assert that the "commissioner of administration is as close as you come to a deputy governor during the transition."[82] Chip Robertson, who handled the budget for the Ashcroft administration during the 1984 transition, commented: "It's ridiculous. They give you sixty days and you can't possibly do it. The budget is the most troublesome. You are at the mercy of the Office of Administration. If it were a hostile transition, they could lie to you and you would be in real trouble."[83]

In many states the official who directs the fiscal and business affairs of the state is among the first to be removed.[84] In Missouri in 1980 and

1984, the commissioners of administration were kept on through the transition. Of course, it is possible that this is a short-term phenomenon, simply attributable to the personalities, interests, and ambitions of the two commissioners, Stephen Bradford during the Teasdale–Bond transition, and John Pelzer during the Bond–Ashcroft transition. There is reason to think, however, that laws and circumstances have combined to create conditions in which we can expect commissioners of administration to be kept on at least through the transition. For example, Missouri law provides that the transition funds are appropriated to the commissioner of administration and requires that he provide office space, equipment, and so on, for the new governor.[85] In effect, law mandates interaction between the governor-elect and the sitting commissioner. Other early interaction between the two includes meetings in which the commissioner briefs the governor-elect about the budget and revenue projections. This interaction casts the governor-elect as a harried official with much responsibility and little time and the commissioner as a professionally competent public official who has the information and resources that the new governor needs so desperately.

The statute that created the Office of Administration contained another provision that helps to account for commissioners of administration being held over. For whatever reason, the original statute provided that the commissioner of administration must have a master's degree "in public administration with major courses in political science, and he must have had at least six years of increasingly responsible experience in governmental administration or comparable managerial or administrative experience in business or industry."[86] The first person to be named to the position was Robert James, nominated by Governor Bond in 1973. Though James had earned a master's degree in business administration and was working toward a doctorate, after a convoluted series of events spanning two years he withdrew his name from consideration, having failed to gain confirmation during two sessions of the senate. The senators contended that he failed to meet the statutory requirements for the position.[87] The Office of Administration statute was modified in 1977 to provide simply that "he must be qualified by training and experience to assume the managerial and administrative functions of the office of commissioner of administration."[88] Even so, all commissioners of administration confirmed by the senate have been persons possessing a master's degree in public administration. So, it appears at the time of this writing that the laws, expectations about competency, and the urgency of budgetary considerations have resulted in delaying the replacement of the commissioner until after the transition.

As the transition works its way, it should be pointed out, the stock of the Division of Budget and Planning, a unit in the Office of Administration, increases relative to that of the commissioner vis-à-vis policy and budget development. Once its office and equipment needs are served, and it gets into its tasks, the transition team finds that the Division of Budget and Planning is the real source of much of the expertise it needs —budget and revenue projections, anticipated costs of legislative initiatives, and so on. Several members of the Ashcroft team came to feel a very close relationship with Budget and Planning. Thus one member of the Ashcroft transition team said that in the early part of the transition he worked more with Commissioner Pelzer, but that later he worked more with the Division of Budget and Planning. He commented that he often went directly to Budget and Planning.[89] Several other members of the transition team also spoke of the close relationship they developed with the Division of Budget and Planning.

The financial state of the state in 1984 was much improved from when Governor Bond began his second term. The state had a $70-million surplus, and Governor Ashcroft projected a growth rate of 6.4 percent in state revenues.[90] The budget that he submitted to the legislature called for $5.66 billion in expenditures. He recommended that $130 million be set aside to satisfy previous legislation mandating a reserve fund and that another $20 million be put into a "rainy day" fund. He further asked that an amount about equal to the surplus from the previous year be set aside to retire high-interest state bonds. Ashcroft reasoned that this amount was from one-time revenue collections and should not be utilized to create new programs that could not be sustained. After these deductions from the projected new funds, and after subtracting another $311 million for the costs of inflation and new programs already mandated, he identified $124 million for program enhancements. This amount was divided to reflect program priorities. (See the section dealing with the policy transition, below.)

Throughout the legislative session, there were differences between the Democratically controlled legislature and Governor Ashcroft about revenues. The legislature projected higher revenues and greater receipts from the newly enacted state lottery. In the end the legislature adopted a budget of $5.76 billion. Pointing out that this represented a 20-

percent increase over previous spending, Governor Ashcroft countered by employing his item veto to slash $50.2 million from the budget the legislature adopted, in order to ward off what he called the "boom and bust, feast and famine policies of the past."[91] The cuts were spread across the board and generally only reduced the size of the increase in spending on programs. State newspapers noted, however, that the governor did not reduce the salary increases for members of the legislature, the governor, and other elected state officials.

An uncertainty that hung over the legislative session was whether Missouri's revenue lid, the Hancock Amendment, had been triggered, requiring a refund to voters. State auditor Margaret Kelly issued a report that stated that the lid had been exceeded.[92] Many officials questioned the constitutionality of the Hancock Amendment because refunds would go only to those citizens who had paid state income taxes; still others pointed out that the amendment was unclear as to what was to be counted as revenue. The issue was still unresolved at the end of the legislative session.

The Administrative Transition

With the exception of Carl Koupal (who was appointed director of the Department of Economic Development), the members of the transition team became the core personnel of the governor's office. Chip Robertson became Ashcroft's chief of staff, Duncan Kincheloe was appointed director of policy development, Tom Deuschle became director of appointments and personnel, and Randy Sissel was selected to become the governor's special assistant for public and press operations. Jo Frappier, who had held public office for over two decades, having served in both the house and the senate as well as in local government and the state executive branch, was appointed director of government operations and legislation. As the only member of the governor's senior staff over the age of thirty-four, his selection was to provide the maturity and legislative expertise that some members of the legislature found lacking in the Ashcroft team.

The position of chief of staff did not exist in the Bond administration and Bond adviser Chip Casteel counseled against it, but officials of the National Governors' Association (NGA) convinced Governor-elect Ashcroft that "he would be crazy not to have a chief of staff."[93] "Casteel said don't have a chief of staff, but he was one—he had all the elements, but didn't have the title as a lightning rod."[94]

As chief of staff, Robertson worked closely with the governor and approved any correspondence that went out over the governor's signature. He took responsibility for any relationships with the federal government that involved the governor. He also sat in on personnel meetings that involved political appointments. Weekly meetings were held between the chief of staff and heads of some especially important government units; meetings were scheduled for alternate weeks with most department directors. Unlike recent Republican presidents, the Ashcroft administration did not come to office with an elaborate administrative strategy for dealing with the bureaucracy.[95] However, a midsummer evaluation of the departments—a sort of strategic planning exercise—was contemplated.

Though a chief-of-staff arrangement implies hierarchy, the hierarchy in the Ashcroft governor's office seems to have been a loose one. The senior staff met every Thursday to discuss vital issues. Votes were taken and once a decision was made, it was everybody's decision. In making decisions, Robertson sought out as many viewpoints as seemed appropriate and submitted them to the governor. Said Robertson: "Many governors' chiefs of staff describe themselves as the governor's gatekeeper. We have a big open door here. Several of us—three or four —have ready access to the governor for big decisions."[96] Robertson, Frappier, and Kincheloe were among those staff members with easy access. Did jealousy develop among the senior advisers when they attempted to operate in this fashion? Frappier answered this way: "When everyone is drowning in work, there is no time for ego involvement."[97]

This mode of decision making fitted well into Governor Ashcroft's chairman-of-the-board style. Tom Deuschle compared Ashcroft's style of delegating responsibility to President Reagan's: "He lets us develop a lot of things and it flows up to him. He's like a chairman of the board and that frees him up to do more things."[98] Governor Ashcroft likened the confidence with which he delegates responsibility to a basketball team whose members have played together for a long time: after a while you know what to expect of each of the other team members.[99]

In Missouri the governor has about 200 good appointments that he makes directly or that are cleared through the governor's office. Among the executive appointments the governor makes directly are those of nine department directors, four division directors, and members of boards and commissions. The transition team, and after the inaugural, a governor's office committee coordinated by the special assistant for appointments and personnel interviewed candidates for such nonmerit positions as department directors and deputy directors, division directors and deputy directors, and such senior staff as fiscal officers, purchasing agents, data processing officers, chief lawyers, and so on. In the case of boards and commissions, each nominee had to be cleared with his or her representative and senator if the nominee was of the same political party as the governor.[100] During the preinaugural, the task of recruitment was divided, with Duncan Kincheloe handling executive appointments and Tom Deuschle dealing with the bulk of personnel interviewing and selection.

Deuschle estimated that the transition team received about 4,500 résumés and that 2,000 to 3,000 persons were interviewed. At the peak of placement activity, Deuschle received about 100 telephone messages per day. The sources of names to be considered for positions, ranked in order of importance, were: (1) the previous administration, (2) self-submission, (3) the business community and party sources, (4) legislative sources, (5) trade associations, and (6) the NGA.[101] An effort was made to have applicants interviewed by a committee of ten to twelve persons. Included were members of the transition team, officials from the Bond administration, individuals from the business community, persons involved in Ashcroft's campaign, and some persons from trade associations. Interviewing began at 7:30 A.M. and continued through the day—indeed, sometimes into the evening—with individual interviews lasting from thirty minutes to an hour.

Because this was a transition in which one Republican succeeded another as governor, a basic decision that faced Ashcroft was whether to retain the Bond appointees in his administration. It was decided that Bond department directors would have to apply for their positions if they wanted to be considered; in doing so, they would be neither advantaged nor disadvantaged. This was referred to as the "level field" policy.[102] A similar policy was followed for other positions. With reference to middle-level nonmerit positions, the transition team and later the assistant for appointments and personnel went department-by-department, posting the open positions and inviting those who wished to be considered to submit their résumés.[103] A problem under consideration in May was what to do about those officials who held patronage positions, but who were also on leaves of absence from merit positions. The feeling ran high among the governor's senior advisers that these persons should give up either the patronage or the merit appointments. In the words of one adviser, "If you don't have the courage, you can't take the credit."[104]

A couple of characteristics of the results of the recruitment process should be noted. In spite of the level field policy of the Ashcroft transition team, many Bond administration officials were kept on. Of the thirteen department and division directors the governor appoints directly, about half were from the previous administration. Below this top echelon a much higher percentage of Bond appointees were carried over. Again the bulk of appointees were from Missouri or had Missouri roots. Though names were collected nationally, there was a strong preference for persons with a Missouri connection. All of the new department and division directors appointed directly by the governor were from Missouri or had some Missouri roots, for example.[105] None of the persons whose names were submitted by the NGA were selected.[106]

Most of Governor Ashcroft's appointments met with wide approval both in the legislature and the state media. Some, however, did cause waves. One Bond department head who wasn't kept on and who had publicly indicated an interest in doing so was Richard King, director of the Department of Revenue.[107] He was widely credited with turning the department around and modernizing its revenue collections. He attributed his ill-fortune to personal considerations: "My problems were my style and my divorce. The divorce was a big problem with Ashcroft."[108] Governor Ashcroft is a religious fundamentalist whose religion influences his own lifestyle. Indeed, capital city chatter suggested that questions of lifestyle might have played a significant part in the appointment process.[109] We have no evidence to address this question directly because we did not raise the matter in interviews; however, an interesting rationale for such an approach was offered by an Ashcroft transition team member in response to a question about what he looked for in a candidate. He indicated that one characteristic was personal compatibility with the governor. This, he noted, was stressed by the NGA. He went on, "If the governor is not comfortable with the appointee, then he will not be interested in having his advice."[110]

Of all the positions, those on the newly created Missouri Horse Racing Commission generated the largest interest—about 350 to 400 applications. In a curious approach to this matter, the governor did not appoint any of the applicants, but instead chose five persons who demonstrated their disinterest by not applying. Some of those nominated, however, became a source of controversy. Chosen to chair the commission was Lawrence K. Roos, former Federal Reserve Bank president, former St. Louis County supervisor, and unsuccessful GOP candidate for governor in 1968. Though the *St. Louis Post-Dispatch* editorialized that Roos was an individual of "unquestioned integrity," it regretted his choice because he was the brother-in-law of William Deramus III, chairman of Kansas City Southern Industries, which contributed more than $420,000 to the campaign to legalize pari-mutuel betting.[111] In addition, the two members nominated to the commission as Democrats were questioned by party brethren about the steadfastness of their party loyalty.

The Policy Transition

When a candidate for governor campaigns, he or she selects issues that will appeal to varied constituencies statewide in the hope of successfully contesting the election. But when that candidate becomes governor-elect, he or she must make choices from among those campaign pledges reflective of limited funds and opportunities. One Missouri Division of Budget and Planning official noted, "Transition for the governor is a tension between limitations and opportunities and much restraint results from revenues."[112] A transition team member commented, "In the budget we look at the top of the iceberg. We fit our campaign pledges into it."[113] Ashcroft, as has been noted, identified $124 million that was available for program enhancements; any new programs had to come from these funds.

Of the many programs advocated during the campaign, some were more attractive than others because they presented windows of opportunity. The governor's program for excellence in education was one such window. As Director of Policy Development Duncan Kincheloe stated, "In preparation for this session, public education was on the front burner. The legislative work had been done on public education so we kept it on the front burner."[114] Kincheloe's reference was to the Joint Committee on Education, chaired by Senator Roger Wilson (D, Columbia); it had laid much of the groundwork for an initiative in this area. At the national level, of course, the report *A Nation at Risk* had added urgency to this policy area. Another such window was that of economic development, an issue on which candidate Ashcroft had campaigned hard. Here a window had been opened by the Bond administration, which had devoted much effort to the issue.

There were other sources of opportunities and restraints. The governor's legislative package includes policy requests from the departments. These, too, must be sifted through budgetary constraints in an effort to match policy initiatives with available funds. A further limitation mentioned was federal compliance requirements. Among other things, in 1985 this meant an estimated $79.5 million to provide for court-ordered busing for St. Louis schools. Then several members of the transition team mentioned the need to keep the legislative package manageable. It had to be kept in focus, and this meant selecting a few issues for attention during the first legislative session.

In anticipation of the 1984 transition, the Division of Budget and Planning prepared twenty to twenty-five position papers ranging from general background studies to those dealing with specific issues.[115] Though the choice of topics was left to those in the division, officials looked to the position papers of the candidates as one source of topics. While work began on the issue papers in mid-October, they were not completed until late November. The entire staff of Budget and Planning worked on them. In addition the division felt free to seek help from the departments. These papers were useful in the policy transition—all of the members of the senior staff commented favorably about them. Soon after the election Assistant Director Tony Moulton met with the members of the staff of Budget and Planning and presented a distillation of Governor-elect Ashcroft's position papers. "Frequent interaction with the transition team—day-by-day, hour-by-hour—started within a week of the election."[116]

The progress of the administration's legislative program was monitored in the governor's office by the director of governmental operations and legislation, Jo Frappier. The policy staff and a large portion of the personnel in the Division of Budget and Planning were assigned bills to follow. They attended committee hearings, tracked the progress of legislation, and prepared scan sheets summarizing legislative activity. Departmental personnel had similar assignments in relation to legislation of interest to their departments. In addition to the governor's legislative package and the departmental legislative packages, there were what were referred to as "significant bills," which had to be monitored. These were bills that the governor did not want to be passed and that the departments were pledged to kill.[117] An assistant on the governor's policy staff was charged with the responsibility of preparing a midsession scorecard on the legislative packets.

Though Governor Ashcroft presented a substantial list of legislative proposals, they were clustered into general policy areas, thus focusing attention on a few major themes. In his legislative and budget address delivered January 23, he clearly emphasized education (especially elementary and secondary education); economic development; programs to protect Missouri's children from child abuse, neglect, and child pornography; and legislative proposals to aid the elderly. Though both chambers of the General Assembly were controlled by Democrats, and there had been considerable apprehension about how the legislatively inexperienced Ashcroft would fare, it was widely agreed that the first session of the legislature was an exceedingly productive one. A beaming Governor Ashcroft told the press that by his count, more than 85 percent of the bills he supported had become law.[118] A *Columbia Missourian* reporter wrote that fourteen of twenty-four pieces of legislation the governor had requested had been enacted.[119] Said Ashcroft, "We asked the General Assembly to concentrate on Missouri's needs and they responded as energetically as we could have hoped."[120] Senator Pro Tem John Scott (D, St. Louis) commented, "He was there if we needed him. I have nothing but praise for the Governor. He let the legislative process take its course."[121] Speaker of the House Bob Griffin, (D, Cameron) agreed that it was a productive session, the most productive in which he had been involved. He, however, felt the governor succeeded by associating himself with a number of bills that had already been introduced. Nonetheless, he saw Ashcroft as "willing to get out on the front line with the rest of us."[122] The *St. Louis Post-Dispatch* editorialized that the 1985 session had been unusually productive: "Indeed, the legislators praise the Republican governor both for cooperation and for allowing them to do their work. The flow of bipartisan praise is about as unusual as the productiveness. But their assessment is right."[123]

Among the laws the legislature enacted was the Excellence in Education Act, which provided a substantial increase in support for public schools, higher salaries and a career ladder for teachers, and more stringent evaluations of both teachers and students. Other important pieces of legislation requested by the governor that were enacted included an omnibus child protection law that dealt with child abuse, child pornography, and missing children; a super-fund bill, which revised the method of taxing companies that generate hazardous waste to provide a fund to clean up waste sites; and a law that tightened the reporting of political campaign contributions and expenses.

Among the biggest disappointments handed the governor were the failure of the General Assembly to pass legislation earmarking revenue from the newly created lottery for education, its failure to enact legislation reorganizing the Department of Economic Development, and its failure to pass a law reducing the size of the vote necessary to pass bond issues.

A late-breaking option that became an important component of the Ashcroft policy transition was the unsuccessful campaign to attract the General Motors (GM) Saturn plant to Missouri. With estimates of thousands of jobs, millions of dollars in annual income, and billions in investments, Saturn fit snugly into Governor Ashcroft's announced emphasis on economic development. The governor sent a letter to business leaders, civic leaders, and mayors of the main communities throughout the state, inviting them to attend a seminar dealing with the Saturn opportunity. Three hundred persons attended and thirty communities chose to compete for the plant. A selection committee was constituted to select the final Missouri sites.[124] Much time during the transition, probably totaling thousands of hours, was devoted to the Saturn project, not the least of which was getting the legislature to pass mandatory seat belt legislation to strengthen Missouri's case with GM to be the site for the plant. When the dust settled, GM chose neighboring Tennessee as the location for Saturn.

Was the effort, then, a waste of valuable time? Not according to Jo Frappier, who spearheaded the campaign in the governor's office. For one thing, he noted, the governor received much good press on his trip to Detroit. More importantly, "Ashcroft established himself as a leader. Detroit required the governor be present to make Missouri's case for the Saturn plant so the urban mayors had to work through him."[125] He could also have added that Saturn provided some early hands-on experience coordinating the people and processes important in attracting industry to the state.

An issue that became more painfully public during the transition was the problem of farm foreclosures. Missouri, with the second largest number of farms of any state in the union, was hard hit. In March 1985 the Farmers Home Administration owned more farmland in Missouri than in any other state.[126] Other midwestern states had placed the crisis on the land high on their agendas. In neighboring Iowa, for example, the legislature passed a bill offering reduced interest farm loans and authorizing the governor to declare a moratorium on farm foreclosures. Programs providing farm loans at reduced interest similarly were implemented in Illinois.[127] In South Dakota the entire legislature flew to Washington to lobby federal officials for farm relief.[128]

Compared to these efforts, the response of the Ashcroft administration during the early winter seemed anemic. Agriculture was not mentioned, for instance, in the governor's legislative and budget address. Ashcroft did support the passage of a bill channeling $200 million in unused state funds into reduced-interest farm loans but opposed the version of the bill passed by the house because it would have included small businesses as beneficiaries. In the end, no program was enacted.[129] In general the administration's stance seemed to be that the crisis on the land was a national problem to be dealt with by national programs. For her part, Democratic lieutenant governor Harriett Woods saw a chance to make some hay: she convened a meeting of agricultural leaders to discuss the farm crisis while Ashcroft was in Detroit making his pitch for Saturn.

Conclusion

The gubernatorial transition that took place in Missouri in 1984 was a tranquil one. Of course, it helped that Governor-elect Ashcroft and Governor Bond were of the same political party and were kindred spirits; however, other considerations were also important. These include the norm of standing aside and the central role played by the Office of Administration.

The norm of standing aside provides that the old administration will stay out of the way of the new. One aspect of standing aside is that the outgoing governor reduces his demands on the time and resources of the Office of Administration. Another is that the old administration does not surprise the new by making midnight appointments. Standing aside may also include such positive acts of cooperation as appointing contact persons, requesting administrative officials to cooperate with appointees of the new administration, and vacating the governor's offices the weekend before the inaugural. It is likely that the norm as discussed in this essay is traceable to the 1980 election. It did not appear to be operative in 1976, for example, though we know little about

Missouri gubernatorial transitions before 1976. We cannot state the conditions under which it will be operative or how long it will last. What is clear is that the norm was generally recognized by officials interviewed by the authors in 1985.

The findings in regard to the norm of standing aside should be evaluated in future studies of gubernatorial transition—in Missouri as well as in other states. It might be especially interesting to focus on the perceptual and behavioral transactions between the outgoing governor, the incoming governor, and the commissioner of administration (or comparable official) as control over the Office of Administration (or comparable office) is transferred. In many respects the most interesting and difficult role is the one played by the commissioner. He will likely be encouraged to seek reappointment by the division directors who work under him (and form an important part of his milieu) because they know that if the commissioner leaves, a successor is likely to want to start with a new team of directors. In addition we can readily imagine that the personal ambition of the commissioner is likely to play a significant part in this decision. The desire to be kept on must be communicated, but the commissioner should be vigilant to maintain a certain amount of "class" throughout. He must not be perceived by subordinates or members of the transition team as wanting the position too badly, as groveling, or his authority as a professional will be called into question. Flexibility is in order because nothing less than a change of employers from one political master to another is taking place. Again, though flexibility about ends is an essential ingredient for professionals in the professional-politician relationship, the commissioner must avoid being seen as lacking backbone. Another point of interest is when the commissioner's transfer of psychological commitment from one governor to another is perceived to have taken place. If it is seen by subordinates to have occurred too early, the commissioner will be thought to have compromised himself.

Of the three Missouri transitions that took place between 1976 and 1984, the 1976 transition was turbulent. Though many factors could explain its roughness, one might bear special scrutiny in comparative studies. In 1976 in Missouri, an incumbent governor was upset in the final days of an election campaign. One can readily imagine the bitterness and low morale among members of a governor's staff who are confronted unexpectedly on election evening with the necessity of pulling their children out of school, selling their houses, finding new employment, and relocating. The various staff members are likely to take their leave when and as they can. In an interview a decade after the 1976 transition, former governor Bond addressed this problem: "At the very end the people who were primary movers in my administration had almost all disbanded. There was stress and a lot of tremendous disappointment, but it wasn't our policy to be disagreeable." [130] Along with such other factors as the personalities of the candidates and the bitterness of the campaign, the upset of an incumbent late in the campaign could contribute to a rocky transition.

This study directs attention to some aspects of gubernatorial transition in Missouri that need improvement. One is the problem of accrued annual leave, created because members of the outgoing governor's staff do not take leave until they vacate their offices, and then a number of them take all they are entitled to receive. The resulting drain on the governor's office budget may force the new governor to reduce the first year's salary of the staff, as Bond did in 1980, or force him to ask for a supplemental appropriation during the first legislative session, as Ashcroft did in 1984. The former course is too Draconian, the latter poses political risks for the image of the new governor. Because this is a recurring irritant, it should be remedied by an automatic appropriation during those years in which a transition is likely, similar to the 1977 transition legislation.

Another strain in the fabric of transition is the role of the outgoing governor. The situation that now prevails sees the incoming governor receiving much direction from the NGA and much attention from the press. The departing governor and his staff are left to themselves to box up their tangible possessions, deflate their egos, turn out the lights (at least temporarily) on their public careers, and find alternate ways to make their livelihoods. Certainly, the responsibilities of the outgoing governor need some elaboration. More discussion and study by scholars and organizations like the NGA are necessary to clarify for outgoing governors what can reasonably be expected of them. New laws may also be in order. The work of the governor does not stop the instant he leaves office; rather it is likely to taper off over a period of months. Legislation should be crafted to provide public support for the former governor for a limited time to defray such expenses as postage, telephone bills, equipment expenses, and part-time secretarial assistance.

The relationship between the governor's office and the Division of Budget and Planning in Missouri is one that requires continual boundary maintenance. As of now, the association appears to center around respect for neutral competence. For example, a member of the governor's senior staff who definitely conceived of the division as the research staff of the governor's office commented, "I feel comfortable working with Budget and Planning. They are career people who don't work by patronage."[131] In a reciprocal way, an official of the Division of Budget and Planning explained, "The role of position papers and the Office of Administration is advice—background. We don't make decisions in any instance."[132] The danger is that although the sort of expertise found in Budget and Planning would be much more valuable if it could be combined with loyal support and employed for partisan purposes, the practical effect of this transformation would be to erode the basis of neutral competence and alter the nature of the division. Another aspect of this problem is organizational. The Division of Budget and Planning is physically located in the Office of Administration. This poses the question, "How can the commissioner of administration be held accountable for the activities of Budget and Planning when it works for the governor's office?"

One of our respondents stated that the Office of Administration is the glue that holds the transition together. If this is true, neutral competence is the source of the adhesion. One can imagine a much different scenario for gubernatorial transitions in Missouri. It might proceed as follows. Shortly after the election the governor-elect, sensing that the Office of Administration houses a nest of partisans, announces he will appoint a new commissioner of administration. The current commissioner performs the duties required in the transition law, then resigns. The director of the Division of Budget and Planning, who sees that his days are numbered, offers only perfunctory cooperation. The personnel of Budget and Planning are demoralized because, though they have been trained as professionals, they have been used for partisan purposes. They are not accorded the status due professionals in their dealings with other agencies.[133] The transition team searches for a new commissioner of administration but cannot find a replacement immediately who will satisfy the governor-elect, the state law requirement for professional qualifications, and the expectations of state legislators. The new administration comes into office in the middle of January. It has still not been able to gain effective control over the budget because the budget process was far advanced at the time of the election and the governor-elect lacks reliable advice from persons inside government who understand what has gone into making the budget. Missouri law requires that the budget must be submitted to the General Assembly within a couple of weeks. This hypothetical situation shows the importance of preserving the standard of neutral competence in the Office of Administration to smooth gubernatorial transitions. Without it, new administrations would be launched figuratively into a numbing winter of harsh Missouri politics.

Gubernatorial Transition
in North Carolina, 1984–1985

)))))

Joel A. Thompson

On November 6, 1984, James G. Martin was elected governor of North Carolina. Martin, who holds a doctorate in chemistry from Princeton, is a former Davidson College professor, Mecklenburg County commissioner, and six-term congressman. He is only the second Republican elected to the North Carolina governorship in the twentieth century.

Martin's election paralleled that of his Republican predecessor, James E. Holshouser (1973–77). Both men were the beneficiaries of popular Republican incumbent presidents heading the national ticket, strong state Republican tickets (Jesse Helms's campaigns for the Senate), and unusually bitter and divisive Democratic primaries. These factors, as well as an unpopular national Democratic ticket, contributed to Martin's election in a state where registered Democrats outnumber Republicans by approximately a three-to-one ratio.

Martin assumed the governor's chair of the nation's tenth most populous state from Democrat James B. (Jim) Hunt (1977–85), North Carolina's only two-term governor in modern history. Hunt was a strong and active governor and unsuccessfully challenged Jesse Helms for his Senate seat in 1984.

North Carolina is a rural, small-town, and small-city state. Historically, the economy has been dependent upon tobacco, textiles, and furniture manufacturing. Despite recent setbacks in these industries, the state has remained financially sound, partly due to the high-tech diversification of the state's economy in the Research Triangle area (Raleigh, Durham, and Chapel Hill).

North Carolina has been traditionally a Democratic state. The Democratic party continues to have a strong base, although the Republicans made significant inroads in the state legislature and at the local level in 1984. At the national level in 1984 the state mirrored contemporary southern political behavior with two Republican U.S. senators and five Republicans of eleven U.S. congressmen. Further, only Jimmy Carter in 1976 had been able to carry the state at the presidential level for the Democrats since 1968. (In 1986, however, the Democrats recaptured two congressional seats and one Senate seat.) Thus, the collision of tradition and history (domination by southern Democrats) and contemporary political realignments (growing Republicanism) creates an intriguing backdrop for analyzing the 1984 gubernatorial transition in North Carolina.

The Campaign and Election

When Martin began his quest for the governorship he trailed his potential Democratic opponents by a wide margin. He believed that 1984 was an opportune time for a serious GOP challenge to the traditional Democratic chair. With Ronald Reagan heading the national ticket and Jesse Helms sharing the state ticket, Martin foresaw the potential for long coattails, and he was able to ride them all the way to Raleigh.

The Democrats contributed significantly to Martin's victory. Like his Republican predecessor, Jim Holshouser, Martin was the beneficiary of a bitter and devisive Democratic primary. His opponent in the general election, Attorney General Rufus Edmisten, had surprised political observers by finishing first in the primary, edging former Charlotte mayor Eddie Knox (who was considered the favorite) and three other challengers (including the incumbent lieutenant governor). Knox was a close friend and former college pal of Jim Hunt. Hunt had appointed Knox to the Advisory Budget Commission, a move designed to give Knox some statewide visibility.

On the other hand, Edmisten and Hunt, while outwardly cordial, had had their differences over budget and policy matters during Hunt's tenure. Hunt refused to endorse any Democrat prior to the nomination, primarily because his transition team found unanimous opposition to it ("you can really get burned") in their interviews with former governors.

This infuriated Knox, and when he lost to Edmisten in the runoff, he refused to endorse the Democratic ticket and openly flirted with the Republican Party.

Martin had token opposition in the Republican primary. In the general election, he campaigned on conservative issues and portrayed his opponent as an ineffective administrator who did not "mind the store." His campaign ads also tied Edmisten to the "liberal Carter-Mondale-Hunt organization." The centerpiece of the Martin campaign was a pledge to cut various state taxes: repeal the sales tax on food and non-prescription drugs; repeal the intangibles tax on money on deposit, stocks, bonds, and accounts receivable; and reduce the inventory tax for business. Martin also pledged to eliminate the state's abortion fund for poor women. Other issues given some emphasis by the Martin campaign included education and highways, traditional issues in North Carolina.

Edmisten attempted to divorce himself from the national ticket ("I'm a North Carolina Democrat") and stress his experience. However, not even a last-minute endorsement from his former boss, retired senator Sam Ervin, could offset the combination of the strong Republican ticket, a popular tax-cut issue, and the innuendos that surfaced concerning Edmisten's personal life and public performance. Martin won comfortably, outpolling Edmisten by 190,000 votes and tallying 54.2 percent of the statewide vote.

The Office of Governor

In terms of formal authority, the governor in North Carolina is one of the least powerful in the United States.[1] It is the only governorship that has no veto authority. Prior to 1977 the governor was limited to a single four-year term. Martin's predecessor successfully spearheaded an effort to allow himself and future governors to run for a second four-year term. However, in 1985 the legislature, faced with the possibility of an eight-year tenure by a Republican governor, placed a repeal amendment on the November 1986 ballot, only to remove it later as a result of charges of partisanship in the effort.

The governor is also limited in his managerial role. He must share executive authority with eight separately elected department heads (the auditor, the attorney general, the treasurer, and the heads of the departments of state, agriculture, labor, insurance, and education) as well as a separately elected lieutenant governor. He shares budget power with an appointed board, two-thirds of whose members are appointed by the legislature. The governor does have significant appointive power, being able to distribute over 1,000 jobs to loyalists, party members, and campaign workers.

Partly because of the institutional weakness of the office, North Carolina governors have not dominated the legislature as has been the case in other southern states. However, traditionally the legislature has looked to the governor for leadership and policy direction. Martin's predecessor, Jim Hunt, did not disappoint them.

During his eight years as governor, Jim Hunt made the office a more forceful center of power and enhanced its position as a center of policy-making. The change in the governor's office was recognized by Martin's advisers. As one noted "It's a different governor's office now than it was in 1972, or even in 1976."

The most profound change in the office of governor was the result of the succession amendment to the state constitution. The possibility of succession in office gives the governor greater political and managerial leverage and removes the extended lame-duck status of the governor during a single four-year term. This provision may possibly help account for the reaction of the Democrats in the legislature to the new Republican governor. For the first time, the legislature was faced with the possibility of a Republican in the statehouse, not for a mere four years, but for a possible eight-year tenure.

Another change in the office has been the growth of the gubernatorial staff. When former Republican governor Jim Holshouser completed his term in 1977, the governor's office payroll listed thirty-one staff members. When his successor Jim Hunt left office eight years later, he left with a seventy-eight-member staff.

Hunt took other steps to strengthen the office. He never organized his office so as to have a pure chief of staff, but rather had several policy advisers reporting directly to him. Hunt's staff members knew that the governor felt a project was especially important whenever they discovered that several of them were working on the same project independently of one another.

In his second term Hunt rearranged his staff so as to give his office more influence in the direction of state government. Four assistants were assigned specifically as policy coordinators in different areas. The governor also had a science adviser and an agricultural adviser. Cabinet meetings included not only the heads of departments appointed by the governor, but also as many as ten members of the governor's staff.

Hunt also made two other important changes in his office. In 1978 he named John A. Williams to the dual role of executive assistant to the governor and state budget director. Although the budget office staff remained in the Department of Administration, Hunt's actions brought part of the budget process into the governor's office and made Williams an agent of the governor. This gave Williams considerable clout in dealing with the legislature and state agencies.

Similarly, Joseph Pell, another special assistant to the governor, had broad authority over state government personnel as well as serving as the political contact person in the governor's office. Another staff member served as state personnel officer and participated in cabinet meetings.

Hunt enhanced the political role of the governor, as well as the administrative and managerial roles. He worked very closely with the legislature—pushing, lobbying, cajoling, and even arm-twisting on occasion—for his legislative program. He provided the legislature with major issues for its agenda: an unpopular but successful move to increase the state gasoline tax in light of a declining highway fund in 1981 and a comprehensive "Safe Roads Act" that restricted alcohol sales and strengthened driving-under-the-influence penalties in 1983.

As a result of the succession amendment and the solid leadership of Hunt, Martin inherited an office that was strengthened substantially. However, this proved to be a two-edged sword for Martin because Hunt's actions created an expectation of gubernatorial leadership and involvement in the policymaking process on the part of the legislature. Unfortunately for Martin, these expectations were not met during the initial legislative session.

Transitioning Out

The Martin administration was the beneficiary of an extensive effort on the part of the outgoing governor to smooth the transition process. As early as January 1982 (mid–second term) key staffers of the Hunt administration began discussing the transition process. Staffers who had been members of previous administrations were concerned about potential problems that might arise in the last year and a half of the phasing-out process of the governorship. They were asked to prepare some material for the next cabinet retreat, scheduled to be held in the summer of 1982. In preparation for the retreat, members of the Hunt staff interviewed all former living governors of North Carolina and members of their staffs, a total of about twenty-five people. They also interviewed staff members of two out-of-state, two-term governors.

Among the questions asked were these: What are major pitfalls that an administration may encounter during its last year? What lessons can be learned from the experiences of your administration? What are the major challenges in finishing up an administration? Are there any unique challenges to the Hunt administration in finishing up? And, what suggestions or recommendations could you make to the outgoing Hunt administration?

From these interviews the staff developed what they called a "framework of challenges," which centered around seven or eight major issues. These issues fell into three broad categories: First, what will be the *legacy of the administration*? For example, how do we complete the programmatic agenda? How do we develop and leave a road map for the future? And, what will be the historical legacy of this administration? Second, how do we deal with *challenges related to management*? In other words, how do we keep the system from deteriorating? Management concerns centered around various aspects of public administration: the tendency of people to jump ship, apathy developing among the work force, and anxieties about changes in personnel. Other challenges to the management function centered around the vulnerabilities of the administration, both legislatively (the lame-duck status of the outgoing governor) and politically (Hunt was attempting to unseat U.S. Senator Jesse Helms). The Hunt staff was cognizant of the "system deterioration" that had plagued other gubernatorial administrations in their waning days. Rather than coasting toward inauguration day, they wanted to "finish in style," as one staff member put it. For Hunt this meant making several key judicial appointments, approving the state highway plan, and putting together a final budget that reflected his priorities and vision of the future for the state.

The third category of the "framework of challenges" dealt with *efforts to smooth the transition process*. These efforts were concerned with such questions as how to deal with the two nominees, how to help current members of the administration beyond the inauguration, and how to assist the incoming administration.

This extensive transitioning-out process by the Hunt administration was interrupted in the summer of 1982 when documents that were prepared for a cabinet retreat were leaked to the press and caused great embarrassment for the administration. The documents had been replete with direct quotes from the staff interviews that were taken out of context. The leak caused the transition process to be put on hold until the summer of 1984, approximately six months prior to the gubernatorial election.

When the media attention subsided, the Hunt staff narrowed their immediate transition efforts to dealing with the two nominees. Governor Hunt wrote a letter to each of the candidates to offer assistance, primarily in two ways: (1) he offered information concerning the programs of the administration, ostensibly to enlighten the debate in the campaign, and (2) he promised to work with the winning candidate to smooth the transition process. He designated a member of his staff to deal directly with any transition questions that might arise, and asked each of the nominees to do the same. Also at this time, the Hunt staff began to develop background materials for the incoming administration.

The transition process in North Carolina had both formal (statutory) and informal (personal) aspects. A state transition act provides nominal funds for the transition and for the inauguration, but the provisions of the act are insufficient. Cognizant of this, Governor Hunt had included a $50,000 appropriation in the Department of Administration's budget to cover additional expenses. The informal support offered by the Hunt administration primarily covered logistical matters—providing state office space and equipment and supplies and placing members of the new governor's transition staff in vacant positions in state government. Vacant positions had been held open by the Hunt administration specifically for that purpose.

The transitioning-out process operated on two fronts. At the departmental level, each department in the cabinet was instructed to prepare background material for the incoming secretary. This effort was coordinated by Jane Patterson, secretary of the Department of Administration. Each department subsequently prepared a background document, or briefing book, of the major activities of the department. Included in this material were an organizational chart, a brief history of the department, budget instructions, a list of individuals who are exempt from the state personnel act, and the major programs and functions of the department. An executive summary of these documents was also prepared for the new governor.

A second front was the gubernatorial staff level. Staff members of the Hunt administration identified twenty-four separate activities carried out by the governor's staff. Each of these functional units was instructed to prepare a profile following a standard outline, which included such items as how the staff was organized, the major functions provided by each unit, budget reporting relationships, and the relationships of each of these units to outside boards and commissions. Staff-level material included information about special issues or special activities that would require attention from the incoming staff, particularly in the first few months of the new administration (such as information about emergency procedures in the case of natural disaster or catastrophe and appointments to boards and commissions).

The Martin administration made use of the material developed by the outgoing administration. Each of the departmental transition coordinators for the Martin administration was asked to review the material and develop a short synopsis of it for the incoming departmental secretaries.

The Hunt administration's extensive transitioning-out efforts were in part due to its experience eight years before. As one staff member said of Hunt, "He clearly remembers [the transition process] where they [the Holshouser administration] went out of their way to be helpful. They did things for us. They took people and put them on the payroll. It was not a large-scale operation like we did here, but they did it." Holshouser's efforts were also a response to the transition that his predecessor, Governor Bob Scott, had staged. Holshouser remembered the courtesies and tried to do better, and apparently Hunt tried to do even better than that. Given the transition efforts of the last three governors, each who left the office to a governor of the other party, North Carolina may have established a tradition of orderly and cooperative transitions.

There was also an altruistic motive on the part of the Hunt administration. As one staffer put it, "I remember when eight years ago, we sat in the new governor's conference and listened to governors talk about their horrible transition efforts, where the outgoing governor did not speak to the incoming governor from election day to inauguration day. Where incoming governors and their staffs stepped into offices and found nothing. No papers, no paper clips, no office supplies, no stationery, no anything. Basically, they had to start from scratch. Our feeling was that this certainly was a disservice to the people of the state."

One problem did occur during the transition process, although it was quickly resolved. Some members of Martin's transition team had gone to incumbent departmental secretaries prior to the inauguration and said, "We've got our marching orders, and they are to locate money in your budget and in all the budgets. We must identify potential cuts in your budget." They asked specific career people in each department who had worked to develop the last Hunt budget to help them identify where their departmental budgets could be cut. This undoubtedly was in preparation for Martin's legislative package and in response to his campaign promise to reduce taxes and trim state expenditures. This created tension between the two camps because employees who had worked to put the Hunt budget together and to establish the priorities of the Hunt administration were now being asked to dismantle these priorities. One member of the Hunt organization summarized it this way: "He [Hunt] has asked us to put together a budget that says 'these are our priorities,' and you [Martin] have asked us simultaneously to go behind his back and identify cuts." The Hunt administration's response was, "Wait until January 5 and they're your people. Then you can go back and ask them to do whatever you want them to do." After a hastily called meeting, the Martin transition coordinator agreed that they were placing these individuals in an untenable situation and immediately ceased the process.

The Martin Transition

Martin moved quickly to establish a transition team. For several days immediately after the election he closeted himself with key advisers on the eighth floor of the Hilton Hotel in downtown Raleigh, in a suite of rooms that was accessible only by a special elevator key. Meeting with Martin were those people often referred to as his "inner circle." These individuals included his brother, Joseph B. Martin, a Charlotte bank executive; former Republican governor James E. Holshouser; James S. Loftin, Martin's long-time congressional administrative assistant; Phillip J. Kirk, the top aide to Republican congressman James T. Broyhill and a former Holshouser cabinet official; and R. Jack Hawke, Jr., Martin's campaign manager.

The transition team began to develop a broad outline of the action they planned to take. This included initial discussions of a legislative strategy and administrative appointments. Early in his administration, Martin planned to push for sweeping, Reagan-like tax cuts, which had been the centerpiece of his campaign. Martin viewed this goal as a mandate from the people and hoped to accomplish tax cuts by working with the legislature, but if his efforts were stymied, Martin aides maintained that the new governor, versed in the political hardball of Congress, would not hesitate to engage in a scrap.

Another concern given priority in these initial discussions was the selection of people to staff the new administration. Former Republican governor Holshouser had encountered some difficulty in finding experienced, qualified Republicans for top jobs in his administration, and Martin's aides, some of whom had worked in the Holshouser administration, wanted to avoid the delays that had plagued their only Republican predecessor.

The Martin transition team began drawing up lists of potential cabinet and subcabinet members, typically jotting down four or five names for each major post. Martin planned to announce his first cabinet officers in early December and hoped to have the entire cabinet in place by the January inauguration.

Martin and his advisers wanted to broaden his political base by appealing to conservative Democrats as well as to the academic and business communities. As one adviser said, "We are looking at the business community, looking at the academic community, to put together an administration that does what Jim Martin has been talking about—building bridges and opening doors."

The structure of the transition team is depicted in figure 1. The overall director of the transition effort was the governor's brother, Joseph Martin. Three other transition coordinators reported directly to Martin.

Phillip Kirk, Jr., was given the title of executive director of Martin's transition team, and his responsibilities included coordinating the transition effort, overseeing the inauguration process, initial considerations of budget and legislative matters, and continuing the recruitment of personnel for the administration.

James Loftin, Martin's executive assistant, was given the responsibility for developing the structure and organization of the governor's

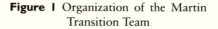

Figure 1 Organization of the Martin
Transition Team

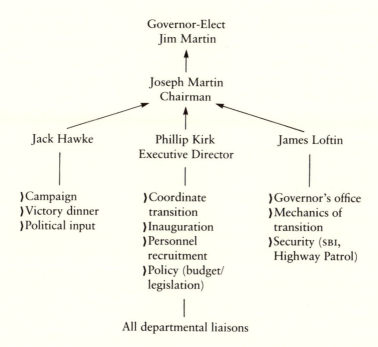

Governor-Elect
Jim Martin

↑

Joseph Martin
Chairman

Jack Hawke   Phillip Kirk   James Loftin
                  Executive Director

) Campaign   ) Coordinate   ) Governor's office
) Victory dinner   transition   ) Mechanics of
) Political input) Inauguration   transition
) Personnel   ) Security (SBI,
                    recruitment   Highway Patrol)
) Policy (budget/
                    legislation)

All departmental liaisons

office. Also under his purview were other matters, such as running the transition team, providing security, and performing liaison functions with the State Bureau of Investigation and the State Highway Patrol.

Jack Hawke, the campaign manager, was given the task of winding down the campaign, preparing the victory dinner, and providing political input to the transition process.

By November 28, three weeks after the election, Martin had his entire transition team in place, structured so that every executive department had a liaison person reporting to Phillip Kirk, the executive director of the transition team. The liaison person for each executive department was chosen for his or her background and experience; most had some familiarity with the functions of the department. They were given the task of researching how departments function and preparing and synthesizing briefing material for the new departmental secretary.

Martin drew from a variety of sources in naming his transition team. For example, one member of the team, the liaison person for the Department of Human Resources, was a former employee of the Division of Health Services and also a member of former Democratic governor Jim Hunt's transition team. A former secretary of natural and economic resources under Governor Holshouser was named coordinator of the overall transition team. Other members included a former secretary of natural and economic resources who was named liaison for the Department of Commerce; a former secretary of cultural resources in the Holshouser administration, who was named liaison for the Department of Administration; a former secretary of transportation in the Holshouser administration who was named liaison person for the Department of Transportation; a former director of the state Office of Marine Affairs, who was named liaison person for the Department of Natural Resources and Community Development; a former state Justice Department official under Republican attorney general James Carson who was named liaison to the judiciary; the eastern coordinator of unsuccessful Democratic gubernatorial candidate Eddie Knox, who was named liaison to the Department of Corrections; a prominent arts patron, who was named liaison to the Department of Cultural Resources; a former GOP state senator and unsuccessful candidate for Congress, who was named liaison to the Department of Crime Control and Public Safety; a law partner of Tom Ellis (the chairman of Jesse Helms's National Congressional Club), who was named liaison to the Department of Revenue; and a Republican state senator from Martin's home county of Mecklenburg who was named liaison to the Department of Education.

The transition process went relatively smoothly. Liaison personnel for most departments utilized the extensive material prepared by the Hunt administration. As one member of the transition team put it, "We found those materials very, very helpful. The whole administration was very thorough in putting it together." Included in the documents were detailed descriptions of the organization and structure of each department, its major functions, and even suggestions on how to improve its operation.

Personal relationships between the incoming and outgoing staffs also went very smoothly with few exceptions. Said one member of the Martin transition team, "We called them on Wednesday [after the election] and we were in business on Friday." He also characterized the

Hunt effort as "tremendous." A similar perspective was echoed by the Hunt transition people.

In late November Martin and a few of his top advisers attended the new governors' conference sponsored by the National Governors' Association (NGA). Most of his advisers agreed that the new governors' conference provided "invaluable information" for the transition team. They also had some contact with the National Governors' Association and utilized some of the material they provided.

The transition effort enabled Martin to have his cabinet in place by Christmas. Martin kept his campaign pledge to establish a nominally bipartisan administration by appointing two Democrats to his ten-member cabinet. He also named two women and one black. His appointments reflected an attempt to secure a broad range of support from all segments of the Republican party, and to extend a friendly hand to conservative Democrats in the state, a necessity for a minority party governor. In general, Martin's appointments drew favorable reaction from most observers of state government, including the state's major newspapers and leaders of both political parties. Three members of Martin's cabinet had served in the administration of former governor Jim Holshouser and the others had served on the transition team. Phillip Kirk, Jr., who was named secretary of human resources, had held the same post in the last year of the Holshouser administration and most recently had been administrative assistant to U.S. Congressman James T. Broyhill. Martin's appointee as executive assistant for budget and management was a former member of the Advisory Budget Commission during the Hunt administration. A former furniture company chairman was named secretary of commerce. A member of the Fayetteville City Council, who had been active in organizing civil rights training sessions for prison inmates, was named secretary of corrections. He was the only black member of the cabinet. A former assistant U.S. attorney was appointed secretary of crime control and public safety. A former Republican candidate for secretary of state and chairman of the Craven County industrial development commission was named secretary of cultural resources. A six-term member of the North Carolina house who had waged an unsuccessful campaign to unseat Democratic U.S. Congressman Charles G. Rose III was named secretary of natural resources and community development. Environmentalists, who had strongly backed Martin's opponent in the election, praised the appointment. The appointee had a pro-environmental voting record in the state house and was one of the few eastern legislators to consistently support the Coastal Area Management Act, which regulated development in coastal areas. A retired bank vice president and supporter of unsuccessful Democratic candidate Eddie Knox was named secretary of revenue. The former secretary of natural and economic resources under Governor Holshouser was named secretary of transportation.

Organizing the Governor's Office

James Loftin, Martin's congressional executive assistant, was named executive assistant and staff director in the new administration, and he was given the responsibility for organizing the governor's office. The organization of this office is depicted in figure 2. Loftin assumed the responsibility of the day-to-day activities of running the governor's office, coordinating intergovernmental activities, dealing with citizens' affairs, and operating as the governor's personal secretary. The governor's education advisers also reported to Loftin.

Jack Hawke, the campaign manager, was named special assistant for policy. Hawke, the political point man of the administration, was assigned the duties of handling media relations, special projects, and organizing the governor's town meetings.

James Trotter was named special counsel, serving as the senior legal adviser to the governor. He was also given responsibility for overseeing the executive mansion, coordinating the legislative efforts of the governor's administration, and patronage.

Three other people reported directly to the governor. These included C. C. Cameron, the budget director; John Higgins, the personnel manager; and Tom Stith, the minority affairs adviser. The structure of the governor's office, with at least six senior-level staff people reporting directly to Martin, was to cause problems for him, especially in dealing with the legislature and political appointees across the state.

While one of Martin's goals in appointing individuals to his administration was to bridge factional, partisan, ideological, racial, and other divisions, it soon became apparent that the governor-elect had a proclivity for naming individuals with ties to his home county of Mecklenburg. When he started assembling his administration, he did so with a map outlining the 100 counties of North Carolina. When he found someone to fill a cabinet post, Martin placed a "C" on the map inside the appointee's home county. For assistant secretaries, the

Figure 2 Organization of the Governor's Office

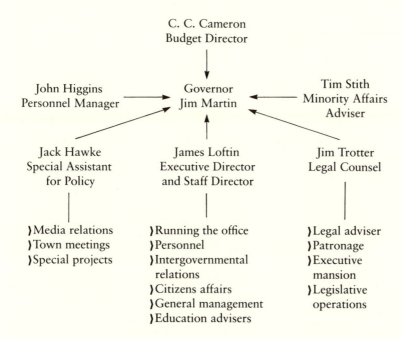

C. C. Cameron
Budget Director

John Higgins
Personnel Manager

Governor
Jim Martin

Tim Stith
Minority Affairs
Adviser

Jack Hawke
Special Assistant
for Policy

James Loftin
Executive Director
and Staff Director

Jim Trotter
Legal Counsel

)Media relations
)Town meetings
)Special projects

)Running the office
)Personnel
)Intergovernmental
  relations
)Citizens affairs
)General management
)Education advisers

)Legal adviser
)Patronage
)Executive
  mansion
)Legislative
  operations

notation was "AS." The governor wanted a geographically balanced administration; however, by inauguration day the area around Mecklenburg County was filled with many letters. Of the top forty positions the new governor had to fill, seven had gone to people from Charlotte (which is in Mecklenburg County). More significant than the number was the prominence of these jobs.

Martin turned to his home town for his top budget adviser, his chief of staff, and his legal counsel. He installed Charlotte bankers as deputy secretaries of commerce and transportation. And the governor called on Mecklenburg County for his chairman of the board to oversee alcoholic beverage sales and the personnel director for the 66,000 state employees. While this arrangement did not sit well with some individuals, others thought it only natural. As one Martin appointee said, "It's normal for people to go back to where they grew up and tap the people they know." Martin's comment, somewhat tongue-in-cheek, was "we've been successful in getting them to share their talents with the rest of the state."

Martin's inaugural address stressed the themes of unity of purpose and bipartisanship—necessary conditions for a Republican governor confronted by rule-proof Democratic majorities in both houses of the legislature (38 to 12 in the senate; 82 to 38 in the house). Martin's statements that "there is a time for partisanship and there is a time for bipartisanship" and "today we're all Democrats and today we're all Republicans" raised the possibility of a good working relationship with the legislature. In return, "the Democratic majority in the General Assembly made respectful and non-combative noises in the direction of the governor's mansion."[2] However, the spirit of bipartisanship was short-lived.

The Legislative Session

In what must be a record for the shortest honeymoon between a new governor and legislature, it took less than two hours after the beginning of the session for the Republican leader in the senate to observe: "I have a strange, strange feeling that the honeymoon is over." The point of controversy was the date for the governor's state of the state address. Martin had indicated that he planned to give the speech on February 19, but would not have his budget (a revision of the Hunt budget) ready by that date. In what was viewed by Republicans as an attempt to embarrass and insult the governor, the senate adopted a resolution that invited Martin to deliver the address on February 28 and *directed* him to provide details of his budget at that time. Democrats claimed there was little for them to do until the governor put forth his budget proposals and felt it was unnecessary for the governor to address them without specific policy directives. Regardless of the rationale behind the move, it set the tone for the remainder of the session.

In his state of the state speech Martin surprised political observers and lawmakers by requesting that the legislature approve a constitutional amendment granting him veto power. The proposal was promptly killed in committee and Martin condemned the move as "an arrogantly repulsive act."

Other partisan disputes arose over legislative attempts to chip away gubernatorial authority. These included a move to freeze 3,087 vacant state jobs, ostensibly an economy measure, that in reality would have temporarily prevented the administration from filling the positions; a measure to limit the governor's control over the State Board of Elections and its chief administrator (a Democrat); a statewide referendum to repeal gubernatorial secession (although it would not affect Martin); a proposal to reduce the authority of the executive branch to draft, approve, and enforce administrative rules and regulations; and a measure to prevent the governor from hiring private attorneys in disputes with other agencies.

The greatest source of partisan rancor and rhetoric centered around Martin's tax-cut package. As proposed, the various cuts would have cost the state an estimated $489 million in revenue. Martin's proposal received little legislative attention in part because most Democrats felt that the proposed cuts were unrealistic and that the state could not afford such a massive reduction in revenue while attempting to upgrade health, education, and transportation programs. Another contributing factor was the long delay before the legislature received Martin's proposals. Although he was the beneficiary of a one-month grace period (the legislature convened in February rather than January in order to give the new governor more time to prepare his legislative package), it was not until seven weeks into the session that Martin's plan was introduced. By that time the legislature was considering several Democratic alternatives. As one influential legislator noted "We've got to do something and he [Martin] is not ready. We've got to plow ahead." The end result was a tax cut (minor changes in sales, intangibles, and inventory taxes with additional cuts in income, inheritance, and gift taxes) that only faintly resembled the governor's original request. The cuts totalled only $171 million, approximately one-third of the total under the Martin proposal.

The partisan pot shots did not end with the close of the session. Martin characterized the session as "as embarrassment" and said that Democratic leaders "may have some tall explaining to do" to the voters. He summarized his maiden attempt to work with the legislature in a tone not designed to engender future rapport: "I had a difficult time draining the swamp with all the alligators in it." To counter the Martin attack, Lieutenant Governor Bob Jordan immediately embarked on a five-city tour to "remove the smoke screen" ignited by the governor's rhetoric.

Although Martin described the session as an embarrassment to the Democratically controlled legislature, it could be considered nothing less than an embarrassment to his administration. Most observers agreed that Martin asked for little and got very little. One major state newspaper was more specific, criticizing Martin for his "lack of vision and leadership." Even Republicans in the legislature conceded that "the governor took his lumps." The end result was a shift toward legislative dominance. In the absence of sizable gains in the 1986 elections by Republicans, Martin fared only slightly better in the subsequent session.

Evaluating the Transition

To evaluate the Martin transition, it is instructive to discuss it in two parts; one covering the period from the election to the inauguration and the second covering the period from the inauguration through the end of the first legislative session.

The first phase of the transition went relatively smoothly. Much of the credit for the success of this phase must be attributed to the thoughtful preparation and extensive efforts of the outgoing governor. The Martin team was significantly aided by the financial resources provided by the Hunt budget, the quick provisions of state office space, telephones, equipment, and other supplies, the placement of Martin personnel on the state payroll in vacancies specifically left open for that purpose, and the use of the background material prepared for new department heads and staff persons. Martin was also judicious in his choice of key Republicans who had weathered a transition process before and who brought some expertise and experience with them to his team. With only a very few exceptions, the Martin transition team was able to establish some degree of order to the chaotic postelection phase and have in place a widely respected cabinet and staff by inauguration day.

The second phase of the transition was largely unsuccessful. Martin failed to establish a working coalition in the legislature and saw his limited legislative program essentially ignored. In the process he alienated many powerful Democrats and lost some of the media support that characterized the pre-inauguration phase.

Given the high hopes and bipartisan spirit that characterized the pre-session period, one is compelled to ask how the prospects of a working relationship between the new governor and the legislature evaporated so quickly. The answer may be found in the status of Martin's can-

didacy, the political nature of executive-legislative relations in North
Carolina, and specific organizational problems and strategies of the
Martin administration in particular.

The Martin administration never really got its policy "act" together
during the first legislative session. This was in part due to the nature
of the campaign. Martin, the decided underdog, was forced to concentrate all of his efforts and resources toward his election; otherwise there
would not have been a transition. In contrast, his opponent had developed a transition and legislative strategy months before the election,
complete with names, organizational charts, and legislative priorities,
and had already initiated contacts with key legislators and state agency
personnel.

As previously noted, the office of governor in North Carolina is
institutionally weak. Because of the weak nature of the office, governors derive their influence with the legislature through political means:
providing leadership and direction, lobbying and logrolling with legislators. Martin's predecessor in office, Jim Hunt, was effective in culti-
vating legislators; Martin was not. One Republican legislator noted the
difference in Martin's style and that of his predecessor: Hunt's letters
to him began with "Dear Frank" and were signed "Jim." Martin's letters were addressed "Dear Representative Rhodes" and were signed by
"James G. Martin." A Democratic leader noted a difference in tactics:
"He [Hunt] would pick up the phone and call late at night, or would
go visit them [the legislators] or have them come to his office . . . to
work out differences. . . . Governor Martin chose a different route; he
chose to talk to the papers."

The administration's formal interactions with the legislature fared no
better. In what most observers would agree was a good choice, Martin
selected former state legislator I. Beverly Lake, Jr., a Democrat turned
Republican, as his chief legislative lobbyist. Lake had been persuaded
in 1980 to change parties and be the Republican Party's sacrificial lamb
to the reelection of Jim Hunt. As a former Democratic legislator, Lake
knew the institutional ways and personalities of the legislature and
could have been an effective lobbyist. However, the inability of the
Martin staff to get its legislative agenda in order severely limited his
effectiveness. He once complained to reporters that he was "frustrated
by having to spend more time in staff meetings than working the legislative hallways." As a result, "the ineffectiveness of Martin's legislative
lobbying effort left even Republicans shaking their heads."[3]

Of course, Martin's predecessor was a Democrat dealing with legislative Democrats. But it would be too easy and misleading to dismiss Martin's ineffectiveness as simply partisan politics. Democrats conceded that, given the mood in Raleigh after the November election, "if he [Martin] had played his cards right he could have been very successful in building a coalition of Republicans and conservative Democrats." However, as one newspaper noted, "From the start, Martin made it clear that he wanted a confrontation."[4] If confrontation politics was a strategic choice, it was undoubtedly a poor choice. One generally plays confrontation politics from a position of power. Martin had neither an institutional base nor a political base of power with the legislature.

Governor Martin's ineffectiveness in the legislative arena also can be traced to problems within his administration. These problems were organizational, strategic, and tactical. The administrative structure of Martin's office was designed to maximize input from a variety of sources. Ostensibly the rationale for this organizational scheme was to make it unlikely that the governor would become isolated. However, in attempting to avoid one problem this organizational structure created several other problems. Without a single chief of staff to coordinate administrative tasks, the four "bull elephants," as the senior staffers were known, battled over administrative and policy turf from the outset. These battles detracted from the necessary organizational matters at lower levels within the administration, prohibited the development of a clear-cut programmatic legislative agenda, and caused catastrophic delays and blunders with the very limited agenda that finally did emerge late in the legislative session. The most frequent complaints were that the staff was inexperienced and unorganized and that there were too many people reporting to the governor. These problems resulted in bills from the administration being introduced with entire pages missing, the tax-cut issue losing momentum because it arrived so late in the session, and several breaches of protocol when the governor made appointments to boards and commissions in legislative districts without first seeking the advice of the district representative.

The organizational problems were significant enough that eleven of the twelve Republican senators requested a meeting with the governor and his staff and, in embarrassing detail, spelled out a litany of "goofs, delays, and breaches in political protocol committed by the governor's inexperienced staff." One senator was succinct in his comments: "It's a damn mess, Governor."[5]

The organizational problems were compounded by strategic and tactical decisions made by the administration. Martin's strategy in dealing with the legislature was to "put all of his eggs in one basket" and "strike while the iron was hot." Whether by choice or necessity (given his organizational problems), Martin's tax-cut package *was* his legislative program. Thus, his measurable fortunes were determined largely by a single issue. The only other issue that generated much attention—gubernatorial veto—had no chance of success and was viewed by legislators as simply a partisan ploy to acquire ammunition for the 1986 legislative elections.

Unfortunately for Martin, the iron had cooled considerably by the time the tax package reached the legislature. Martin decided to incorporate the tax package with his revised version of the outgoing governor's budget. Rather than making quick and marginal adjustments to the Hunt budget, the Martin staff made a rather comprehensive review —a time-consuming and subsequently costly decision. The administration failed to recognize the important and central role of the budget in legislative decision-making, and as a result much of the momentum was lost.

As the session progressed and the frequency of legislative setbacks increased, Martin's favorite tactic became the press conference. Martin's comments were often harsh, using words like "partisan intransigence," "cavalier disrespect," "arrogantly repulsive," and "insulting" in reference to legislative actions. Martin also committed an unusual if not unpardonable act—he criticized the legislative leadership directly. After one typical Martin press conference the speaker of the house responded: "Statements like this don't do much to strengthen relations."

What continued to rankle legislators was the combination of Martin's lack of personal involvement in legislative proposals and his determination to "go over their heads" by taking every setback directly to the people. As one legislator put it, "He has sat in his office and talked . . . only to himself, God, and the press. . . . I'm getting tired of it."

Democratic legislators perceived Martin's tactics as attempts to gain political ammunition for future elections. Martin did little to dispel this perception. At one press conference, hastily called after another setback to this tax-cut package, Martin stated: "We took these questions to the voters in 1984 and, if necessary, we can ask them again in 1986." On two occasions during the session Martin hopscotched the state, holding a series of news conferences asking voters to demand that their representatives support his programs. These tactics increasingly alienated Democratic legislators and exacerbated an already poor relationship. A statement by one legislator summarized their feelings: "This governor doesn't care what the legislature thinks. He says, 'I'm going to talk to the press. I'm going to talk to the people. I'm going out to elect Republicans in 1986 and defeat a few Democrats.' Well, that might defeat a few Democrats, but it sure won't get any legislation passed."

In summary, organizational problems and inexperience among key staffers limited the development of a clear and comprehensive policy agenda. The limited agenda was either perceived as an unrealistic partisan ploy (the veto and, to some extent, the magnitude of the tax-cut package) or was so late in reaching the legislative floor (the tax-cut package) that it had clearly lost valuable momentum. As the legislature began to hew at the governor's limited program, Martin's rhetoric became more partisan and his motives more political. As a result, the schism between the governor and the legislature grew wider and the legislature assumed the policy initiative.

Martin's inability to establish and cultivate a better relationship with the Democrat-controlled legislature may have its origin in the nature of the governor's previous political experiences and in the inexperience of his staff. Until his election as governor, Martin's political career consisted of a stint as a Mecklenburg County commissioner and six terms in the U.S. Congress. In these positions Martin had always been in a position of *responding* to proposals developed elsewhere—either from citizen's groups or the executive branch. During his congressional service Martin never established a reputation for himself as a policy initiator and, in fact, rarely was involved in major policy debates. As a result, Martin had never developed or refined his policy process capabilities prior to his election as governor.

Martin and his staff were also relatively unfamiliar with North Carolina politics, especially the legislative process. Only one of the four bull elephants had previous experience in state government (C. C. Cameron, the budget director, who was the newcomer to the staff and probably the least influential with Martin). The administration underestimated the power of the legislature vis-à-vis the office of governor and the tradition of gubernatorial leadership (both personal and programmatic). One legislator summed up the result of Martin's initial legislative actions this way: "He's beginning to see the legislative process in

Raleigh is different from Washington. I believe you'll see him working through the committee process next time, not just lambasting it when things go wrong."

Martin also overestimated his ability to go over the head of the legislature and take his case directly to the people. This strategy too may have been the result of his previous experience in Congress. Martin was a member of Congress during the "Reagan Revolution" and the parallels between Reagan's strategy with Congress and Martin's strategy with the General Assembly are striking. Both were swept into office by Republican landslides and with significant Republican legislative gains. Both ran on conservative campaign issues that centered around major tax cuts. Reagan was quick to seize the momentum, establishing a coalition of Republicans and conservative southern "boll-weevil" Democrats and ramrodding his tax cuts through Congress. When Congress appeared recalcitrant, the "Great Communicator" would remind them of his "mandate" and threatened to take his case to the American people.

Martin's strategy was much the same. However, Martin's election was less of a mandate and more a function of Reagan and Helms's coattails, a bitter Democratic runoff primary, and an opponent burdened by personal innuendo and the national ticket. Although Martin is personable and telegenic, his speeches are more reminiscent of a college lecture than a fireside chat. Reagan was able to prod Congress through a combination of lobbying and personal involvement, and utilized his perception of the public mood to back him up. Martin and his legislative liaison personnel, whether because of inexperience or unfamiliarity with the state legislative process, were unable to establish a personal rapport with legislative leaders. And, instead of being a truly viable alternative, his continued threats to take his case to the people only further alienated Democrats and widened the gap between the statehouse and the legislature.

Conclusion

Analysis of the Martin transition effort is somewhat tentative and specific to North Carolina. One of the questions that this study leaves unexamined is to what extent a governor's transition and initial legislative efforts set the tone for his administration. Is it possible for governors who have been disappointed with their initial lack of legislative success to sufficiently recover the lost momentum, mend legislative fences, and subsequently offer future direction for the state? Or does the legislature continue to fill the leadership vacuum and relegate the governor to the status of a noisy lame duck?

On a positive note, the one-upmanship that a succession of North Carolina governors have played with their transition efforts, culminating with the extensive Hunt effort, has probably institutionalized a tradition of orderly and facilitative transition in the state. Given the chaotic nature and frenzied pace of transition, such a tradition can significantly aid a new governor and his administration as they begin the complex task of governing.

North Dakota's Gubernatorial Transition, 1984–1985: "Battling It Out in the Budgetary Badlands"

)))))

Theodore B. Pedeliski

The Campaign

The election of George Sinner, a Democrat, to the governorship of North Dakota in the 1984 election represented an anomaly in terms of national election trends. North Dakotans demonstrated their reputation for split-ticket voting by giving Ronald Reagan his mandate to serve another four years, by voting in a number of Democratic statewide officials, by voting for a majority of Republicans in both houses of the state legislature, and by ousting an incumbent and politically secure Republican governor.

Allen Olson, the incumbent Republican governor, enjoyed a measure of political advantage as the campaign began. While his four-year term was not particularly noted for grand achievements or sweeping new policies, he played a good game of maintenance politics. He was a strong promoter of the state and its resources. He applied his influence in Washington, stressing his ties to Reagan in terms of protecting those federal programs that were vital to the state's interests (farm supports, transportation, rural electrification, agricultural trade, water policies).

Olson had also preempted what North Dakota politicians are usually obligated to embrace to gain approval by the state's political culture —a position of fiscal stringency. After the 1982 legislative session he rescinded pay raises of 4 percent that had been scheduled for state employees. In the 1983 legislative session the legislature and Olson blocked any further raises (exclusive of some fringe benefits) for state employees for the 1983–85 biennium. The action strongly alienated state employees, a small but vocal minority, but was applauded by state taxpayers.

Olson also registered personal appeal. His speaking style improved during his first years in office. He projected a gregarious and optimistic attitude, and he conveyed a strong sense of concern for the state and its interests.

If Olson had any liabilities, they involved a number of incidents in his administration that raised issues of judgment, personal patronage, and integrity. Early in his administration, Olson took steps to procure a new limousine, redecorate his office, and acquire a new plane for his use. Under a flurry of criticism Olson withdrew the request for a $1.3-million airplane. But the basis was laid for labeling Olson a "luxury governor." Olson's appointments were also criticized in that he appeared to favor very close friends and associates or highly partisan Republican party officials and supporters in patronage.

In 1983, the year before the election, several of Olson's appointees were forced to resign because of integrity issues. His director of human services was charged with shoplifting. His director of management and budget also resigned because of problems with the Internal Revenue Service. In addition, two Republican-endorsed officials, the insurance commissioner and the superintendent of public instruction, did not seek reelection after integrity issues were raised against them.

In North Dakota's moralistic political culture, such a rash of incidents caused voters to question the "Republican sweep" of 1980. Luckily Governor Olson was able to move quickly to see to it that his "embarrassments" were removed from the administration.

On balance, Olson's position was strong and the polls indicated that Olson had a comfortable lead. A University of North Dakota Bureau of Governmental Affairs poll in May saw Olson leading Sinner 47 percent to 36 percent.[1]

George Sinner, the Democratic challenger from Casselton, North Dakota, made his living as a farmer. He was involved as a president and as a lobbyist for the Red River Sugarbeet Growers Association. His political experience included terms in the state senate (1962–66) and the house (1983–85). From 1966 to 1973 he was a member of the State Board of Higher Education, and he was also a member of the 1970 State Constitutional Convention. He made an unsuccessful bid for Congress in 1964. His political service was in positions of relatively low visibility and his recognition outside the Red River Valley was low. Sinner's personal appeal to a political public left much to be desired. His low key, professional, and often digressive speaking style, laced with chalkboard statistics, did little to fire up an audience's enthusiasm. He was also characterized as being overly pessimistic. Earl Strinden, the Republican house majority leader, called him "Mr. Gloom and Doom" for his dire assessments of the state's fiscal well being.

Others saw Sinner as having certain strengths as he entered the campaign. In winning the Democratic nomination he had conducted a well-organized, well-timed campaign, winning the endorsement over Art Link, a prior two-term governor who enjoyed a warm relationship with the electorate. Sinner's style—low keyed, reasoned, and concerned —also reminded voters of William Guy, a former governor (1961–73) held in wide respect. Finally, his candor and integrity were unquestioned.

While Olson maintained a significant lead in the polls, a poll commissioned by the state Democratic party revealed that Olson's support was soft. Some 47 percent of the respondents could name something they didn't like about the incumbent.[2]

Following the conventions, the campaign took off slowly. Sinner stressed what he termed a lack of leadership in the administration and an inability to handle the budget. He used the first part of the summer to raise a credibility issue. In the beginning of the campaign Olson had saturated the state with a series of billboard messages. Sinner claimed that the billboards were gross distortions. This issue was stressed time and time again, but the electorate never did react to it as important.

Three substantive issues stressed in the early phase of the campaign were taxes, the budget, and education, all important to the voters. Each candidate attributed the large increase in state expenditures in 1981, the financial shortfall of 1982, and the subsequent large tax increases in 1983 to the other. Because Sinner as a legislator and Olson as chief executive both had worked for and voted for the outcomes, the attempts to attach responsibility for the budgetary condition of the state fell on deaf ears.

The tax issue also failed to illustrate or sharpen differences between the candidates. Both candidates were opposed to any new taxes. Sinner left open the possibility that taxes might have to be raised to provide state employees with salary increases—but only as a last resort.

In respect to education, in particular higher education, Olson thought that a 5-percent increase in salaries would be reasonable. Sinner supported an 11.5-percent increase that had been recommended by the State Board of Higher Education.

The three issues of budget, taxes, and education became intertwined and stayed so even into the legislative session. In terms of the campaign, they conferred no advantage to either candidate. The differences between the candidates were never really clear and they appeared to be haggling over nuances in position.

Sinner's position on salary increases did help align his interest-group support. Even before the convention his most active supporters appeared to be state employees and faculty members. During the summer Sinner received the endorsements of the North Dakota Educational Association, the North Dakota branch of the Association of Federal, State, County, and Municipal Employees, and the state organization of the AFL-CIO. In addition Sinner scheduled a series of approximately thirty meetings with civic and business leaders in communities throughout the state. These meetings were public but aimed at opinion leaders, who were ordinarily Republican. Backed up by his chalkboard, Sinner painted a picture of the state's deteriorating economy and the necessity of stringent and innovative measures to meet the problems of state government under such changing conditions—a tactic to persuade even Republican voters that he could be a credible governor with a reasoned and conservative approach to the state's fiscal problems.

At the Labor Day mark, Sinner was the acknowledged underdog. According to polls taken at the end of August by the Bureau of Governmental Affairs at the University of North Dakota, Olson was ahead with 52 percent to Sinner's 33 percent, with 15 percent undecided. As Mike Jacobs of the *Grand Forks Herald* reported on September 15, "George Sinner looked like a beaten man. He acted like one too."[3]

The change in the character of the campaign came in a speech that Sinner gave to a meeting of the North Dakota Broadcasters, a speech that Mike Jacobs characterized as one of the meanest in recent North Dakota politics. Sinner made it clear that the main issue in the election was that of "moral" leadership. Olson had failed to set a moral tone for state government or for his appointees. His people had been a series of embarrassments to the state.

On September 28 Sinner charged that Olson had broken state law by not explaining $3,600 worth of out-of-state travel vouchers. What was more damaging to Olson than the technical omissions in the case was the fact that the reimbursement was for five nights at the Hyatt Regency in Washington, D.C., at $275 a night. To many North Dakotans the governor's action could only be interpreted as extravagant and "at their expense."

Polls now showed that Sinner was moving up rapidly. A Bureau of Governmental Affairs poll taken in early October showed Olson with 45 percent of the vote, Sinner with 41 percent, and 14 percent undecided. The campaign was in a dead heat.[4]

The Sinner campaign had timed its expenditures to increase media exposure (television spots) at this critical stage of the campaign. The Olson campaign had instead concentrated on exposure in the early part of the campaign. The cost of each campaign was roughly equivalent for the two candidates. Sinner reported that his campaign cost $300,000. Olson reported that his campaign cost roughly $330,000. Olson received about $125,000 in out-of-state contributions, including a sizable allocation from the Republican National Committee, while Sinner received only some $12,500 from out-of-state political action committees (PACs) and contributors.

One ad nearly undid the Sinner campaign: a newly introduced Sinner spot depicted a farmer talking about all the "bull" that the Olson campaign was throwing around, whereupon the farmer dug his pitchfork into a manure pile and dispatched some manure in the direction of the camera. That week every cafe and small-town watering hole buzzed with talk about how dirty the campaign had become. Sinner was interpreted to have sunk to a new low. The ad was withdrawn.

Polls conducted by the Bureau of Governmental Affairs on October 29–November 1 and by James Lauer and Associates on October 24–26 showed Olson with 49 percent of the vote and Sinner with 41 percent of the vote, with 11 percent undecided.[5]

On October 27 Sinner and members of his campaign revealed to the public that Olson had secretly taken a general pay raise that he said he wouldn't take. When Olson rescinded the legislatively directed pay raise that had been scheduled to go into effect in 1982, he stated, "I'm going to sacrifice my four percent because I'm governor and I expect to be affected equally or greater than other state employees." Olson explained that in collecting his back pay he was only following an attorney general's opinion. But he had not revealed this acceptance publicly and the picture of "the check for $4,907" printed in newspapers across the state had as much impact upon the election as any other incident in the campaign.

Then, on November 2, another issue emerged, revolving around Olson's role in a land sale involving industrial commission loan approval. The complexity of the sale and the failure to candidly and publicly reveal the full facts behind the Bank of North Dakota loan fueled further suspicions of the Olson administration.

Finally it was revealed that Governor Olson had not filed his federal and state income taxes for 1983. Olson tried to deflect the issue by noting that he had paid his estimate of taxes for the year—but the damage was done and at a time when it could not be reversed by the Republicans.

The election results, particularly the magnitude of Sinner's win, surprised North Dakotans. Sinner won by a convincing 10-percent margin (55.3 percent to Olson's 44.7 percent), or better than 42,000 votes. Sinner won a majority in forty-one of the state's fifty-two counties. With the exception of Minot, he carried all of the state's major cities (populations of more than 15,000) including Fargo and Bismarck, which are traditionally Republican. Olson carried only the far-western counties and three counties from the conservatively oriented German-Russian triangle.[6]

Olson's support eroded very rapidly in the ten days prior to the election, with Sinner moving from 41 percent to 55 percent in about twelve days. The erosion was also general, his margin in rural areas equalling those margins he received in the cities. The integrity issue appeared to transcend geographical, occupational, and economic divisions in the state.

An analysis of the election reveals that Olson had lost the election more than Sinner had won it. But Olson and his colleagues had done more than shoot themselves in the foot during the final weeks of the campaign. The defeat can be attributed to Olson's misreading of North Dakota's strongly moralistic political culture. Political traditions and constituents in North Dakota support a concept of political service as a sacrifice.[7] Power does not come with perquisites. The combination of the governor's airplane, the appointment of close friends to positions, the expensive hotel rooms, the land deal, and the acceptance of a pay raise all indicated the use of official status as a conduit to aggrandizement. Mike Jacobs in a *Grand Forks Herald* editorial characterized the Olson administration as having exhibited an excess of hubris: an attitude of exclusivity (to members of Republican inner circles), an attitude of arrogance (particularly to the press), and an attitude of moral insensitivity.[8]

The character of the campaign actually had very little impact on the transition. Despite the negative nature of the campaign, particularly in its final phases, the two sides moved to effect a cordial and cooperative transition. A major hang-up would occur on the issue of the date of taking office. But that would likely have occurred regardless of the intense, aggressive, and negative aspects of the campaign.

The Transition

The transition began with a staff meeting at the Sinner headquarters in Fargo ten days after the election. Present at the meeting were Governor-elect Sinner and his wife, Jane; Charles Fleming, his campaign manager; Carole Siegert, treasurer of the campaign and director of field operations; Dick Gross, a state government lawyer; Joe Lamb, long time friend and rural banker; and Lloyd Omdahl, political scientist at the University of North Dakota and director of administration for former governor Bill Guy.

The general direction of the transition was addressed at that time. Lloyd Omdahl indicated the range of problems that needed to be addressed by the transition—everything from a policy of press relations to relations with elected officials, appointed officials, party officials, and agency heads. The transition group agreed this wide range of issues and problems could not be handled by a single unit. Issues of the functions of the office and legislative and political relations might best be handled by different teams. It was important to recruit the best and the brightest to those teams and the two former Democratic governors with whom the governor-elect was on good terms were natural choices to chair these committees. Former governor William Guy was chosen to head the administrative functions committee. Former governor Art Link was chosen to head a transition committee on policy and legislative relations.

The committee also made several important decisions at that meeting. Sinner put first priority on selection of a director of management and budget. Richard Rayl, a corporate executive and close acquaintance of the governor-elect, had prior consideration for the post, but it was important to get him on the team immediately. Governor Olson was scheduled to release his proposed budget on December 8, and work would begin immediately to render this the Sinner budget.

Another important decision was to move the transition process to Bismarck. This was important in establishing an atmosphere of taking charge and putting a new face on the governor's office.

A third decision was made in regard to the personnel recruitment and selection process. Another transition committee, headed by Joe Lamb and Carole Siegert, would take on this task. It was decided that outside the governor's immediate staff, all appointments would be handled through personnel selection committees whose members would be precluded from appointing themselves to positions. The personnel selection team was to consist of a cross-section of prominent party people from throughout the state. It would direct itself to a search and screening of candidates for the 16 key positions in state government in which officers serve at the pleasure of the governor.

By this time Sinner had also decided on his immediate staff. Charles Fleming was to be the chief of staff, Richard Gross was to be the governor's counsel, and Carole Siegert was to be the administrative assistant to the governor. She was also to deal with party matters and serve as liaison to the Department of Public Instruction and the State Board of Higher Education.

The logistics of the transition left much to be desired. The statutes provided only for a $5,000 appropriation to cover expenses of the transition, a totally inadequate amount.[9] It served to cover the cost of rental and telephones for a warehouse structure on the east edge of Bismarck. There was no money for staff salaries; a lot of work was volunteer work. The Sinner-Meiers campaign paid for the bulk of the salaries of the staff core. Joe Lamb served without remuneration. Furniture, carpeting, and office equipment were donated.

The governor and male members of the staff took up quarters in an apartment house next to transition headquarters. Living conditions were spartan. There was no furniture except for cots.

The lack of equipment and personnel put the staff at a severe disadvantage. One of the problems was information processing. The deluge of job applicants and accompanying references required a great deal of sorting, classification, and filing of material. Handling the correspondence was a horrendous burden for the skeletal staff. Hundreds of letters arrived each day dealing with every conceivable problem. Many inquiries dealt with issues that would be better handled by local or federal officials. All seemed to demand an answer. Not only was it difficult to find time to answer the correspondence, but there were no research resources that would allow the staff to find answers for these inquiries. It was "mindboggling," as one staff member recalled, and the staff worked terribly long hours. The governor-elect also became ill during this period and was briefly hospitalized, which further complicated matters.

On top of all of this was the need to attend to inaugural arrangements. Invitations had to be sent out for a "Victory Reception" for the governor's supporters and prominent Democrats, and some 10,000 invitations were sent out for the inaugural reception and ball. The Democratic-NPL Party did furnish a group of volunteers to assist in the latter.

Most of the inaugural planning is traditionally done by the North Dakota National Guard working with the party of the incoming governor. The guard has a meager appropriation of $3,600 to be spent on inauguration activities, most of which is used for printing and the rental of a civic center. Expenses above that limit were funded by private party donors. The guard also furnished the band for the event and drew up the ceremonial protocols for both the joint inaugural session of the legislature and the inaugural ball.

Administrative Functions Committee

The first transition team was the Administrative Functions Committee. Former governor Bill Guy was named chairman—also on the committee were Ruth Meiers, the lieutenant governor-elect; Woody Gagnon, who had been former governor Art Link's director of administration; Jim Kusler, who had been Link's research and information assistant; Harlan Fugelsten, former counsel for the Highway Department; Lucy Caulutti, U.S. congressman Byron Dorgan's Bismarck office head; and Charles Fleming, the designated chief of staff for the governor's office.

The basic mission of this team was to make recommendations to the Governor in regard to the following areas:

) a process by which major budgeting, legislative, administrative, communications, and personnel decisions were to be made.
) mail and constituent service functions.
) legislative relations apparatus.

⟩ liaison with the press and public.

⟩ liaison with agencies of state government and elected officials.

⟩ governor's relations with the federal government and political sub-divisions.

⟩ relations with the party.

Within this broad framework each member brought an agenda or in-ventory of proposals.

The first meeting largely dealt with the basic plan for getting the governor's office structured and functioning. It included the delegation of portfolio tasks among Sinner's staff and the relations that would be established with Olson's outgoing staff.

Subsequent meetings focused on how to exercise power through the governor's office and how to structure relations with all the political actors with whom the governor must deal. Governor Guy set the tone. He felt that Sinner should be a strong governor with a hands-on ap-proach. The objective was to appoint very good people and work with them on a personal, one-to-one basis.

Guy also indicated that Sinner should not allow the staff to serve as a buffer between the governor and agency heads. Chuck Fleming suggested that the chief of staff be liaison between the governor and agency heads, thus allowing the governor to travel, to lobby, to address himself to planning issues, and to interact with the public. Guy's views prevailed and appear to have prevailed in application.

Questions were also raised about the status of the chief of staff and the counsel in the office. Should they be coequals or should one be the dominant figure? The transition team reached no consensus on this issue but Governor Sinner appears to have kept counsel and chief of staff as coequals. He has stated that he is not put off by disagreements among his staff. In fact he welcomes divergent views. "I strenuously seek variations in position and I'm not afraid to make a decision if they're at odds."[10]

The issue of Lieutenant Governor Meiers's role in the new adminis-tration was also explored. North Dakota's statutes do not delineate any administrative duties for the lieutenant governor. Guy indicated that delegation of governor's powers should proceed slowly. Once power is delegated it can rarely be retrieved. Because one of the lieutenant governor's duties was presiding over the state senate, it was felt that this duty would really preclude any other responsibilities and issues of her permanent role were deferred until after the session.

Since the end of the session Meiers was increasingly called on to stand in for the governor at public appearances, ceremonies, and commission meetings when he was unavailable. She also carried a portfolio in human services and was a first-rate consultant on such issues.

Communication issues were the object of much discussion. There was a general consensus that the governor's office should be as accessible as possible to all parties. In terms of political liaison it was decided that Carole Siegert would handle such matters in the governor's office, including campaign and campaign finance issues, political meetings, and matters of appointments.

In terms of legislative liaison between sessions it was agreed that the legislative leadership of both parties would be invited to attend task force meetings dealing with issues that would require legislative action.

One communication issue that caused a great deal of argument concerned relations with elected officials and agency heads. One agenda item centered on cabinet meetings. During Governor Link's tenure, cabinet meetings were held every Monday morning. Most members concluded that these meetings never were effective. There was a suggestion (by the governor-elect himself) that regular meetings be held with all elected officials, regardless of party, but this proposal was disapproved.

Another proposal was to schedule luncheon meetings with elected Democrat officials on an ad hoc, "need basis" to discuss the administration's policy strategy. This would include the lieutenant governor, the attorney general, the tax commissioner, and the director of management and budget. It could include the chairman and the legislative leaders of the Democratic party.

Similar luncheon meetings were proposed for the heads of agencies— the governor's appointments. Again they would not be a regular feature but would be scheduled around broad-ranging issues affecting state government in general: budget procedures and forecasts, management and personnel policies, reorganization issues. The head of the Office of Management and Budget and the tax commissioner would likely be in attendance at such meetings. After assuming office, the governor scheduled luncheon meetings on an ad hoc basis for elected officials and his cabinet about once a month.

The Administrative Functions Committee also discussed relations with the state's delegation in Washington. Sinner had close personal ties with Congressman Byron Dorgan and indicated all communication with Dorgan would be through himself. In terms of the North Dakota senators, Sinner surprised some members of the transition team when he indicated that he would reach out to both Senator Burdick, the Democrat, and Senator Andrews, the Republican, with equal favor. Sinner intended to transcend political differences when state interests were at issue.

The matter of communication with the public was also considered. Accessibility was to occupy a high priority. In a small state like North Dakota the public maintains a sense of closeness with their highest officials and expects easy and personal access.

Lucy Caulutti felt strongly that the staff should involve a caseworker (staff assistant) to deal with constituent problems. A director of constituent services was established, whose office was to handle all of the correspondence, ensure an expeditious response to mail, and also serve as a referral service.

Former governor Guy set the tone for the functioning of a "strong" governor—an activist who would have a direct line of authority to all the units of government under his control. He also made the point that in taking power a governor should assume control as soon as possible. The importance of this observation would soon be clear as events unfolded that led to the state's constitutional crisis.

Finally, Guy made the point that it was acceptable to take one's time in effecting a transition; not every problem needed to be solved, not every appointment had to be made. The proper time frame for taking power allows the deferral of many problems.

Governor Sinner later agreed that a great many organizational and personnel issues might be deferred. But Governor Guy did not experience the budget dilemma that faced this administration. Budgetary crises presented Sinner's office with unavoidable and immediate pressures.

Policy and Legislative Action Committee

The second transition team formed was the Policy and Legislative Action Committee. Sinner selected former governor Art Link to chair the committee. Representing Sinner's staff on the committee was Dick Gross, the governor's counsel. Also represented were the Democratic Party legislative leaders, selected rank-and-file legislative members, and the Democratic–NPL party chairman.

The committee explored various policy themes that would require gubernatorial and legislative action. The thrust was to establish legislative priorities, provide gubernatorial and legislative consensus, and identify legislative sponsors and floor managers for specific pieces of legislation. The committee intended to look at three areas: economic issues, human services, and education. In this endeavor the committee used as a basis for discussion the Democratic party platform.

What the committee did was to express concerns, identify issues for action, and propose suggestions in the areas of agriculture, natural resources, and education. The most attention was given to the human services area.

The Policy and Legislative Action Committee also recommended approaches that the governor might take with the legislature. Composed for the most part of legislators, the committee naturally recommended that the legislature have maximum accessibility to the governor. They recommended daily meetings with party legislative leaders, possible weekly breakfasts (a Link tradition) with leadership and staff, and biweekly meetings with both Democratic and Republican leaders. They suggested an open-door policy enabling legislators to drop in on the governor during the session. This approach represented a change from Olson's policy, which was criticized by his own party for his lack of accessibility to legislators. It also reaffirmed the traditional contention of legislators that they have prime demands upon the governor during a legislative session.

The group raised a controversial issue that was given publicity by the press. Article 11 of the state's constitution prohibits use of any official influence, use of the appointment power, or threat of the veto in influencing the course of legislation. As a result, in North Dakota governors cannot state in advance any intentions of vetoing legislation. The committee suggested that an attorney general's opinion be obtained on the question. It suggested that the threat of a veto might well be constitutional and could well be a significant weapon. Sinner disavowed this suggestion, indicating that it was confrontational and most likely a counterproductive approach.

The governor-elect himself submitted an inventory of proposed legislation that had not been on the committee's agenda. Some proposals dealt directly with the transition itself—a change in election to allow for either the odd-year election of governors or meeting of the legislature in even years. There were a score of other proposals to which the committee reacted. In most instances possible sponsors for the legislation were identified and other legislators were tagged to obtain and develop information on the issues.

The Policy and Legislative Action Committee was effective not so much in terms of framing a total legislative program as it was in establishing a basic rapport with the party's legislators. It is also significant that the committee did not deal in any way with the budget or revenues. There was an implicit understanding among the Democrats that the matter of the budget and budgetary priorities required the governor's leadership.

The Personnel Search Team

The original personnel search team was composed of Joe Lamb as chairman, Carole Siegert, Lieutenant Governor-elect Ruth Meiers, and seven other individuals. These included a former house majority leader, a mayor, a lawyer, a labor union representative, and several people with experience in personnel. The committee included four women and representatives from every region of the state. The task of the committee was to screen applicants for the sixteen agency heads who attain office by gubernatorial appointment.

Lamb and Siegert began by preparing a position synopsis for each position. It was a shock to discover that many major positions had no job descriptions or skill requirements. Statutes provided no guidance whatsoever.

The inquiries for jobs came in a flood. Governor-elect Sinner was surprised by the number of applicants "who wanted jobs, who expected jobs and needed jobs." Some 500 applications were received. After screening out the frivolous and unqualified applications, Lamb and Siegert reviewed a hundred applications to be given serious consideration. Then, following a matching of applicants to jobs, the applicants were reduced to five for each position.

During the campaign Sinner had indicated that he wanted input from both state employees and clients in making key gubernatorial appointments. A mechanism was developed to allow agency employees and a client/consumer/public representative to be on the final interviews as ad hoc members and to assist in making the final recommendations. The team then conducted interviews for the assigned positions over a three-day period. After the interviews the full committee (without adjunct members) suggested preferred candidates to the governor. The governor then made his selection. He scheduled his own private interviews with a few recommended selections.

Political considerations were avoided. Joe Lamb set a priority on finding people who had experience and training in budgets, personnel, and management. Policy positions didn't come out until the interviews. Some administrators were chosen without a political identification, much less a political test. "I still don't know to this day if our director of institutions or our parks and recreation director are Democrat or Republican. And we did choose three agency heads who came from the Olson administration."[11]

The personnel selection system was a most useful mechanism for dealing with the "prominent" party office-seeker. Old party warhorses were told to submit their applications with everyone else. One prominent Democrat learned that the only position the screening procedure matched him with was motor vehicle registrar (a largely ministerial post) and he was beat out by candidates with better administrative qualifications.

The personnel selection team was invaluable to the transition process. Sinner reported that it relieved him of a tremendous burden at a time when higher priorities, such as the budget, occupied his time. It served to deflect many job seekers, and it sent a signal to the political types that appointments were to be made on the basis of proper qualifications, not political currency.

The personnel search teams disbanded after making fifteen top appointments. But a major task remained: appointments to the state's 100 boards and commissions, which ranged from a Blackbird Depredation on Sunflower Board to a Board of Examiners in Watchmaking. Of these 100 boards there were 26 for which the governor had the authority to appoint a majority of members. The statutes provide that all members of these boards are to be considered resigned effective January 1 in the first year of each four-year term of governor. The governor must acknowledge those resignations and appoint successors within six months.

The Sinner people took the view that this appointment process should be not solely centered on partisan considerations. If Republican incumbents were seen as doing a proper job on their commissions they might be retained. Lamb and Siegert sent out evaluation sheets on board members to Democratic state legislators, district chairmen, prominent Democrats, and Sinner supporters asking them to rate and comment on those incumbent board members who resided in their district. Certain boards invited turnover because of the highly visible public policies that were the responsibilities of those boards. Some boards attracted as many as ten applicants for every vacancy. Such boards included the North Dakota Arts Council, the Water Commission, and the Game and Fish Advisory Board.

The final selections for these boards were left to Siegert and Lamb. Many of the appointments had to meet very specific statutory requirements as to occupation and interest-group membership. Statutes on the boards and commissions were replete with "one-eyed, bald headed, red moustached man with a limp"—seemingly overly specific—requirements. Most of the twenty-six key boards and commissions were staffed by July 1.

The transition experience in staffing boards and commissions provided several lessons. The sheer logistical requirements of the search and personnel screening indicated the need for computerization and possibly a larger staff or special commission team to deal with the number of appointments. Also the restraints of special statutory qualifications raised questions of whether many of these boards needed such interest group representation. And finally questions were raised as to the necessity for the existence of many boards and commissions. As a result, the director of management and budget embarked on a survey to determine the costs of these boards and commissions.

Cooperation to Confrontation: The Constitutional Crisis

After the election Bill Wright, Olson's chief of staff, contacted the incoming Sinner people. Olson also appointed Lee Stenehjem, his OMB director, and Al Lick as transition liaisons.

Most of the contact was between staff members and involved housekeeping matters, screening of archives, office procedures, familiarization with the governor's office budget, the travel voucher system, and so forth. Both sides reported that cooperation was excellent.

Cooperation between budget directors was delayed about a month. The executive budget is held to be so sensitive and controversial that its details are kept confidential until officially delivered to the legislature in mid-December. Once that date passed the incumbent OMB staff instituted an open-door policy to Sinner's budget people (see section on the executive budget, below).

There was only one personal meeting between the outgoing and incoming governors, which took place in the office of the director of the OMB. It began as a private meeting but turned into an open meeting with the media present. The discussion was very formal and dealt with the budget in the most general terms. There was some talk about the Garrison Diversion and a discussion on proclamations.[12] There was really no discussion of when the formal transfer of power would really take place.

Had tradition been followed, the inauguration would have taken place on January 8, the opening day of the legislative session, with the outgoing governor giving the state of the state address followed by the new governor taking the oath of office and giving the inaugural address. Fleming, the chief of staff, took the position that tradition should be respected, and that a delay in taking office until January 7 would give the staff more time to get the governor's office organized.

The events that prompted the constitutional crisis originated in the judiciary. On November 8, the day after the election, Justice Pederson of the North Dakota Supreme Court resigned from the court—effective January 7, 1985. In-term vacancies of the supreme court are filled by gubernatorial appointment, but in 1981 the legislature put a significant check and balance on the governor's powers by dividing the process into a nominations process handled by a Judicial Nominating Committee and then final appointment by the governor. The Judicial Nominating Committee (for supreme court recruitments) consists of six permanent members—two selected by the governor, two by the chief justice, and two by the State Bar Association. Upon being notified by the governor of a vacancy the committee would submit within sixty days a list of not fewer than two nor more than seven nominees for the vacant position.

The statute is unclear as to whether the selection process is to commence on notification of a vacancy or on the first day of the vacancy. The Judicial Nominating Committee took the position that the sixty days began with receipt of a letter of resignation. Owen Anderson, chairman of the nominating committee and a University of North Dakota Law School faculty member, set a schedule for the committee, establishing a deadline of December 19 for nominations and applications for the vacancy, with interviews of candidates to be held on

January 3 and 4. Because the vacancy would not occur until January 7, the nominee would be considered by the new governor.

Then, on December 8, Justice Paul Sands of the supreme court died, which created an instant vacancy that could in fact be filled by Olson if the nominating committee supplied him the names. The new development brought to a head the suggestion by former governor Guy that Sinner should take office as soon as possible to forestall any "midnight appointments" by exiting governor Olson. The Sinner people were particularly concerned that the Judicial Nominating Committee might arrange a partisan outcome. The Judicial Nominating Committee was composed of five acknowledged Republicans and one "Independent." Charles Fleming said the committee was "out of our control."

Anderson, the chairman, indicated that the committee was under no one's control, certainly not Olson's. He said that had the committee been partisan in its outlook it could well have supplied Governor Olson with three names on December 20 because three of the nominees had been reviewed and interviewed by the committee in previous nomination actions. But such a grossly political action on the part of the committee would have transgressed the strong nonpartisan norms of the state's judiciary.

With the death of Sands, the committee did decide to supply names for both vacancies at the same time, a procedure allowed by law and followed previously. The committee decided to adhere to its original schedule and submit its names to the governor after interviews were concluded on the January 3 and 4. Meanwhile the chairman of the committee was to conduct a bar survey evaluation of the twenty-two candidates.

The transition team approached Olson aides before Christmas with the proposal that the governor-elect might want to take office January 1, 1985. Olson had been assuming that the transition would take place when the legislature convened. The outgoing governor would then have the final honor of delivering the traditional state of the state address to the legislature. Olson also later indicated that he too saw the "importance" of the judicial selections. The two administrations could arrive at no agreement as to the proper date when power was to be transferred in the governor's office. A constitutional crisis was upon the state.

The constitutional crisis was really an incipient legal bomb waiting for the proper occasion to explode. The date for North Dakota's gubernatorial inaugurations was not clearly specified in either the constitution or the statutes. The relevant statute was NDCC 44-01-03 (S.L. 1975, Ch. 45), which in 1975 changed the *qualifying date* of elected officials from the first Monday in January and ten days thereafter to January 1 and ten days thereafter. The date for taking office was now open to any one of the first ten days in January. There was no guidance as to who had authority to select the date—the governor-elect or the secretary of state.

In addition to the statute providing for a variable date on which to take office, the official transition was governed by election laws requiring certification of election results by the State Canvassing Board. The secretary of state transmits to each of the persons elected a certificate of election that prescribes the term of office and the commencement date. The certificate of election issued to Sinner stated that the term of governor would be four years commencing on the first Monday of January 1985. Sinner did not legally challenge the validity of the certificate. One reason why the certificates of election prescribed the first Monday in January irrespective of statutory change in 1975 was that the printed forms for the 1976, 1980, and 1984 elections specified the term commencing on the first Monday in January. Secretary of State Ben Meier, renowned for his frugality, had continued to use old forms and actually had not technically departed from the requirements of the law because the 1975 amendments still allowed the taking of office within ten days of January first.

Historical precedent on taking office provided little light on the subject. Governor Olson had taken the oath of office on January 6, 1981. Governor Arthur Link's second term began on January 13, 1977, three days beyond the time allowed by law.

Both sides dug in their heels. Olson and Sinner talked by phone to determine if there was some way to compromise on the issue but compromise was rejected as both sides opted for a legal resolution. Sinner opted for a direct petition to the state's supreme court. Events moved quickly as Sinner filed to take his oath of office on December 31 along with an intention to take office on January 1, 1985. Governor Olson then informed Sinner by letter that his term had not expired, that the Sinner term did not begin until January 7, 1985, and that gubernatorial activity is not transferred until the day the legislature convenes. On January 1, 1985, the attorney general and other state constitutional officers took their oaths and moved into their offices vacated by the outgoing officials.

On January 2, 1985, Democratic representative Serenus Hoffner requested an attorney general's opinion as to whether a newly elected governor may take office on the first day of January. Nicholas Spaeth, the new Democratic attorney general, was ready with an opinion. He noted that the state's constitution was silent on the matter, although common law interpretations presupposed that a calendar year began the first day of January. Legislative history of the 1965 bill also revealed legislative intent to transfer power on January 1.[13]

Olson received the opinion and disagreed with its conclusion. As Olson saw it, the opinion attempted to deal with constitutional issues not within the attorney general's purview: he considered it nonbinding.[14]

Faced with a noncompliance with his opinion, Spaeth filed a suit in original jurisdiction in the nature of a quo warranto before the North Dakota Supreme Court. Sinner's brief supporting the action developed support from an attorney general's opinion written by Allen Olson himself in December 1980 (before the Link-Olson transition), when the director of accounts and purchases requested a clarification of the exact date when constitutional officers assume office—a housekeeping opinion to determine when the signatures would change. Olson said that qualified state officers shall, at the earliest moment of January 1, become incumbents to the office to which they were elected. Olson was hoisted on his own petard.[15]

Upon the filing of the suit, three of the court's four surviving justices disqualified themselves. They had either served under Olson in some capacity or been appointed by him. Chief Justice Ralph Erikstad then drew the names of four district judges from a hat and scheduled a hearing for 10 A.M., January 4, the next day.

At this time Sinner moved into the governor's mansion. (Olson had not lived there because he preferred to reserve it for ceremonial occasions.) While allowing Sinner to move into the governor's residence, he resolutely continued to occupy the governor's office.

The conflict of two governors' contending for the governor's chair provided good copy for the state's humorists and cartoonists. "North Dakota was now the only state in the union with a bicameral executive." "No wonder Virgil Hill, the Olympic boxer, couldn't remember the name of the state's governor." "Letters to the Governor" were to be addressed to "occupant." North Dakotans, already overly sensitive about the state's perceived national image and their portrayal in the media, wrote to their editors, blaming both governors for taking stances that disgraced the state.[16]

Meanwhile the Judicial Nominating Committee was conducting its final interviews. Charles Fleming, Sinner's chief of staff, contacted the chairman of the Judicial Nominating Committee and suggested they read the attorney general's opinion. Owen Anderson, the chairman, resented this gesture. "It doesn't make any difference to this crisis who we select, or who we put on the lists. We're furnishing a list to the governor and which governor it is is going to be determined by the supreme court, not by us. In any case if Sinner doesn't like the list of nominees he can request a new list."[17]

January 4 was marked by the hearing before the supreme court and by the issuance by the Judicial Nominating Committee of its recommendations for the supreme court, a list addressed to both gubernatorial claimants. Of the eight nominees who had been recommended for the two vacancies, four were Democrats. The committee had scrupulously avoided the partisan thicket. As Owen Anderson noted, "Common knowledge might indicate that a particular nominee was Republican or Democrat but no one paid a whit of attention to that in the process."

The supreme court's morning hearing lasted less than an hour. Nicholas Spaeth's major appeal was that the court should make a quick decision, that there would be vast confusion if an emergency were to crop up and two people claimed to be governor. He said the court would be wise to make its decision before either Sinner or Olson had selected his court appointees. Otherwise the court might be put into the awkward position of adjudicating which slate of appointees was the valid slate. Malcolm Brown, who argued for Sinner as affected party, concentrated on attacking Olson's claim that he was entitled to serve four full years. Brown said, "He can take office whenever he wants but in doing so, he can't affect the term of his successor." Spaeth and Sinner let the materials in the briefs, especially Olson's own earlier opinion as attorney general, speak for themselves.

Olson's attorney, Tom Kelsch, argued a governor cannot serve less than four years. Kelsch also argued that in signing the certification of election Sinner agreed with the date for commencement of office that was printed on the form.

In its unanimous decision the court agreed with Spaeth and Sinner on two key points. The certificate of election was not the crucial document that Olson had claimed it was. The certificate simply acknowledged the right of a person to possess and exercise the functions of a given office and was not determinative of the term or date indicated on the form. In terms of Olson's claim that he was entitled to a term of four full years, the court said that Olson failed to make a distinction between the term of his office and the tenure of his office. "When Olson as incoming governor elected not to assume the duties of his office until January 6, 1981, the choice did not affect the term of his office which commenced on January 1, 1981. It merely shortened the tenure." The court decision also supported its conclusions with Allen Olson's opinion as attorney general, which stated that the powers of the office of governor and other state officials commence at the earliest moment of January 1. The decision also noted that Olson received a full month's salary for January 1981 and that his pay records indicated his employment commenced on January 1, 1981, and terminated on December 31, 1984. The court then enjoined Olson not to take any further actions as governor. It was silent on whether actions taken from January 1 through January 4 were valid. Olson said he had engaged in routine functions only.[18]

Within an hour of the court's decision, Olson greeted Sinner in the reception area of the governor's office and offered his congratulations. In a press conference immediately following the meeting Olson made the point that the open question of the date of taking office was of such importance as to require a decision by the supreme court. Sinner thanked Olson for keeping this issue on a theoretical plane and not letting it descend to anything personal. The crisis was over.

The last scene in the transition crisis was played out on January 8, when Olson gave the state of the state address and Sinner gave his inaugural address before the opening session of the legislature. The state of the state address was an anticlimax. It served principally to highlight the difference in style and political perception between the outgoing and incoming governors. Olson's address highlighted his accomplishments as governor and indicated an optimistic view ("I am pleased to report that the state of the state of North Dakota is very sound indeed"). He saw his most important accomplishment as keeping North Dakota "in the black" and leaving office with a projected $140 million general-fund balance at biennium's end.

In contrast, Sinner's inaugural address painted a bleak picture. "Much of our rural economy is in trouble. Our energy industry is far from prosperous. Jobs are in short supply. Revenues to run state and local governments are far from adequate. . . . The macro-economists who say the liquidation of family farms is inevitable have not seen the faces of the families who are going under. I have seen those faces. It is a wrenching experience."

Sinner saw the state at a crossroads. With shrinking revenue and shrinking federal support it was necessary for the state to reassess priorities, reduce bureaucracy, and look at new ways of delivering services. Politics was also to become less contentious and more oriented to finding solutions.

The supreme court decision did not foreclose future inaugural issues. To permanently resolve the question, a move for a constitutional amendment was begun during the legislative session by Senator Ray Holmberg, a Republican. An amendment to Section 1, Article V, of the constitution was proposed, which stipulated that the term of governor shall begin on December 15 following the governor's election, the change beginning in the year 1988. This amendment was to provide a significant transition reform allowing the governor-elect to obtain hands-on authority to change and modify the budget much earlier in the game.

Earl Strinden, house majority leader, stressed that the Olson-Sinner experience had taught the legislature that it could not afford to wait a whole month before receiving a transitional governor's revised budget recommendations. It also gave the responsibility for a state of the state address to the new governor.

The concurrent resolution proposing the amendment sailed through the senate by a vote of 50 to 2 on March 21. In the house it had the sponsorship of both majority and minority leaders and passed 80 to 21. The electorate voted on the transition amendment on November 4, 1986, and passed it 171,766 to 93,220 (64.8 percent).

The Executive Budget

Before 1965 the state of North Dakota did not have an executive budget. The budget was devised by the State Budget Board, which consisted of the governor, the secretary of state, the state auditor, the chairmen of the House and Senate Appropriations Committees, five members of the house chosen by the speaker, and three members of the senate chosen by the lieutenant governor. In 1965 during the term of William Guy, the state legislature established an executive budget, giving budget-making authority to the director of accounts and purchases (now the OMB), who serves at the pleasure of the governor. Guy found the change a great improvement and an advantage to transition.[19]

However, the executive budget mechanism did not solve the issue of an OMB budget that had been shaped by an outgoing governor, particularly one of the opposite party. Governor Olson experienced that in his transition in 1980. With only a few weeks to review the Link executive budget, he chose to accept the Link figures as reasonable and acceptable. He did call for some minor adjustments and some increased expenditures in the governor's office (e.g., the airplane), which were not well received.

When Sinner won the election he determined that he would not follow Olson's example. Sinner intended to recast and reshape the budget according to his own economic analysis and set of priorities. However short the time available, the budget people would work day and night to restructure the budget. There was a growing awareness that the Olson budget was obsolete and unrealistic in its projections, and Sinner was committed to administer a budget that was as far as possible his own.

The first appointment Sinner made was the director of the OMB. He chose Dick Rayl, a close acquaintance who had been president of Westgo Industries (a farm equipment manufacturer) and vice president of marketing for Mayrath, an Illinois agribusiness firm. At the same time that Sinner appointed Rayl, he also brought on board Dave Haring, who had been an analyst for Kent Conrad, the tax commissioner.

Sinner made his objectives clear to the designate director. Sinner would maintain full charge of the budget, which would be completely reorganized to fall in line with general objectives that included a readjustment of expenditures to balance decreasing revenues, preservation of a healthy general-fund balance, and no new increases in taxes.

The Sinner people did not get the budget until December 8, when Governor Olson formally announced it. The tax commissioner's office had already indicated to Sinner that revenue forecasts were falling behind expectations and that Olson's projections on revenues were already $30 million too high. Olson's projections were based on an unrealistic assessment of developing economic trends. By December Olson's revenue estimates appeared to be $100 million too high.

Rayl and Haring contacted Lee Stenehjem, the outgoing director, immediately after December 8. For the next two weeks Rayl and Haring met with Stenehjem and each of the four area analysts in the OMB to obtain full information on the budget. Cooperation could not have been better as the two familiarized themselves with the protocols and the fiscal impact statements. Sinner and Rayl had no authority to direct in any way the work of the department, but their statements to the press on a pressing need to reform the budget alerted the staff of the approaching need to update fiscal impacts and document the basis for any cuts.

Upon taking office on January 1, Rayl put into effect a system for downscaling budget expenditures. He directed each budget analyst to create decision packages in his area—proposals for obtaining savings by cutting back programs, merging functions, and operating at less than optimal levels.

The analysts prepared over 300 decision packages, each highlighting an area for dollar-saving. Most helpful in putting together these decision packages was Olson's three-tier budget proposal plan. In 1982 Olson directed all agencies submitting their budgets to the OMB to prepare three budgets: a maintenance budget, an enhanced budget that would include expenditures above that of the biennium, and a basic services budget allowing for up to a 10-percent reduction in expenditures. The system allowed the budget analysts to prepare decision packages allowing drops from one level to another. In other areas savings were achieved by means of modifications in accounting systems. In collating the decision package savings the OMB attempted to get a minimum of an 8-percent reduction in agency budgets. However, general government and regulatory function reductions were insufficient to bring the $30 to $70 million in reductions that the Sinner people were mandated to obtain. The greatest reductions would come from three areas in the budget: the foundation aid program for elementary and secondary education (a $500 million item in the Olson budget), higher education ($347 million) and human services ($660 million).

Rayl and the governor personally went over all the decision packages. And from January 5 on, the major agency heads and their own budget officers paraded in a steady stream to meet with Sinner and Rayl and review their budgets. Most came to defend their budgets but realized the money wasn't there. Rayl noted that the cooperation was tremendous.

The greatest problems were with the State Board of Higher Education, which has independent administrative and spending authority over all of the state's institutions of higher learning. As Rayl reported,

"The Board of Higher Education had different goals; they had the goals of meeting needs and not the balancing of income and outgo." As a result the Sinner budget people reworked the higher education budget with little input (except submitted budgets) from higher education.

The Sinner modifications needed legislative support for passage. No matter how carefully the budget was devised and documented, it represented only a set of recommendations. Sinner did not want to spring his budget on the legislature, at least not on the legislators of his own party. Beginning in January, Sinner, Fleming, and Rayl met with the two legislative minority leaders every day, generally from 4:00 P.M. to 10:00 P.M. after the legislative houses had adjourned. The leaders were presented the spending options and the decision packages and asked to register their approval or disapproval. They questioned the practicality of some cuts, and the degree of others, but in most cases the leaders agreed with the cost-cutting initiatives. In five or six major decision packages the controversy of the cuts led the leaders to say to Sinner, "This is the time for you to call the shots."

There was one budgetary item that raised more controversy than any other—the issue of faculty pay raises at the state's institutions of higher learning. Sinner recognized that faculty members had received no paycheck increases for three years during a period in which the state's general fund balance was $20 million over projection. During the campaign he made the promise that salary increases of 11.6 percent were required for the state's faculty, who had become one of his most active support groups during the campaign.

Olson had provided only an immediate 5 percent annual raise for faculty in his budget. While Sinner was downscaling all of Olson's budget recommendations, this was one area where he was bound by campaign commitments. The solution he chose proved to be the worst solution in terms of political reaction. In following the egalitarian ideology of the party the Sinner budget people set a priority in dealing with the needs of the faculty at the lower end of the economic scale. They indicated that their faculty salary recommendation would be an 11.6 percent increase as promised, but that a cap of $200 a month should be placed on anyone's raise. The device was arrived at without consultation with the affected interests.

When Sinner's salary recommendations were finally announced they met with disbelief and anger on the part of faculty. Sinner had effected "the great betrayal." The 11.6 percent raise in reality applied only to those faculty members earning less than $25,000 a year. Sinner was faced with a storm of protest. To explain the decision Sinner went to the major universities and attempted to explain the cutbacks to stone-faced audiences. He apologized for the lower recommendations but stood his ground in not altering his plan.

Sinner was acutely pained by the response of a group that had included some of his most ardent supporters. "But he was glad that he did it, even though it involved a great embarrassment," said Joe Lamb. "He learned that as governor, there are times when criticism comes from friends rather than enemies."

Another group that received a shock from the Sinner budget were the elementary- and secondary-education interests. Sinner and Rayl reduced the foundation aid program to local school districts eight percent from the Olson recommendations. The education people were stunned.

In spite of cutbacks in most areas, there were a few instances where he added or increased appropriations. For example, he recommended an appropriation of $800,000 for American Indian community colleges and an initiative costing $3 million for the state's mental health program.

It is of interest to note that throughout the budget process there was no serious consideration of tax increases. The large shortfall of state revenues had occurred in the oil and gas gross production and extraction taxes—an area of taxation painless to the state's constituent taxpayers. Sales taxes had been raised in the 1983 session, but the state's income-tax structure remained one of the lower such structures in the nation. Political consensus opposed any change in this area.

The Sinner budget arrived at a reduction of some $72 million from the Olson budget. It contemplated an ending cash balance of $40 million. Sinner would now become an outside player as the legislature reacted to his recommendations.

Legislative Relations

Governors in North Dakota have always found the state's legislative assembly a formidable institution. Earl Strinden, the Republican house majority leader, made a point of publicly stating that "the legislature is the policy-making branch of government." Strinden's comments simply express the political realities of the state that has seen the legislative branch maintain its position as the dominant branch of government.

Legislative leaders often ignore the executive budget in favor of their own initiatives.

Sinner had been a member of the senate and the house. During the 1983 session he was chairman of the House Finance and Taxation Committee. The experience provided several lessons. One was that the governor cannot dictate to the legislature. The other was that the legislature approached its budgetary responsibilities with a high degree of professionalism. Members of the Appropriations and Finance and Taxation Committees of both parties—some of whom had twenty years' service —had considerable expertise in budgetary matters, bargained in good faith, and were realistic pragmatists. If the governor was to effect any influence upon the legislature, that influence would depend upon good lines of communication.

In terms of communications mechanisms to be established for the session, Sinner decided against former governor Link's morning breakfast meetings with both majority and minority leaders and key committee members held every Tuesday during the session. Sinner initiated a practice of meeting almost daily with the Democratic floor leaders (minority leaders). He also utilized Richard Gross, his counsel, as a legislative liaison to the "calendar caucuses" that were held over the noon hour in each house. If there was a particular bill on which the governor had a position, Gross presented the governor's recommendations and reasoning. There were few efforts to lobby the rank and file. That was left to legislative leaders and the floor managers. There was never any pressure to follow the governor's direction. That followed the long-term tradition of Democrats being free "to vote their consciences." Formal caucus votes were taken only when the governor had vetoed a bill and the Democrats were put in position of sustaining his veto.

On six or seven occasions both house and senate Democrats met jointly with the governor's people after their calendar caucuses to discuss elements of the governor's program. There were also three Sunday night joint caucuses that involved a general discussion of the party's main programs. The governor, the budget director, the tax commissioner, and other Democrat elected officials made personal appearances. This followed Democratic tradition. A Republican caucus, on the other hand, would never tolerate such "intrusion" by the executive branch. No caucus votes were taken, but discussion was open, and extensive, and often heated.

Sinner also maintained an open-door policy for the legislators of his party. Members of his transitional Policy and Legislative Action Committee had easy access to the governor and Sinner met on several occasions with such special caucuses as the Women's Caucus (bipartisan) and the Southwest Legislative Caucus.

The test of the governor's influence came in the reaction of the legislature to his program. Because the Republicans had a majority in both houses, Sinner limited his legislative objectives. Most important were the budget and the farm-relief bill. He also sponsored some initiatives in the human services area (mental health), and he supported some tax exemptions for the oil industry.

Even before Sinner released his budget the Republicans were receiving the reports on declining revenue projections. In fact Strinden, the house majority leader, presented to the Republican legislative caucus on January 17 a program and budget document that anticipated reductions.[20]

When Sinner announced his budget on February 5, he struck a responsive chord with the fiscally conservative Republicans. Bryce Streibel, a veteran legislator who had been Republican minority and majority leader and a strong partisan throughout his career, gave Sinner's decision to trim $73 million from the budget an "A."[21] Strinden was reservedly complimentary. He agreed on the revenue projections, the degree of budget reductions that had to be made, and the $30-million general-fund balance. But he voiced his disagreements. He felt the budget was substantially out of balance in the human services area. Strinden felt that the Sinner budget neutralized the "big spenders" in the legislature—an allusion to the Democrats.

Within ten days Strinden produced his own fiscal plan, which reallocated the cuts that were to be made. He produced a budget that reduced spending in the human services area by $12 million, cut back $13 million on energy development impact aid,[22] and reduced cuts in medical education, experiment stations, and junior colleges. He also made a $2-million cut in the judiciary's budget. He would later introduce legislation that would increase the salary levels for college faculty.[23]

When all thirteen of the major appropriations bills had been passed it was evident that the contours of the budget followed neither Sinner's model nor Strinden's model but presented a syndrome of compromises that was acceptable but not totally satisfactory to both sides.

The human services budget was hammered out in the human services section of the House Appropriations Committee. In effect the process on the human services budget involved a deference to committee expertise with final figures some $5 million under those recommended by Sinner.

In regard to salaries of state employees and higher education faculty, there was a confrontation of caucuses. The Democrats stuck strongly to their egalitarian principles and advocated salary caps. In the Republican caucus, Strinden, concerned about salary compression and morale of higher-paid professionals, argued for raises to be made according to merit. The situation stood at an impasse until Sinner and Strinden arrived at an accommodation that allowed the governor with direct control over personnel in sixteen major agencies (comprising two-thirds of the state's employees) to have the flexibility to put into effect any personnel policy or compensation standards he might favor. The next day the governor's office announced a "compromise" on the salary issue.

In some areas Sinner and Strinden found themselves in agreement. Sinner vetoed a $44-million political subdivision's revenue sharing measure, feeling that it was at least $12 million too high, and Strinden supported him on the veto. The papers talked of a topsy-turvy legislature, with conservative Republicans recommending more spending for state and local subdivisions, elementary and secondary education, and higher education and Democrats favoring fiscal stringency.[24]

There was one area where Sinner suffered a significant defeat. He had pinned considerable hopes on passage of his Farm Relief Bill, which called for the Bank of North Dakota to sell up to $500 million in bonds to help farmers restructure long-term debts. The Republican caucus came out strongly against it, citing uneasiness about the state being a surrogate lending institution for federal credit agencies. The full senate voted on party lines and killed the bill. In the house, a Family Farm Survival Act was also vastly down-scaled. The appropriation was cut from $50 million to a mere $500,000. The farm credit measures were probably doomed from the beginning. Sinner could not be consistent with his austerity measures for state government in other areas and still be generous in loaning out the state's assets to the desperate farmers. Also, mail and constituent response indicated as much farm resistance to the credit measures as there was support for them.

Sinner won a significant victory in terms of the "Trigger" tax. Reluctantly he proposed that with the uncertainty of the economic picture over the next two years, the legislature should vote a contingent increase in the sales tax, with the tax to go into effect if state revenues fell below $400 million on July 1, 1986. Two days before the end of the session, the bill was introduced at the request of the OMB. The house passed the measure on the basis of a coalition of the Democrats and prudent Republicans, but it was defeated in the senate by one vote, only to pass again on a vote to reconsider.

In assessing the outcome of the session both sides claimed some victories. The Sinner people wanted some $72 million in cuts. They obtained $73 million. The Republicans could claim a success in budget reallocation. Toward the end of the session when many of the bills, including the appropriations bills, were in conference, a channel of communication opened between the governor and the Republican legislative leadership. Strinden noted that his leadership did not enjoy the open-door policy extended to Democrats, but contact was close—generally through Dick Rayl, the OMB director acting as liaison. Strinden and Dave Nething, senate majority leader, registered a great deal of respect for Rayl, his understanding of the fiscal problems, and his flexibility. Sinner also said that working with the leaders of the opposition party was not a constraint on his goals. Fiscal realities were the constraint.

Sinner's Gubernatorial Style

Upon taking office Sinner suggested various steps to eliminate, consolidate, and decentralize certain services within the state, and his suggestions ran into hard and immovable opposition. He suggested alternate uses for some of the state's institutions of higher education. He suggested regional consolidation of farm extension services. He suggested a freeze on construction of new nursing home space (the state leads the nation in beds per capita). The proposals were characterized as heresy. What Sinner ran into was a historical framework that supports these institutions. Decades of legislative support, strong alumni support, and local pride combined to maintain institutions even where the historical framework was obsolete.

Sinner's values and gubernatorial style fit in with the state's political culture as described by Daniel Elazar. As Elazar has indicated, in a moralistic political culture "there is a general insistence that government service is public service which places moral obligations upon those who participate in government which are more demanding than the moral obligations of the marketplace. There is an equally general rejection of the notion that the field of politics is a legitimate realm for private economic enrichment." [25] The Sinner people who were involved in the transition assumed great financial sacrifice, many serving without pay. The members of the personnel search teams were not paid their expenses, and the highest-paid professionals in state government were expected to accept a "bearable sacrifice" in terms of salary increases. Also, in many of Sinner's austerity measures cost savings were to be achieved by attrition in number of personnel, which often involves an expectation that remaining personnel will assume duties of those leaving.

The other feature of Sinner's style compatible with the expectations of official behavior in the state was accessibility to all constituents. Sinner was particularly conscientious in regard to correspondence: "To give a constituent a substantive and reasoned answer is one of my compelling instincts."

Sinner also expressed a particular sensitivity for the constituent and for the human dimension of an issue. One commentator characterized him as "achingly sensitive." When Sinner made his decision on state employee salaries, he knew that many employees whom he characterized as dedicated and professional would be greatly disappointed. The decision troubled Sinner and pointed up an interesting paradox in his political personality: the commitment to making the hard choices and personal difficulty of living with decisions that might force loss of jobs, displacement, and community disruption.

Sinner's concept of the governorship fit in with his political perceptions. As he noted, "In my judgment, the chief executive in North Dakota must be an initiator. He must take significant initiatives and lead in a clear and unequivocal manner. It is not necessary to pursue all the details. But if change is to be achieved he must signal to all the major players that change must come even if hard decisions are to be made."

Sinner's approach in office was interventionist. His first eight months in office saw a continuing series of initiatives involving the governor's office on a wide range of issues. He set up task forces and made suggestions on the functions of the smaller colleges whose missions were being questioned. He set up ad hoc committees to deal with small industries threatened with bankruptcy. He reacted on a grand scale to deal with the Great Plains Synthetic Gas Plant default. He implemented reforms and reorganizational plans for the Bank of North Dakota. He proposed a $60-million fund to aid troubled banks by the use of Bank of North Dakota capital injection funds. He sent a message to the Public Service Commission on a carbon dioxide pipeline issue. He sent a message to the Health Council on cost containment.

This activist role has raised its own set of problems. The higher education task forces Sinner established competed with State Board of Higher Education studies under way and with the Special Legislative Council Committee on Higher Education addressing those same problems. His efforts to create the Great Plains task forces were criticized as "grandstanding." His initiatives on the bank and health services issues alienated bankers and hospital administrators. Communities where he suggested a change in institutional missions were up in arms. His letter to the Public Service Commission met with a cold reaction that charged "intrusion of the executive into the affairs of a board of elected officials." Sinner was discovering a political reality of the state. Independently elected officers and independent institutions like the Public Service Commission or the State Board of Higher Education zealously guard their grants of power.

One comment frequently heard as Sinner's term extended was that the governor's office may have been overextending itself in resources as well as jurisdiction. One commentator, noting that the whole governor's office consists only of a half-dozen staff members, said, "with its frenzied involvement in crises, near crises, and crises looming on the horizon, the office may well become overwhelmed." A larger staff might be in order, but that would place the office in a dilemma. Larger staffs and involvement in methodical long-range studies may be seen as redundant to similar efforts being made in other branches and independent offices. Also, staff expansion is antithetical to the nature of the executive who is the one official in a position to act expeditiously, immediately, and decisively.

Sinner and the Transition

The transition experience provided the Sinner people with some reassurances as well as some lessons. On attending the seminar for new governors held at Hilton Head, South Carolina, Sinner noted that the first advice they received was to immediately select a budget director. Sinner's response was, "We have done that." The second decision the sponsors advised was to have an appointment-committee structure in place. The governor could confidently say, "We had them already in place. Instinctively we set out on the correct course."

Sinner noted that the transition produced its own shocks. One was the deluge of office-seekers. But luckily the transition staff had a system for dealing with them. The other was the discovery of how badly the economic condition of the state had deteriorated. The implications were staggering. Of the problems that emerge with transitions, Sinner listed three salient problems, the making of the executive budget, dealing with office-seekers, and handling the huge volumes of correspondence and providing meaningful personal responses.

Actually all these problems were simply manifestations of an omnibus problem—the time factor—the compressed period in which hundreds of administrative, organizational, budgetary, and policy questions had to be decided. According to Sinner, the entire transition period must be restructured and the chief executive must come in early. While newly adopted constitutional changes allow the governor to come on board a few weeks earlier (i.e., December 15) this still does not provide enough time to plan for a legislative session or do justice to the executive budget. In fact, Sinner would like to see the legislative session moved to commence in even-numbered years to allow an incoming governor a full year's head start on the executive's legislative responsibilities. This would have the governor function a longer time under his predecessor's budget, but as things now stand, the incoming governor functions with the old budget until the new fiscal year begins in July 1.

Such a radical change in the scheduling of sessions seems unlikely. Legislative opposition appears unavoidable; while the change would provide for immediate exercise of a new governor's official role, new legislators would lie fallow an entire year before having their first legislative experience. Also, under the present system the transitional governor experiences a "reverse honeymoon" in his first legislative session. He is inexperienced, he must work with his predecessor's budget, he has not had any time to build an image and base of support with the public as a governor in charge. The legislature can exert its dominance more easily. The legislature may not be willing to accept a situation that allows the governor to have a full year's head start on the legislature for image building and strengthening of the office.

Gubernatorial Transition
in Rhode Island, 1984–1985

)))))

Elmer E. Cornwell, Jr.

From 1932 until 1984 there had been only three Republican governors in Rhode Island, serving a total of ten years. Special circumstances caused the election of each of these: a party split, a feeling that a four-term governor had overstayed his time, and the issue of a state income tax. The 1984 Republican win resulted not from one incident or factor, but a cumulation of things that seemed to suggest that the Democrats had become complacent and arrogant.

The popular disaffection had its roots in a long, drawn-out battle over legislative reapportionment in the wake of the 1980 census. The legislature had enacted house and senate plans during the 1982 annual session. Both were challenged in court on grounds of gerrymandering and other constitutional violations. The house plan was at length upheld, but the senate plan, the focus of the major battle, was ruled unconstitutional. Efforts to remedy its defects in time for the 1982 November election failed, and as a result the house elections went forward on schedule, but the senate held over until a special election in June 1983.

The resulting popular perception was of an arrogant Democratic party attempting to protect its own in the redistricting. When Rhode Islanders went to the polls at the June special senate election they increased the Republican share of seats in the fifty-member senate from seven to twenty-one. This was read as a staggering vote of no confidence in the majority party.

Background

Against this background, some of the events leading up to the 1984 general election themselves contributed to the public's disenchantment with the Democratic Party. During the last two or three years of Democratic Governor J. Joseph Garrahy's eight-year tenure in office, his relations with the Democratic General Assembly leadership had ranged from cool to frigid. Personality clashes, rivalry for power, and a variety of other factors accounted for this breach. Filling a vacancy in the Democratic state chairmanship turned into one of the culminating face-offs between the governor and the legislative leaders, with the latter winning. Not long after this, Governor Garrahy, who may well have wanted a fifth term, announced that he would not run for reelection in 1984.

This announcement had several consequences. Garrahy, who had served four terms as lieutenant governor before election as governor in 1976, was a popular and extremely well-known figure in the state. Many people took offense at what appeared to have been a power play by his factional opponents in the party that caused him to withdraw. At the same time his decision, by heading off one prospective primary confrontation in September 1984, laid the groundwork for another one, which proved disastrous for the Democratic Party. Joseph Walsh, the popular mayor of the state's second-largest city, Warwick, had long eyed the governorship. He would certainly have run in 1982 if Garrahy had decided to return to private life, but stepped aside when the governor sought his fourth term. In 1984 he probably would not have been willing to wait any longer, and a bruising primary with the governor likely would have resulted.

As it turned out, there was a bitter primary struggle anyway. The contestants were Walsh, long allied with the legislative leaders and the party's officially endorsed candidate, and General Treasurer Anthony Solomon. Solomon had also had his eye on the governor's office for some time. The theme of his campaign against Mayor Walsh grew naturally out of the events of recent months and the image they projected. Solomon linked Walsh with the "bosses" who headed the Democratic majorities in the legislature. He portrayed himself as the "independent" candidate who was fighting for the rights of the rank-and-file Democrats and against bossism. In the September primary, Solomon defeated Walsh by winning 58 percent of the vote.

The Republicans naturally watched all of this with glee. After years in the wilderness (John Chafee, currently U.S. senator, the last Republican to hold the governorship, had left office in January 1969) they sensed victory. They had reached their nadir in the last two elections in which Governor Garrahy had taken 74 percent of the vote against Mayor Vincent Cianci of Providence in 1980 and 76 percent against an unknown named Vincent Marzullo in 1982. Frequently, as in 1982, the GOP had not been able to find any credible candidate to represent the cause. The election of 1984 was to be different. Various names had been bruited about, but the best possibility seemed to be Mayor Edward DiPrete of Cranston, a city bordering on Walsh's Warwick and similar to it in many ways. The two mayors actually resembled each other also, in that both were enormously popular in their respective communities, and both had reputations as successful administrators and managers of city finances. At first DiPrete expressed reluctance to run but was persuaded to do so. He formally launched his campaign February 21, 1984.

Mayor DiPrete's running mate for lieutenant governor was Senator Lila Sapinsley, who had been one of the chief intended victims of the gerrymander that had triggered the furor over the senate redistricting plan. The Republican ticket was further strengthened by the candidacy of former nun Arlene Violet for attorney general. She had lost narrowly to incumbent Dennis Roberts II, two years earlier. Republican Secretary of State Susan Farmer, who had gained office in 1982, was almost certain to win reelection, as was Second District Representative Claudine Schneider, who was just completing her second term.

Buoyed by this strong slate, the obvious problems of the Democrats, and its successes in the 1983 special senate election, the Republican party exuded optimism. The large number of women on the GOP slate was not the result of any overall strategy; all four had come forward on their own. Party leaders were not unaware, however, of the poor Democratic record in fielding women as candidates.

The Campaign

Providence Journal columnist Tom Walsh, writing a few days after the Solomon primary victory, captured neatly the essence of the campaign that was now underway. "DiPrete is now trying to do to Solomon exactly what Solomon did to Walsh—link him to Democratic party bosses. DiPrete's handlers believe political independence is what Rhode Island voters care most about this year, and they believe they can turn Solomon's big gun around and use it on the Democrat."[1]

In more specific terms, Mayor DiPrete sought to capitalize on the disillusionment abroad in the state and the desire for change, as well as on the specific grievances he felt people had against the Democrats. He interwove this general theme with a series of specific promises that had the effect of reinforcing, as it were, by illustration his critique of the Democrats. Using the big-spender line of attack, he promised to cut taxes immediately by cutting the income tax obligation of Rhode Islanders. At the same time he insisted there was at least $100 million in waste in state government, though he was forced to back off and say he meant that he could make actual savings of up to $35 million.

Still on the theme of waste, he stressed the need for better and fairer personnel practices. There were, he claimed, 2,700 temporary civil service appointees, many of whom had held that status for long periods of time. He promised that all would be given the examinations they should have taken, and implied that many would be let go. He cited specific examples of jobs given to political cronies or even created for friends and relatives of elected officials. In general, he sought to support his bossism charge by painting a picture of rampant patronage.

On more positive notes, he promised a $10-million revolving fund to help lure business to the state and special assistance to small business through an advisory council. He and his opponent were not far apart in this area, nor in regard to necessary services to the poor and handicapped in the population. Actually, the Republican seemed more liberal here than the Democrat—who questioned how much more could or should be found for that kind of program.

Candidate Solomon seemed to spend a good deal of his time on the defensive. He had been endorsed by Governor Garrahy. Moreover, not long after the primary, he held a well-publicized meeting with the legislative leaders whom he had recently been labelling as back-room bosses. Most agreed to rally round the primary winner. All of this of course provided DiPrete with ammunition with which to use, as columnist Walsh put it, Solomon's own gun against him. How could Solomon have it both ways—be independent of what had gone on before, and yet welcome the support of the Democratic incumbents? It is worth noting that DiPrete and Garrahy had long been personal friends, which meant that the mayor had to aim his criticisms of the past administration in a way that would not be too hard on the governor. The latter in turn, did not do much to actively assist Solomon, nor did Mayor Walsh.

The campaign was, to say the least, hard fought, and became bitter and personal at times. The cost soared, topping any previous Rhode Island statewide campaign. Each of the two contenders spent at least $1.5 million, and with the approximately $1 million spent during the primary by Mayor Walsh, the total was $4 million or more. It is probably true that Solomon had a lead early in the campaign, but by the first week in October a well-publicized DiPrete poll showed the two even at 42 percent. When the votes were finally counted on election night, DiPrete had won with 60 percent of the vote.

Arlene Violet also won in her contest with the incumbent attorney general; Secretary of State Farmer gained reelection handily; Roger Begin, running for general treasurer to replace Solomon, was the only statewide Democrat to win comfortably in the traditional manner. The contest for lieutenant governor between Senator Lila Sapinsley and Senator Richard Licht was a cliffhanger until Licht was finally declared the winner by less than 3,000 votes out of nearly 400,000 cast. An interesting footnote to this contest was that Licht also, as a liberal maverick in the senate, had been targeted for elimination under the senate redistricting plan. In fact, the architects of that plan had arranged that he and Sapinsley would end up living in the same district!

In short, the Republicans won a resounding victory at the top of the state ticket, carrying three of the five offices and narrowly missing a fourth, a record they had not made since 1938. In the legislature, however, they did not do nearly as well. In the house, to be sure, the Republicans picked up seven seats, lifting their total from fifteen in the previous legislature to twenty-two, out of one hundred. But in the senate, having gone from seven to twenty-one in the June 1983 special election, they dropped back to twelve in 1984. Governor DiPrete's coattails had not been particularly effective.

The Democratic legislative leaders were quick to issue a conciliatory statement the day after the election. They called for cooperation between the new governor and themselves, promising to examine all of his proposals carefully and "make a good faith effort to reach an accommodation." But they also reminded the Republican victors that "the public quite clearly has given the General Assembly a mandate to continue to play the constructive and innovative role in the government of the state which it has played [in the past]." [2] Unlike many statements of this kind made under similar circumstances, this one proved to be prophetic. The ensuing legislative session was marked by a surprising degree of cooperation, compromise, and good feeling between the two parties and the two branches.

Transition Personnel and Process

The transition from the administration of Governor J. Joseph Garrahy to that of Edward D. DiPrete was a very smooth one. No thanks were due to preexisting statutory provisions or budgeted funds, however. The state has never made any standing provision for the process, leaving it up to each incoming governor to make do as best he can and to secure as much unofficial assistance as possible from his predecessor.

The outgoing governor had been giving thought to the transition well before election day. He instructed each of his department directors to prepare a transition briefing document describing his or her department's functions and highlighting upcoming problems. He instructed the budget staff to prepare briefing material on the current (1985) budget for the information of the incoming administration. He also made it a point to have as little as possible to do with the preparation of the budget of 1986, in order to allow free rein to the new people.

Immediately following the election, the two principals were in contact by phone. Governor Garrahy invited Governor-elect DiPrete to meet with him, and the latter agreed, urging that they meet as soon as possible. In fact they sat down in the governor's office to discuss the transition on Thursday, November 8. According to Maureen Massiwer, head of the Garrahy policy staff, she and the governor's legal counsel, Bill Brody, met with them for a while and then were excused so the two could have a private chat.[3] During the next hour or so they discussed the department directors, immediate problems that would need attention, and the budgetary situation, among other things. They then called the staffers back in, and the governor asked Massiwer and Brody to represent him on the transition team. DiPrete had designated Robert Murray, who was his campaign manager and former director of administration in Cranston, to head up the team.

The National Governors' Association publication *Transition and the New Governor* advises that the campaign manager not be appointed to head up the transition.[4] When this injunction was recalled to Murray during an interview, he indicated his and the governor-elect's awareness of it.[5] He felt that his selection had posed no problem, however. Recalling that he had been both executive assistant to DiPrete as mayor and then director of administration, the choice had been a natural one. He said his role in Cranston had been largely on the political side— dealing with issues of image and perception on behalf of the administration. His point was that quite possibly a campaign manager who had not had prior governmental experience might well be ruled out, but one who had had such experience, and, as in his case, had worked intimately in prior governmental roles with the candidate would be well qualified for the job.

On the Garrahy side, people from the budget office and others on the staff of the Department of Administration were made available. They knew the departments intimately and could provide the incoming people with detailed information. For other purposes such as protocol questions and inaugural planning, allocations of space, and the like, appropriate members of the governor's staff would also be ready to assist. On the DiPrete side the key figures were Murray and Michael Doyle, who had succeeded Murray as Cranston director of administration. Murray had overall responsibility, and Doyle was in charge of the personnel process to fill directorships and other key positions. There is little question that the transition developed as smoothly as it did in part because of the longstanding personal friendship between Garrahy and DiPrete. Also, the incumbent wanted his administration to go out, as Massiwer put it, "with a lot of class."

Of particular importance in helping with the mechanics of the transition was Betty Hannan, who had been office manager in Governor Garrahy's office. She had worked for two prior governors, and Garrahy kept her on when he took office. Before the election, she had been placed in a job at the Department of Transportation. (Other Garrahy staffers had left too and taken state or private sector positions.) She returned to help the outgoing administration go through the files, which she had been responsible for setting up originally, and to decide what to leave for the DiPrete people and what to pack up for Garrahy to take. In the end she was asked to return and join the new governor's office in her former position.

A final word is in order on the role of Governor Garrahy. He and DiPrete met on a few other occasions after their initial session. During the interim period, some issues did arise that Garrahy simply referred to the new governor. Questions came up in the course of the work of the transition team about whether or not information that the new people wanted could be turned over to them. Garrahy's representatives would normally consult him on those matters. In regard to one important project in the city of Providence relating to an ongoing redevelopment of parts of the downtown area, the incumbent governor personally met with his successor. The state was committed to involvement in that project, and Garrahy felt he should brief DiPrete personally regarding issues that could not wait until January for resolution.

By the weekend following the election, the governor-elect had made several of his key staff appointments. Murray was designated executive assistant and chief of staff; Doyle, director of administration; Jeremiah S. Jeremiah, Cranston city solicitor, his legal counsel; and Nanci Martin, his campaign press secretary, was to serve him in the same capacity as governor. These appointments were obviously ones that had been long planned. They also laid the initial basis for later criticism that far too many members of the new administration were carryovers from the Cranston mayor's office and were hardly representative of the state as a whole.

At the first meeting of the two governors, Garrahy had promised to make available statehouse space for the DiPrete transition people and to help with the costs by placing at least Bob Murray on his payroll. Accordingly, a three-room suite on the third floor, just above the large suite of offices that the governor himself occupies (until then used by his legal counsel) was turned over to the Republican transition team. The salary issue seemed easy to solve because the departures from the governor's staff left a number of vacancies. Actually, instead of following up on the first suggestion that Murray fill the vacant federal coordinator slot, it was decided that would be undesirable since the title was remote from what Murray would actually be doing. Other funds were found and used instead. This courtesy to the new governor was of considerable help, but the DiPrete people still decided that they must hold a mid-January fundraiser to clean up campaign debts and pay other transition payroll costs.

The governor-elect, as far as announced activities were concerned, spent the interim before January first working to wind up his tenure as mayor and meeting with various groups, including the house and senate leaders, in quest of a cooperative relationship for the session. He also attended the seminar for new governors and found it very informative and useful. Murray says that he still consulted his notes from the seminar months into his term. DiPrete had been particularly struck by the thoroughness of the coverage of the agenda, and the fact that much of the discussion was led by actual governors. The wives' program was very helpful to his wife.

In overall terms, the seminar may not have fundamentally changed DiPrete's thinking about the office he was soon to assume. He had, after all, been the chief executive of one of the larger cities in the state and obviously had a sense of what the role of such an official entailed. It is probably true, Murray feels, that the seminar did allow the new governor to see things in a broader perspective, and to gain a better sense of how a governor, as contrasted with a mayor, influences policy. He probably also changed his view somewhat as to how much control the governor can have. As mayor he could know what was going on in a particular public works garage or other facility. As governor, the scale of the operation over which he presided was much too large for that kind of detailed knowledge and control.

Murray said of the interim period that DiPrete and his advisers were concerned to have the governor-elect touch bases with the various constituencies with which he would have to deal once in office. They also were concerned to insure that an impression of movement and activity was conveyed to the public, a sense that things were being done during the weeks prior to January and that DiPrete was ready to move forward as soon as he took office. DiPrete himself used the phrase "hit the ground running." Accordingly, he appeared before a small business organization, the Chamber of Commerce, representatives of the black community, and other groups. The blacks had criticized the lack of minority appointees.

Much of DiPrete's time was also devoted to agency briefings and to the making of plans for the budget he must submit to the General Assembly. In addition to the previously prepared briefing documents mentioned above, a series of oral briefings was put together with the department directors for the new governor and his chief aides. These obviously dovetailed with his concern about how to implement the many specific promises he had made during the campaign. The oral briefings, besides providing information on agency structure and programs, gave them advanced warning of immediately pending problems and, as Massiwer noted, gave DiPrete a chance to meet the Garrahy directors, many of whom would have been happy to remain at their posts. The briefings varied in length from an hour or two for very small departments to half a day for the giants. Directors, at their discretion, brought some of their top management people with them.

The budget itself, and how to handle it, had been a concern for DiPrete's people. The budget staff in the Department of Administration is civil service, and in theory was available to serve the new people with as much loyalty and discretion as they had served under Garrahy. Because, no doubt, of the strong partisan tradition in the state and the atmosphere it seemed to generate throughout state government, and because the Democrats had been in office without interruption since 1969, the DiPrete transition group wondered how much of their sensitive plans they could discuss with these staffers without risking leaks. The problem was solved when Governor Garrahy gave the budget officials permission to develop a confidential relationship with the newcomers, and instructed them for budget preparation purposes to treat DiPrete as if he were actually governor already. He himself stayed strictly away from the process.

Bob Murray stressed how helpful this move by the governor had been, and how good the cooperation was in budget preparation. He said that Ken Kennerson, the chief state budget officer, and his assistants went to the Cranston City Hall on Saturdays to work with DiPrete and his aides. The decision (discussed below) to place in the overall budget act, in addition to the actual appropriations, the bulk of the new administration's agency, personnel, and program reform agenda was doubtless made possible by these arrangements. Without the budget staff to do the necessary detail work, show what legislation had to be amended, and how to achieve the desired changes, time would have been far too short to produce the comprehensive reform package that was eventually sent to the General Assembly.

Other than the budget formulation process as thus broadly conceived by the new administration, the critical concern was of course the selection of department directors. The governor-elect had known for some time that there were individuals among the Garrahy directors that he would want to keep, and that there were people he had worked with in Cranston he would be taking to the statehouse with him. For other positions, there was a kind of blue-ribbon advisory group composed of business and community leaders, including a former state party chairman who had been a campaign adviser throughout, that helped identify people who might be considered. There were not many qualified candidates who applied for high-level positions.

For any particular job a list of perhaps a half-dozen names would be put together and then gone over with the governor-elect. He would indicate the individuals in whom he was most interested. Then Mike Doyle and Bob Murray would interview all the people who were under consideration before they were seen by DiPrete.

The team of department directors had not been completed by inauguration day. The new governor had a total of fourteen appointments to make. Two departments, health and education, did not figure in the process of selection because, in the first instance a relatively recent appointee had just begun to serve a statutory five-year term, and in the second, the governor is not the appointing authority. Of the fourteen whom he does appoint, eleven had been named by the first of January. Four of those were reappointments of serving directors, and four more were individuals who had served with Mayor DiPrete in Cranston. The remaining three, including the one black in the group, were appointed during January.

The reappointees tended to be individuals who had been especially successful, like the director of Corrections, who was widely credited with turning around a prison system that had been under federal court order to correct major deficiencies; the director of the Department of Environmental Management, who seemed to enjoy very broad support, including especially that of the environmental community; the director of Mental Health, Retardation, and Hospitals, who made a considerable impression on the governor as a thorough professional; and the head of the tiny Department of Library Services. The new appointees ranged widely in the view of observers, from one or two with obviously superb qualifications to Cranstonians for whom the governor seemed anxious to find a place.

As to the process and timing of the filling of these key positions, one could probably say that the new administration's record, though not a model of speed and efficiency, was commendable. This was true especially in light of the long hiatus since there last was a Republican governor. A new generation of office holders, so to speak, had to be recruited.

Part of the transition process is obviously the development of the governor's own staff and the working out of appropriate divisions of labor and structural arrangements within it. Bob Murray, whose early designation as chief of staff has already been noted, was responsible for these decisions with less direct involvement from the governor than was the case in the selection of directors. Murray and DiPrete had been very close for several years, both in terms of their political/governmental collaboration and also as personal friends. Some have suggested that it was almost a father-son relationship. Murray's father died when he was ten, and his mother a dozen years later. The governor described him as far more mature than his twenty-eight years would suggest. His intimate knowledge of his boss's work habits and preferences, born of this kind of relationship, made it possible for Murray to put together without detailed instructions the kind of staff setup that would be most acceptable.

Here too, staff construction began with the personnel of the Cranston mayor's office. Murray himself, Jeremiah, and Martin, as already noted, made the transition to the statehouse. On the last day of December the governor announced some further key staff appointments. Frederick Vincent, city plan director, was to be state director of policy; James Malachowski, director of community development, was appointed director of intergovernmental relations; and Norman DeLuca, an administrative assistant at city hall, was to be Murray's deputy. These six constituted the group of senior aides.

Below that top echelon a number of other professional appointments were made with titles of analyst, executive aide, special assistant, and so forth. As of inauguration day, a total of twenty-five positions had been filled, including clerical and secretarial people. That total would rise to thirty-eight by midyear. Mike Doyle, also from the Cranston City Hall, though technically a department director, as chief of state staff services (budget, personnel, planning, taxation, audits, etc.) was a short step removed from, though clearly a member of, the governor's office inner circle.

Organization of the Governor's Office

There are two principal dimensions along which one can analyze staff structure and operation. The first has to do with how the governor relates to his principal aides, and the second with how he relates to his department heads. As to the first, there are two theoretical alternatives. There is the chief-of-staff arrangement under which one individual is the primary contact between the staff and the chief executive, and that individual presides over a hierarchical structure encompassing the rest of the personnel, both senior and junior. The other model is often described as the "spokes of a wheel," suggesting that a number of senior staffers report directly to the governor.[6]

The other major dimension, how the governor relates to department heads, also has characteristically broken down into two models. On the one hand there is the cabinet model under which the governor makes his primary contacts with department directors and deals with their problems in the setting of regular cabinet meetings and individual appointments with directors as needed. The alternative is to use the policy staff, essentially, as intermediaries. In this case, the policy people would each have an area of special concern—education, environment, economic development, or the like, and would deal with issues, departmental or otherwise, that came up in that realm. This would involve taking departmental problems to the governor with suggested solutions, or monitoring programs on the governor's behalf.

When asked, Bob Murray said that the structure of the DiPrete governor's office was basically the chief-of-staff model. Under Murray functioned the five specialized areas indicated in the listing of senior staffers above. Specifically, Martin dealt with press and related matters, and Vincent had a five-member policy staff under his supervision, which handled all policy areas except economic development. This was assigned to DeLuca, along with taxes and tangential concerns, because of the central focus on development that DiPrete wanted for his administration. The responsibilities of Malachowski and Jeremiah were as their titles indicate.

Even these five did not apparently have what used to be called "barging-in rights" during the Kennedy administration, though they did have more access to the governor than more junior staff personnel. They met with Murray each morning for an informal staff meeting to make sure that each knew what the others were doing. No one got to see the governor without going through Murray, and most issues that were presented to the governor went via Murray also. He was responsible for managing the governor's time, for deciding what invitations were to be accepted, and who would get appointments to see DiPrete. If a key person had an appointment, Murray decided which other staff people should be present at the same time. How tight the hierarchy will prove to be, or has proved to be at the time of this writing, in practice, may be open to some debate, but the structural theory involved was clear.

It will be useful to describe the Garrahy governor's office system to sharpen up the important features of the DiPrete model. Maureen Massiwer said that the Department of Administration under DiPrete did many of the things that were done by the governor's staff in the Garrahy years—setting up programs, personnel matters, and the like. The policy office under DiPrete seemed to have a more limited role, though it did facilitate and mediate. In general it had not been as much a consensus process as it was under Garrahy, Massiwer felt. This may in part be the result of the fact that the DiPrete staff was new, while the Garrahy people had been around and had gained maturity over a long period of time. As to the departments, Garrahy tended to deal with them through the policy staff rather than through cabinet meetings. He was, however, accessible to directors if they needed to see him.

As to barging-in rights, the three people who clearly had them were the press secretary, Massiwer in her capacity as head of the policy staff (and therefore in overall charge of the policy side of things), and the governor's executive secretary, who dealt with political matters. A director who had a problem would typically call the policy staffer who had responsibility in that area. The latter would then go in and see the governor about it as intermediary. And yet Garrahy did not want to shut anyone out, because he felt that good ideas might be lost as a result. Staff meetings were held, but about once a week, with the policy staff, the press secretary, and Massiwer presiding. On occasion there would be broader meetings of all of the senior staff, with the governor at times presiding.

A late development should be noted before leaving this staff discussion, which may have important long range consequences for the DiPrete style of operation. The shock waves from an investigation of favoritism in the granting of low interest mortgages by the Rhode Island Mortgage and Home Finance Corporation, felt by many people in public life and their relatives, finally reached the governor's office itself. Bob Murray was accused of making misstatements on a mortgage application. Because Governor DiPrete based much of his campaign on accusations of corruption, patronage, and favoritism leveled against the Democrats, they in turn responded to the Murray revelations with calls for his resignation, or at least for him to take a leave of absence until doubts were cleared up. Finally, in early August DiPrete felt compelled to give his chief aide a leave of absence. Fred Vincent was appointed to act in his place.

As to departmental relations with the governor and vice versa, DiPrete at first restored the kind of cabinet meeting pattern last used extensively by Governor Frank Licht from 1969 to 1973. The new governor even experimented with cabinet meetings open to the public. Actually, during the first eight months of the administration, there were no more than three or four full-cabinet sessions. The pattern that took form in fact resembled the Garrahy approach to a considerable degree. That is, the policy staff did play the role of liaison to the department directors for the governor. But at the same time, DiPrete was concerned that the directors have access to him.

In practice, a director would call Bob Murray and say that he had things he needed to talk with the governor about. Bob would go over the list and in effect decide whether the governor needed to deal with the issues directly or not, on the basis of importance. If he decided to schedule the director to see the governor, he would then brief DiPrete on the issues to be raised, in advance. He went on to estimate that during a given week, perhaps a half-dozen of the directors would see the governor directly. Some from minor departments would be in very rarely, but others, such as the director of the Department of Economic Development, might be in two or three times in a single week.

At one early point in the administration, there was an extensive article in the *Providence Journal*, the gist of which was the dissatisfaction of some of the division people in the Department of Environmental Management at the way the director of the department was usurping or overriding their decisions on permit requests and that sort of thing.[7] When a reporter asked the governor about this, he was told that the governor fully supported the director and would discipline bureaucrats that dragged their feet or were insubordinate. This evidence of an intent to exert strong administrative leadership was communicated to all the directors at one of the cabinet meetings. A part of the DiPrete campaign theme had been to make government more sensitive and responsive. Inordinate delays in acting on requests for wetlands permits had been a major problem for some time.

In overall summary of the 1984–85 transition process, it seems clear that it went well. It was probably the most carefully and deliberately planned such shift in the history of the state. There were special factors that help account for that smoothness. Governor DiPrete was not displacing a defeated opponent. The fact that he and Governor Garrahy were long-time friends obviously smoothed the path. And mention should be made of the high level of professionalism displayed by civil servants who were involved, particularly those from the budget office. Most observers would probably agree that such a high level of professional neutrality would not normally be expected from the state's administrative corps. This is not a criticism in the least. Rather, when the atmosphere of a state is highly partisan and political like that in Rhode Island, it is less likely that one will find, at the same time, a deeply rooted civil-service ethic.

The Legislative Session

The Rhode Island constitution requires that the General Assembly convene for its annual session on the first Tuesday of January in each year. The first Tuesday in January 1985 happened to be New Year's Day. Each odd-numbered year, the swearing-in of new state officers is combined with the opening of the General Assembly. Governor-elect DiPrete let it be known that he planned to deliver his state of the state address on Wednesday evening, rather than in conjunction with his swearing-in on Tuesday. He suggested to the General Assembly leaders that the swearing-in and the opening of the session were enough for the holiday, and that, moreover, he wanted to have his speech covered in prime evening television time. The leadership acquiesced willingly to his proposed schedule.

The speech clearly had been written to take advantage of the momentum that the governor's successful campaign and hefty margin of victory had set in motion. He began by telling the joint session and the television audience, "I stand before you this evening as an agent of the people of the State." The overall theme of his campaign had been the importance of ousting the arrogant Democratic majority and replacing it with a more responsive, reform-oriented administration. After stressing again and again his popular mandate for change and his promise of a new era, he shifted to some of the specifics of his program. He had campaigned for a two-percentage-point reduction in the state's piggyback income tax and now called for the enactment of legislation to accomplish this as quickly as possible. He also called for relief to overburdened payers of property tax and for a general overhaul of the state's tax system.

DiPrete, as had his predecessors for years, promised vigorous efforts to attract jobs to the state and improvements in the economic climate that would make Rhode Island more attractive to business. He then turned to his reform agenda. This comprised tightening up the administration of the civil service system (he had accused the Democrats of patronage mongering), a general policy of spending restraint, and administrative reorganization that would consolidate or eliminate services, and in particular, do away with independent commissions like that in charge of the state lottery in favor of departmental administration of such programs.

He concluded his address to the assembled legislators and the people of the state by assuring all of them that he was committed to adequate social services to deal with human needs and was also pledged to protect the environment. The first of these promises was doubtless felt to be essential to reassure a traditionally Democratic and blue-collar state that there would be no conservative counterrevolution. Rhode Island Republicans have in recent decades been reasonably liberal, even on bread-and-butter issues, but their image, harking back to the years before the New Deal, was of hard-faced mill owners and Yankee disfranchisement of the urban immigrant masses. The governor's reference to the environment reflected the rising tension that had come to surround the enforcement of environmental protection policies, especially in beach and shore areas. DiPrete promised increased support for these state programs.

Overall, the infant DiPrete administration clearly felt it had been "on a roll" up to the election, using its line of attack on the management of the state under the Democrats—especially the Democrat-controlled General Assembly—and promises of reform and openness. The next logical step was to develop a carefully constructed set of program proposals stressing tax and spending reduction (to counter the wasteful practices of the past) and the need for reforms to insure that there would be no return to the bad old days. The campaign themes, in other words, would become the themes of the first year, during which a governor with a two-year term must make his mark.

This thrust of the new administration made excellent political sense, but would it work in the face of a General Assembly that, though smarting under the months of criticism and abuse it had endured, had retained its overwhelming Democratic majorities? Observers in January tended to assume that the Democratic legislative leaders would feel that they must go along with at least some of the program of a governor who had beaten their party so badly. But it was also plausible to speculate that the bitterness of the campaign would not disappear overnight and would poison executive-legislative relations before the session was over. Confrontation seemed almost certain, especially when the governor sought to disestablish independent agencies like the Lottery Commission and fold their functions into the regular departmental structure under his control.

The legislative leaders, those in the house in particular, were indeed angry at the whipping-boy role they had been forced to play. They could point to a number of major programs that they had initiated in recent sessions, and they could take considerable credit for the prudent way in which the state's finances had been managed during the late 1970s and early 1980s. Even so far as the reapportionment cause célèbre had been concerned, the house leaders could note the fact that their plan for realigning house districts had been upheld in the courts, though challenged on grounds similar to those that had been used successfully against the senate scheme.

They had long been troubled by the low esteem in which the General Assembly as an institution was held by the public. With this in mind, the leadership decided to build on their past achievements and, hopefully, improve both their image and their bargaining power with the new Republican governor by putting together a legislative program of their own. This they called their "Blue Print for Progress." A key proposal in it was to bring property-tax relief to the homeowner.

In light of all of this, observers could be pardoned for thinking that the session promised to be a rough ride at best, and a real cat-and-dog fight at worst. The fact that it turned out quite differently not only confounded the experts but brought considerable political benefit to both sides. This latter result is rare in politics, which so often is a kind of zero-sum game, in which if Side A wins, Side B automatically suffers a corresponding loss.

Most of the governor's appointments of directors sent to the senate for confirmation encountered little opposition. However, the heavy stress on elevating former DiPrete subordinates in Cranston city government to fill state-level positions generated criticism. One such individual was found not to have the educational qualifications required by law, and her name had to be withdrawn for that position. She was later nominated for another directorship that posed no qualifications problem. Only in one instance did the senate raise serious questions about an appointee, a former Cranston school department administrator who was nominated for state director of employment security. In 1981 there had been a scandal over the improper use Cranston school committee members had made of travel funds. Upon being reminded of this by the *Providence Journal* and of the fact that the nominee had been in a position to blow the whistle, the nomination was sent back to the senate Judiciary Committee.[8] In a few days the matter was cleared up to the satisfaction of the senate, which voted approval 48 to 0.[9] Blamed for laxness in state government throughout the campaign, the Democrats were letting nothing slip by them.

The Governor's Budget

By all odds the most important piece of legislation introduced by Governor DiPrete during his first legislative session was his 436-page budget bill. It is trite to stress the importance of the executive budget as a management tool or note the potential inherent in the budget process for a new governor to place his imprint on policy. The DiPrete administration sought to take full advantage of this potential. In addition, however, they had early made the strategic decision to use the budget act as the principal vehicle for securing the reforms and agency/program reorganizations that the governor had campaigned for in the fall and promised in general terms in January.

Typically the budget act in Rhode Island, besides containing the department, agency, and program line item appropriation breakdowns and any proposed tax and revenue changes, includes policy matter that may or may not be closely related to the budget itself or the fiscal policies of the state. The last budget bill submitted by Governor Garrahy, for example, was thirty-three pages long, including the pages that dealt with actual appropriations. Governor DiPrete's huge bill dealt with appropriations per se, taxes and revenue matters in approximately its first thirty pages. The remaining 400-plus pages incorporated a massive array of proposals to abolish, transfer, consolidate, and otherwise restructure programs, agencies, and activities across the face of state government.

The *Providence Journal* noted that the budget, if enacted as presented, would, among other things, abolish 554 state jobs and eliminate 183 more as state functions were let out to private contractors, as well as cut out most agency legal counsels and replace them with a legal pool, with overall promised savings of $21 million. This would represent a major portion of the $30 to $35 million in savings DiPrete had promised during the campaign.[10] In scope and comprehensiveness, this budget document was a veritable tour de force for a brand-new administration that had been in office less than three months. As noted in the earlier discussion of the transition period, it was made possible both by the very clearcut objectives that had been developed during the campaign and by the hard work put in, and advantages enjoyed, during the period from election day to January 1 by the DiPrete people.

Chief of Staff Robert Murray, when interviewed and asked about the strategy involved in the budget, said that the apparent purpose was indeed the one they had in mind: to try to insure that as many of their reforms and restructurings as possible went through. A single piece of legislation, albeit a massive and complicated one, would have a better chance than the sixty or more bills that would have had to be introduced individually if they had taken that alternative route. Whether intended or not, the strategy chosen may also have had the beneficial effect of drawing attention away from the actual appropriation total.

Governor DiPrete had won office by promising savings in state expenditures, elimination of unneeded jobs and waste generally, and tax cuts. He was able to deliver on all of those. As to taxes, the budget included two further one-percentage-point cuts in the piggyback income tax: one to take effect on July 1, 1985, and the other January 1, 1986. On the other hand, the total spending package that the governor had sent to the assembly was headlined as the state's first billion-dollar budget. It represented a 6.5-percent increase over the previous year's total, or 1 percent higher than the mandated cap established by the legislature. (DiPrete claimed it did not exceed 5.5 percent if the deficiency appropriations for the year were added to the original total.) Either way, the governor obviously had not cut the rate of expenditure increase.

Actually, this substantial (and of course quite normal) rise in spending was in itself likely to dampen potential hostilities within the General Assembly. Had the governor made substantial program cuts, they would almost of necessity have been in such areas as social services, which the Democratic majority would have insisted on restoring. Clearly the legislative leaders were in a position from which it would have been difficult either to criticize the overall increase or berate the governor for claiming to cut waste and the state payroll, while giving the total as hefty a boost as any Democrat would likely have done. Negotiations between the two branches were thus almost certain to involve no more than marginal changes in spending totals.

The Assembly leaders' reactions to the budget focused naturally on the reorganizational aspects. The governor was clearly attempting to carry out through many of the detailed changes proposed his promise to place programs and independent agencies, over which the Assembly had influence in one way or another, in a direct line of responsibility to the governor. Trading on recent scandals pertaining to issuance of plumbers' licenses by the board with authority to examine candidates in that profession, he sought to abolish a number of such semiautonomous professional boards and assign the responsibilities to line departments whose directors he appointed. The Democrats were right, therefore, when they insisted that these requests if approved would result in a substantial centralization of power in the executive at the expense, in some cases, of the legislative branch. DiPrete also planned to abolish the Department of Community Affairs on the ground that the same functions could be assigned elsewhere and performed just as well, with considerable dollar savings.

After the initial claims and counter-claims about the budget, there followed a lengthy period of study by the staff of the house Finance Committee, and later, by the committee itself. The governor vowed when he sent up the bill to fight for it: "DiPrete said yesterday he does not seek confrontation with the Democratic General Assembly. But he was as scrappy as ever about his budget proposals, and held out hope he ultimately can prevail, even on proposals that directly challenge the Democratic power structure." [11]

Things were relatively quiet on that front until late May. One assumes the intervening weeks had been used on both sides to think through priorities and get ready for serious bargaining. Because the battle was to be over a large number of discrete "reforms" and statutory changes rather than over broad spending philosophy, bargaining was the obvious approach. Neither side could afford, or at least seemed to have assumed that it could afford, to simply adopt a take it or leave it position.

The word began circulating that there was to be a summit meeting between the leadership of the Assembly and the governor. Such sessions in fact began very early in June. As midmonth approached the rumors were that agreement had pretty much been achieved. The *Journal* of June 13 carried an account of a serious though brief last minute hitch, showing that the cooperative atmosphere of recent days was fragile: "DiPrete bid to take credit nearly sinks plan to cut R.I.'s income tax rate . . . But meeting with legislators seemingly defuses flap." Then on June 14 an extraordinary joint press conference was held in the house lounge. There, on legislative turf, surrounded by the Assembly leaders of both parties, the overall compromise on the budget package that had been hammered out was presented and explained by the governor—with comment by Democratic leaders—amid "a glow of bipartisanship." [12] Clearly both sides had made major concessions, but equally evident was the general satisfaction felt by both.

On June 16 the house engaged in an unprecedentedly amiable budget debate of some three hours, and passed the bill with a vote of 90 to 0. Even the most veteran statehouse observers could not recall any such unanimous budget vote in the past. The senate offered no obstacle to final enactment, and again the governor affixed his signature with the bipartisan leadership group gathered around him.

The rest of the story of the session can be recounted in brief terms. The Assembly property-tax relief measure was argued back and forth during much of the session and was finally compromised as part of the overall agreement on the budget. The leadership lost the expanded aid to the elderly they sought, but property tax assistance to homeowners was provided along with a commitment to move by annual steps to 50–50 state-local funding of education.

At the same time, one of the longest running controversies in recent Rhode Island legislative history was resolved as amicably as one could have imagined possible. The elimination of unemployment compensation benefits for strikers was high on the governor's list of business climate improvements that he felt it vital to make. In the past this had been a highly partisan issue that found most Democrats lined up with organized labor in support of the existing law and the Republicans and the business community stridently demanding change. This time the Assembly Democratic leadership, with much soul-searching and not a little reluctance, had concluded that the time had come to repeal strikers' benefits. This placed them on the side of a Republican governor and of most of the Republican rank and file. Many rank-and-file Democrats followed their lead, but a substantial number stuck with labor to the bitter end.

There were a few cases of frayed nerves on the last day of the session, but they did not seriously mar the general sense of euphoria. The *Journal* headlined its story the next day "General Assembly ends long, friendly, productive session."[13] A day later one of the few editorials the paper had ever printed that lauded the legislature in nearly unqualified terms was entitled "Assembly deserves 'A' for cooperation."[14] Any session that could cause the state's major newspaper to dole out praise in such unmeasured terms had to have been historic. And as noted earlier, it appeared that both Republican governor and the Democratic Assembly majority gained politically from the session's record.

Conclusion

Any recounting of the story of the 1984–85 gubernatorial transition in Rhode Island must leave the strong impression that on the whole, things went well. As a transition process it was a success by whatever standard could reasonably be applied. Even the Democratic Party and the Democratic legislative majority, who in theory might have benefited if the Republican administration had stumbled or could have been tripped up, in reality probably came out ahead.

Looking at the way things developed from the point of view of the governor—the chief actor in a transition—Edward DiPrete was probably the principal beneficiary, as he would have been the one to suffer most had things gone badly. The fact that Rhode Island still clings to the two-year term may make the state, and its executive transitions, almost unique in the nation. A four-year-term incoming governor needs a smooth transition, but has considerable "searoom" to recoup if things do not go well during his first six months. He or she still has three and a half years during which to solidify a position, gain control of the executive establishment, and push the gubernatorial program through the legislature. By the end of the third year, when it is time to gear up for the reelection campaign, the governor's rough passage into office will be ancient history if all has gone well in the interim.

The two-year governor, by the end of the first six months, has not only used up a quarter of his or her tenure in office, but has quite possibly either succeeded or failed irrevocably to make a mark as chief administrator, and especially as chief legislator. In dealing with the legislative branch, there is no second or third chance. By the time the governor's second January session rolls around, the next campaign is about to begin if it has not already. An election year, everyone knows, is not the time to seek legislative innovations that might be controversial or to attempt needed action that might be unpalatable.

In short, the two-year governor has only that first legislative session to make his or her mark. This being so, the transition process becomes not merely important, but critical. If it could be isolated from the process of governing and legislating, the damage of a poor transition might be acceptable. But it cannot be. The process of taking over office feeds imperceptibly into the process of dealing with a governor's first legislative session. The one is part and parcel of the other. Thus if there is, effectively, no second chance—no second session free of impending election restraints and inhibitions—the transition phase indeed must be critical.

The 1984–1985 Gubernatorial Transition in Utah: A Textbook Case

)))))

Lauren Holland and
Robert Benedict

The game was a friendly one, despite the fact that the contestants had just finished jousting for the highest political prize in Utah, the governorship of the state. On one side of the tennis net were Democratic governor Scott Matheson and Raymond Sheppach, the director of the National Governors' Association (NGA); facing them were Republican governor-elect Norman Bangerter and his executive assistant, Jon Memmott. The spirited game at the 1984 New Governors' Conference in South Carolina produced one of the few Democratic victories of the year, as the Matheson-Sheppach pairing prevailed. From then on, Bangerter joked, "We're not going to give them those without a fight."[1]

Political pundits agree that only someone like Scott Matheson, an individual with great personal magnetism and record-high public approval ratings, could have preserved the Democratic party's grip on the governor's office in Utah. Yet during the election period the Democrats double-faulted, as Matheson decided not to run for a third term and the party's candidate for the office was defeated at the polls. Indeed, the election marked the first time since 1963 that the Republicans had won game, set, and match, as they swept all federal and 90 percent of the state legislative offices.[2] Moreover, despite the declining fortunes of the Democratic party, Matheson avoided the temptation of luring the new administration into a rematch during the transition period. Rather, Matheson committed himself and his staff to making the tran-

sition to the Republican administration of Norman Bangerter the "best
... transition in the history of the United States."[3]

The tennis match was amicable, and so was Utah's gubernatorial
transition. Is this typical of Utah? Or was the 1984 transition unique?
In its "textbook" quality, does the Utah transition further our understanding of the nature and direction of gubernatorial transitions in the
United States? These questions frame our study of Utah. The response
to these questions requires an exploration of the political, cultural, institutional, economic, and behavioral factors that form the backdrop
for the transition.

For purposes of this study, the transition period constitutes that
period of time before the election when the key actors begin anticipating the consequences of winning the governor's office and the adjournment of the newly elected state legislature. Thus, the length of the
transition can be measured on one end by the confidence with which
the candidates gauge their electoral chances and at the other end by the
prescribed duration of the legislative session.

Length is but one means of characterizing a transition. William
Gormley has designated three separate transitional phases: logistical,
administrative, and policy.[4] During the logistical phase of the transition period, the new administration is faced with the task of instituting
a functional and viable administrative machine. Selecting personnel
and institutionalizing decision-making processes compatible with the
personal style of the governor-elect are tasks that constitute the administrative phase. The policy phase forms that period of time when
the governor delineates those goals, principles, and programs that he
or she expects to pursue during the administration. The distinction is
particularly useful in this study. Moreover, by distinguishing three transitional phases, we have yet another methodological device for isolating
relational phenomena.

Finally, this analysis is further informed by the scholarly findings
from the studies conducted on the 1980 and 1982 gubernatorial transitions. In brief, these studies demonstrate that (1) while politics is still
the major factor influencing transitions, they are becoming more professional; (2) the fiscal situation frames the transition; (3) transitions are
longer than in the past; and (4) the personal management and political
leadership styles of a newly elected governor are critical in determining
the nature and direction of a transition.[5]

Utah: A Most Western and Conservative State

Any political event of consequence is more understandable when the interplay of cultural, economic, and political factors is examined. Certainly a preeminent cultural factor explaining the unique character of Utah is the predominance of the Church of Jesus Christ of Latter Day Saints (Mormons). Since the arrival of Mormon pioneers in the Salt Lake Valley in 1847, the LDS church has impacted the state in direct and subtle ways. Church doctrine has been instrumental in the particular character of economic development and the fiscal prescriptions of the state. Promoting the notions of self-sufficiency and a belief in the free enterprise system, the Mormons developed an economy based primarily on agriculture and the provision of goods and services by small retailers.[6] When extractive industries became the primary revenue producer for the state, church leader Brigham Young cautioned members about the dangers of becoming involved with "outsiders." Throughout the late nineteenth century, however, it became increasingly more difficult to preserve the isolation of the community in the face of national economic realities. Development of the mining industry catapulted Utah into the national economic infrastructure, and until recently this sector has been a critical component of the economy. In the 1980s, however, the mining and mineral industries (such as Kennecott Copper), along with heavy industry (such as U.S. Steel), have fallen on hard economic times.

The tension between increasing federal influence over the economy and the state's beliefs in self-sufficiency and the free enterprise system has been a persistent theme in Utah's economic development. In the aftermath of the Depression federal assistance was reluctantly accepted.[7] By the 1950s the Utah congressional delegation could push for additional spending in public works programs (particularly for water projects) and social security benefits. Similarly, the expanded welfare programs of the Great Society, viewed with initial suspicion, were later accepted by all units of government. This pattern of state officials raising philosophical objections about the extent of federal spending while accepting more aid dollars than the state paid into federal coffers has persisted in recent years. Indeed for fiscal 1984 a study by the Tax Foundation indicated that Utahns paid out seventy-four cents for every federal grant dollar the state received.[8]

An examination of the demographic factors impacting the economy finds the state has much in common with other western states. In the distribution of its relatively sparse population (1,652,000 in 1980) the state is predominantly urban (84.4 percent). The population is overwhelmingly Caucasian, with minorities accounting for only 3 percent of the total. Paralleling other states in the region, the federal government owns a large share of the total acreage in Utah (72 percent), while the state's portion is small (7 percent).[9] Most of the state's land is productive only for grazing usage or for raw-material extraction industries.

While rapid population growth is characteristic of states in the West, Utah exhibits some unique elements. For theological reasons Mormons, who constitute two-thirds of the population, are encouraged to have large families, contributing to the highest birth rate in the nation.[10] Thus while economic development is a priority in all states, in Utah it becomes the critical component to stem the tide of the "best and the brightest" who have been forced to seek jobs outside the state. In recognition of the problem, within the last two decades LDS leaders have provided land for a civic complex in downtown Salt Lake City and have tacitly endorsed attracting industry into the state, the presence of professional sports teams, and two bids to host the International Winter Olympics.

The state is also faced with an overburdened educational system. Moreover, Mother Nature has been decisively uncooperative, and paying for the ravages of two years of flooding has exacerbated the state's fiscal problems. Finally, Utah politicians, in addition to facing the challenges of flooding, educational innovation, fiscal expansion, and the generation of new jobs, must deal with the considerable conflict over land-use management and regulation problems, given the state's resource wealth.

A greater understanding of the relationship between cultural and political factors can be gained by the use of the concept of political culture. Although the concept is not without its faults, Utah does exhibit traits characteristic of a moralistic political culture. In theory, the prevailing attitudes of citizens in such a culture are an orientation toward the commonwealth, a view of politics as a vehicle for collectively realizing the public good, and support for a restrained but selectively interventionist government.[11] In the last case the more common pattern is to prefer intervention and restrictions on social (read sexual) behavior rather than economic behavior. Citizens in these cultures also exhibit an ambivalent view of political parties. On the one hand, they believe public officials should deemphasize partisan leanings and avoid party pressure if the demands are contrary to the public interest. On the other hand, they consider parties useful vehicles for airing issues and winning office. Finally, the growth of the bureaucratic state is viewed as a two-edged sword: it may pose a threat to communitarian values, yet size may be necessary to achieve the benefit of governmental efficiency. Consequently, an extensive merit system is favored to depoliticize and democratize the public sector.[12]

In practice, in states with a moralistic political culture there tends to be a high rate of voter turnout, a willingness to run for office, and a high rate of amateurism in politics (i.e., citizen politics). Moreover, a tendency exists to place service to the community above partisan loyalties and friendships and to promote community and self-help projects as solutions to public problems.[13]

In fact, Utah does exhibit a high level of voter turnout. In the percentage of voting-age population casting votes for presidential electors, Utah ranked first in 1976 and sixth in 1980.[14] Members of the state legislature are proud that theirs is a "citizen's body," although there is now a trend toward professionalization.[15] Finally, on issues ranging from flooding to welfare, Utah politicians, in conjunction with the LDS church, frequently have sought citizens' assistance in addressing problems, while also employing existing governmental channels. For example, church and civic groups were able to turn out thousands of volunteers on very short notice to assist governmental agencies in coping with recent flooding.

The predominance of the LDS church has also affected Utah politics in other ways. For example, church leader Brigham Young served as the territorial governor from 1851–57. Four decades later when the primary obstacles to Utah's admission to the Union were the absence of a competitive two-party system and the practice of polygamy, a revelation denying the doctrinal validity of multiple spouses occurred and church leaders arbitrarily divided congregations of faithful into Republican and Democratic groups.[16] Perhaps reflecting that original balance, in the ninety years since the first popularly elected governor in 1895, the Democrats and Republicans have split the prize, with partisan control of the executive branch being held six times by each party. During the first two decades of Utah statehood, the Republicans controlled the executive office. In the 1920s the Democrats took over power for twenty-four years under three different governors. Following this period the Republicans gained the statehouse for sixteen years prior to the twenty years under Democrats Calvin Rampton and Scott Matheson. Multiple terms in office have also been the Utah norm, with only three governors (Cutler, 1905–09; Bamberger, 1917–21; and Mabey, 1921–25) serving a single term in office.

Since the late 1960s there has been a growing feeling that the national Democratic Party image has been less and less acceptable to Utahns who are predominantly ideologically conservative. Conversely, the Republican Party has been growing in strength, peaking in 1984 when the party succeeded in winning the last remaining political prize, the governorship.

The role of the LDS church in accomplishing this shift has been the subject of debate. According to Kent Shearer, former chair of the Utah State Republican Party, "[t]here is a perception among some people in Utah that it's difficult to be a good Mormon and a Democrat at the same time." [17] Public opinion polls have discredited this assertion, and church leaders contend they only become involved in "moral issues." [18] Nonetheless, the definition of "moral issues" has been broad enough to unofficially involve the church organization in such issues as the Equal Rights Amendment, right-to-work laws, pornography, and the siting of the MX missile system in Utah. Unfortunately for the future of the minority party, the national Democratic Party and the LDS church too often have been on opposite sides of such issues.

Political Background to the Transition of 1985

When Governor Scott Matheson announced in February 1984 that he would not seek a third term, many eulogized the passing of the Democratic Party. A relatively unknown railroad lawyer when he first ran for office in 1976, by 1980 Matheson was the only Utah Democratic candidate to win in a statewide or federal-level race. In fact, public opinion polls showed him to be the most popular politician in the state, with an approval rating from five to ten percentage points above that of President Reagan.[19]

To explain Democrat Matheson's success in a sea of Republicanism one must refer back to the impact of political culture on Utah politics. During his eight years as governor, Matheson exhibited the right combination of antipathy toward "big" government, nonpartisanship, fiscal conservatism, and strong advocacy of the public good. He was a leader in the state's defense of its large water projects when the Carter administration sought to cut such "wasteful" projects in 1977. He stood up to the federal government when it sought to deploy the MX missile system in the Great Basin region of Utah and Nevada, and he battled against nerve gas shipments from Colorado to Utah. Moreover, his visibility as a national leader was secured when he became chair of the NGA in 1982–83.

On state issues Matheson utilized the same combination of advocacy and managerial skills rather than partisanship. Faced with Republican majorities of over two-thirds in both houses of the legislature during his last term, his relations with that branch of government were far from tranquil. While Republicans complained about what they perceived to be a "dictatory" rather than a consultative style, on the vast majority of issues Matheson nonetheless was able to prevail.[20] Throughout his tenure, he was perceived by the people as a strong leader and a "citizen governor" in a culture that responds well to authoritative leadership and nonpartisanship. At no time during his retirement announcement in February did Matheson mention that he was a Democrat. Even in his choice of staff, Matheson claimed to be guided by the qualifications, rather than the political experience, of prospective job holders. As such, Matheson frequently found himself in contention with major elements of the state's Democratic party.

While the decision to retire did not come as a total surprise, it still shocked Democrats who clearly understood their party's desperate plight.[21] Without Matheson, the party would face a nearly impossible task to retain the governorship and its wealth of appointive executive jobs and judicial posts. The only hope was to discover a candidate with the same "correct" combination of qualities as the governor: the candidate must be charismatic, ideologically attractive, and morally "clean," with just the right political distance from the party organization.

Even the two announced candidates for the Democratic gubernatorial nomination in 1984, former congressman and lawyer Wayne Owens and businessman Kem Gardner, exhibited a decided lack of enthusiasm for the rigorous task ahead. Of the two, Owens was the more familiar figure to Utahns as the liberal Democratic congressman from Salt Lake City during the tumultuous 1970s. After serving one term (1973–74), Owens gave up his safe seat in Congress to run for the Senate, losing by over 25,000 votes to Salt Lake City mayor Jake Garn. Kem Gardner's most visible public role was as chair of the State (universities) Board of Regents (Owens also shared board membership). Importantly, however, he has been the most successful fund-raiser for the state Democratic party from the mid-1970s through the early 1980s.

At the state Democratic convention in June, Owens edged Gardner in the delegate vote but failed to gain the 70 percent of the delegates necessary to secure the nomination without a primary. By failing to agree on one candidate at the state convention, the Utah Democratic party followed an informal rule established by the national party in recent years: when the electoral situation appears hopeless, exacerbate the situation by having a nasty fight for the nomination.

In fact the primary did sharply divide the Democratic establishment. Governor Matheson remained neutral, but his wife and son favored Owens; while Gardner gathered the endorsements of former party officeholders Governor Calvin Rampton, U.S. Senator Frank Moss, and Congressman Gunn McKay. Formidable organizations supporting the Democratic party were also deeply involved in the contest. The state AFL-CIO, the Utah Education Association, and the Utah Public Employees Association all endorsed Owens. Just before the Democratic primary, Gardner was involved in a messy legal case as one of a group of businessmen accused of financial improprieties. Owens went on to win clear victory in a primary race characterized by an unexpectedly low turnout.

Even before Matheson declined to run again, the Republican gubernatorial nomination was viewed as a very valuable prize. Early in the preconvention period, the two most formidable candidates were four-term congressman Dan Marriott and speaker of the Utah House of Representatives Norman Bangerter. Marriott was viewed as the stronger candidate by Republican party professionals because of his previous campaign organization skills and his name recognition. However, he had angered or alienated some key factions in the party. For one, Marriott had delayed his announcement, while he kept "both ears to the ground"; and, second, even among Republicans there was divided sentiment over his effectiveness as a congressman.[22]

Norman Bangerter was in many ways the antithesis of Marriott, but a man with the "proper" combination of features for a Utah governor. Born into a Mormon family of ten children, Bangerter had served in the Korean War and attended Brigham Young University for a short period of time before entering the construction industry and working his way up to management status. With the same determination, Bangerter worked his way up through the ranks of the Utah state Republican party, eventually becoming his party's nominee for governor.

Bangerter's first attempt at public office was in 1974 when he won a seat in the Utah House of Representatives by defeating the only incumbent Utah Democrat to lose in the "Watergate election." Four years later he was elected majority leader of the house; two years later he won the speakership. As a legislative leader, Bangerter had developed a reputation for a moderate, consensus-building style that earned him many allies and few enemies.

Were these qualities enough to make Bangerter competitive with Marriott's name familiarity and his better-financed campaign? Only if it could be demonstrated that Marriott was in fact politically vulnerable. This goal became the essence of the campaign strategy devised by Douglas Foxley, Bangerter's campaign coordinator. As the first step in the strategy, Bangerter met with his legislative colleagues in November 1983 to solicit their support and to anticipate who among them would serve as delegates to the county and state Republican conventions. With this information, over one hundred meetings were organized by the Bangerter team for potential delegates; and legislative allies were enlisted in the lobbying task. Once the delegates were actually selected at the May mass (caucus) meetings, they were inundated with mailings lauding the virtues of Norman Bangerter. In fact, one piece of mail was sent to each delegate every five days from the time of the mass meetings until the state convention in mid-June. The strategy paid off, as Bangerter was able to hold off Marriott by a slight margin among the 2,500 delegates guaranteeing a primary election.

The August primary election once again saw the preeminently organized and oiled campaign of Dan Marriott arrayed against the grassroots machine of Norm Bangerter. Marriott stressed his leadership, experience, and Washington, D.C., connections, while Bangerter emphasized his knowledge and experience in state government. There were very few policy differences between the two conservative Republicans; therefore the election centered around personality and political organization. Once again, the strategy was to demonstrate that Bangerter was in fact a viable candidate at the same time that the campaign organization was "groveling for every $100".[23] After the release of the first *Deseret News*/KSL-TV poll showing Bangerter running close to Marriott and closing the gap, the momentum snowballed, and Bangerter surged to an easy victory in the August primary, aided in part by Democrats who took advantage of Utah's open primary to assist in the completion of Marriott's retirement.[24]

For many observers the gubernatorial election was decided on the night of the primary election. With the exception of the closely contested second congressional district, predictions were for a complete Republican sweep of the state. This vision was realized when Ronald Reagan gained his most lopsided victory by garnering 74 percent of the state's popular vote while Republican candidates won all three congressional races, captured 84 of the 104 seats in the legislature, and secured three-quarters of the places on the various county commissions. As predicted by the polls throughout the campaign, Norman Bangerter won 56 percent of the vote, securing 350,000 ballots to 274,000 for Owens. This political devastation gave the Republicans cause to celebrate on election night, although a few activists found their gathering to be dull. "It's boring over there," one commented. "They're too quiet. All they do is drink red punch and eat pretzels."[25]

With the election behind him, Norman Bangerter, Utah's thirteenth governor, embarked on his official transition to office. To what extent, if any, does an election anticipate the nature of the transition? In other words, does understanding an electoral race enhance our understanding of the nature and direction of the transitional period?

Electoral Characteristics and the Transition

Previous studies have found that such electoral characteristics as the margin of victory, the nature of campaign issues, and the occurrence of a party or factional shift do have an effect on a transition.[26] More specifically, a landslide offers a clearer "mandate" to the victor that either his or her issue positions and/or personal attributes have wide support than if the election is "competitive" (i.e., where the governor-elect wins by less than a 10-percent margin). In Utah, however, the mandate theory needs to be qualified, suggests political writer LaVarr Webb, to acknowledge that in any given general election, a good competent Republican can *expect* to get at least 56 percent of the vote against a good competent Democrat.[27] Thus, the fact that Bangerter garnered 56 percent of the vote is not remarkable. In addition, although he won twenty-five out of the state's twenty-nine counties, Bangerter ran significantly behind President Reagan's statewide landslide. The governor-elect's margin in the state's most populated county, Salt Lake, was only 5,000 votes, for example.

A second factor with a direct effect on the nature and direction of a transition is the degree to which issues are discussed in the campaign and the type of issues that prevail. Studies of the 1982 gubernatorial transitions indicate that taxation, the budget deficit, reducing the size of government, and more generally the record of the incumbent predominated.[28] In 1984 there were few big issues shaping the Utah vote for governor. When one poll asked the electorate which issue was most important in deciding how they voted for governor, the top three were the ability to work with the legislature (21 percent), education (13 percent), and two-party balance in government (13 percent).[29] Seconding the notion of a quiescent electorate, an early poll conducted by the Bangerter organization demonstrated that a strong stand on the issues would do little to add to the existing Republican margin, while a serious misstep on one or more issues could lose the election.[30] Thus, a critical strategic objective was, in the words of one legislator closely connected with the campaign, to "avoid the landmines."[31]

The popularity of the Matheson administration clearly precluded an attack on its record as a means of discrediting Democratic candidate Owens. Conveniently for the Bangerter campaign, the governor's role in the election tended more toward that of elder statesman than zealous partisan, although a stronger Owens endorsement did come from former governor Calvin Rampton.

Aficionados of rough-and-tumble politics could not even count on a clash of personalities between Bangerter and Owens to enliven matters. Not only was a determination made by each side to avoid such clashes, but each candidate held the other in esteem. While this development undoubtedly contributed to the general lack of public interest in several televised debates between the candidates, it removed one potential obstacle to a smooth administrative transition.

The Owens campaign, working against a Republican and a conservative political tide, developed a campaign strategy that combined an arduous walk by the candidate through the entire state, a plea for political balance, and persistent opposition to the placement of a nuclear waste repository in southern Utah. The walk, intended to be a media event and demonstration of Wayne Owen's determination, energy, and grassroots proclivities, did not ignite the electorate. In the interim, Norm Bangerter was able to cover more political territory by employing an airplane.

For Democrats at all levels, a critical strategy was employment of the political balance argument. Utahns had to be convinced that a Republican sweep would jeopardize democracy; that is, the political balance necessary to preserve the system of checks and balances and separation of powers would be swept away. While some 13 percent of the electorate did rank this issue as their first concern, most Utahns, accustomed to a shared set of economic and cultural concerns, did not find this argument convincing enough to support the Democratic party.[32]

The nuclear waste repository issue ignited one of the few rhetorical sparks in the campaign. The federal government had originally proposed two sites in southeastern Utah, Davis and Lavender canyons, as candidates to store high-level nuclear waste. Both sites are in close proximity to Canyonlands National Park. Subsequently the Department of Energy had narrowed the list to nine sites nationwide, which included the site at Davis Canyon. Reflecting the attitude of Scott Matheson, Owens strongly opposed the proposal. In contrast Bangerter took a very cautious attitude, refusing to rule out the possibility of a waste repository, but insisting that the matter receive additional study.

In keeping with his overall campaign strategy, Bangerter did manage to complete the campaign without committing himself to many promises. One promise he did make, not to raise state taxes for the first two years of his administration, was safe in light of a projected $100-million surplus in the 1985 state budget. Another tactic, which followed the suggestion of the NGA to limit the policy agenda to no more than three issues, was to build the campaign and his subsequent administration around the "Three E's": education, economic development, and efficiency in government. In a state with an extraordinarily high birthrate, at a time when the LDS church was sympathetic to development, in a political culture as conservative as Utah's, and given the trends in long-term population growth, realizing the "Three E's" was imperative.

According to Bangerter's game plan, as a prerequisite to attracting the needed industry to facilitate economic development, a highly educated workforce was necessary. Therefore a marked increase in educational spending would be sought. The state also would have to adopt a more prominent and aggressive role in attracting new industry, which presented an intriguing dilemma: how could the state act to facilitate economic development without risking a conservative reaction that state funds were being used to usurp the responsibility of the private sector?

To implement the third issue of efficiency in government Bangerter proposed what would later become the Utah Commission on Efficiency. While the philosophical predecessor for the commission was a federal task force chaired by Peter Grace, the Utah version would not concentrate primarily on where dollars were being wasted but would examine programs to see if they were being carried out according to executive and legislative guidelines.

Although Bangerter did not enter office with a strong public mandate when measured by aggregate voting statistics, by avoiding the pitfalls of making unrealistic political promises and by pledging to enact widely embraced policy goals the incoming administration greatly enhanced the chances that the transition to office would be a smoother one than if major disruptions in state policy had been endorsed. Bangerter ran a safe campaign, and it appeared that his transition to office would be safe as well. A contentious legislature or lieutenant governor could prove formidable even to a man who had won comfortably and was entering office relatively unencumbered by policy promises. However, in this instance Bangerter was assured of Republican majorities in both statehouses, and because of a recent constitutional change, the governor and lieutenant governor would be of the same party. In fact, the 1984 election merely completed Utah's transition to a one-party state. By capturing the governorship for the first time in twenty years, the Republicans had eliminated the last Democratic stronghold and were now in complete control of Utah state government and the federal delegation. All the signs predicted a smooth and safe transition.

The Logistical Transition

In establishing a functioning office for the governor-elect, the attitude and behavior of the serving governor are critical. That demeanor in turn is related to whether the incumbent governor voluntarily retires from office or is forced to step down by the voters. "The short term tensions of a political campaign," Gormley has suggested, "are greater than the long term tensions between the two political parties."[33] Finally,

institutional and structural factors are important in framing the logistical phase of the transition period—in particular, the time parameters
for accomplishing administrative tasks and the availability of financial
assistance in advance of the formal inauguration into office.

From a behavioral perspective, the transition was destined to be
orderly. Matheson had not only voluntarily retired but had ordered his
staff to assist the newly elected governor in accomplishing his transition
in as smooth a manner as possible. Because of this, certain institutional
and structural factors, such as the absence of any transition mechanisms
and the existence of time constraints, which otherwise would have
complicated the transition, were compensated for.

Elected on November 6, the new administration would assume
formal power a mere two months later (January 7). In addition, the
Utah legislature historically has not seen fit to guarantee that the
governor-elect will have the tools and support necessary for preparation
during this interim period before the inauguration. In fact, Utah is one
of only eighteen states that have no legislation specifically pertaining
to gubernatorial transitions.[34] There are no provisions for making state
personnel available to the governor-elect or for familiarizing staff with
office functions and procedures and no specified means for transferring such information as records and files. Moreover, the incumbent
governor must determine what funds will be allocated for transition
purposes, with the moneys originating from existing operating budgets
—or through supplemental appropriations if they can be obtained.[35]

With this leverage a disgruntled incumbent in Utah can disrupt the
transition to a new administration. Had Matheson been a stronger
partisan, perhaps he would not have been so accommodating. More
importantly, Matheson consistently emphasized his own transition experience as the reason for a cooperative attitude.

When Matheson received the mantle of government from retiring
incumbent Cal Rampton, he was the handpicked successor. Yet despite
this auspicious setting, and Rampton's efforts to smooth the logistical
transition by providing Matheson access to all of the budget, planning,
and policy heads, the process was far from systematic. Not surprisingly
a major problem was funding. Rampton was only able to secure $5,000
from the governor's emergency fund to hire a staff person to attend
the budget hearings. All other staff served on a voluntary basis until
the beginning of the year. The result, Matheson suggests, was that his
budget was "made out of a briefcase."[36] A second problem was that

of office space for the incoming staff, which proved inadequate. The Planning Office in the state capitol was commandeered and converted into two offices, divided only by a screen. Indeed, in this rustic setting Matheson contends that those in the front office could hear what the governor-elect was saying in the back office better than those who were closest to him, greatly inhibiting discussions about hiring and firing. This experience fueled Matheson's determination to accomplish an extremely professional transition "no matter who won."[37]

Key staff members indicate that Matheson was also motivated to accomplish a smooth transition by his sense of obligation to serve the public good. The transition would flow as smoothly as possible because Matheson's attitude was to "do what is right."[38] As a first step, in January 1984 Matheson requested a $50,000 appropriation for transition expenses. Because the governor had not yet announced whether he would run for reelection, a proviso was added that the amount would revert back to the general fund if it was not used. Having determined that he would run for governor, Norman Bangerter felt uncomfortable using his position as speaker of the house to support the appropriations measure. Moreover, by postponing action until the 1985 session, with a supplemental appropriation as an option, Bangerter would avoid even the appearance of a conflict of interest.[39] Consequently, no funds were appropriated during either the 1984 regular or a subsequent special session.

Even without money, planning for the transition had begun in earnest in early May 1984 with the search for a transition coordinator. At that time it was determined that the person selected must have total credibility with the leaders of both political parties, a high degree of integrity, and a track record of involvement in state government issues. The appointment of Robert Huefner to the position met the requirements in several respects. For one, Huefner brought to the position extensive managerial and political experience in state and local government. As the director of the Center for Public Affairs and Administration at the University of Utah, Huefner had written several articles for professional journals on the subject of gubernatorial transitions.[40] Matheson saw in Huefner a "squeaky pure professional person"[41] who could avoid the taint of politics. However, Republican state party chair Charles Ackerlow's spontaneous reaction was to remind Matheson that "the incoming administration is ultimately responsible for the transition," and Huefner would function as a liaison.[42] All of the gubernatorial candidates, however, found Huefner to be an excellent choice, ending plans for immediate party control over the transition.

Given the criteria set forward in the establishment of the position, Huefner's role was clear. He would facilitate the logistical transition by accumulating information on personnel and procedures from the Matheson team and passing it on to the gubernatorial candidates. Further, he would act as a sounding board, relaying the personal concerns of department heads as well as procedural information. However, the coordinator would not offer political advice or suggestions about policy or appointments.

To establish a functioning office, Matheson's overriding goal was to have all of the phones, office space, and the necessary information about the operations of state government ready to go the day after the general election. During the interim period from the nomination of candidates to the primary election, the decision was made to keep briefings or other information in abeyance, in order to decrease personal or political conflicts among the candidates and reduce discord between them and state agencies.

Huefner's first task was to establish a working relationship with Matheson's transition "Steering Committee": executive assistant Kent Briggs, director of the Department of Administrative Services Jed Kee, budget director Mike Zuhl, planning director Ralph Becker, and press secretary Malin Foster constituted the committee. Following the primary election, the candidates for lieutenant governor were selected as transition directors to serve as liaisons with Huefner. As running mates, Republican Val Oveson and Democrat Dale Carpenter had the necessary formal linkages with the gubernatorial candidates but hopefully would not be totally immersed in the day-to-day details of campaigning.

Given the lack of formal provisions for acquainting the governor-elect with office procedures, in the first week in October Matheson and Huefner held separate meetings with the candidates and with department heads. An outline was given of the budget preparation process and schedule, and each candidate was invited to have a representative attend the October budget hearings. Material from the NGA on preparing for the transition was distributed as well.

The meeting with department heads centered upon establishing both the timetable and the type of information to be conveyed to the incoming administration. Departments were instructed to have each agency under their jurisdiction prepare a transition document that would provide basic knowledge about running the government. In order to spare the incoming administration acute information overload, strict guidelines on document length were set. A maximum of four pages per agency could be produced, which meant a page apiece to discuss key personnel, budget issues and themes, other legislative issues, and long-term program opportunities. The personnel office prepared a transition document that would make information available to incumbent personnel on the procedures for applying for unemployment or retirement benefits. While the information had a pragmatic purpose, it produced the unintended consequence of heightening anxiety levels among those it was supposed to assist. Agencies were given two weeks to prepare their documents, while departments were allocated one week to review the results. As the political campaigns approached their zenith in the last week of October, departments quietly turned in the transition documents to Robert Huefner.

With the November election of Norman Bangerter, the logistical transition rolled into a new phase. Governor Matheson utilized his emergency fund to make money available for the hiring of staff members. The governor-elect immediately appointed Jon Memmott to fill three roles as executive assistant, chief of staff, and special counsel. Memmott, an attorney, had gained widespread knowledge of the workings of state government while serving as the director of the Office of Legislative Research and as the legislature's general counsel. His appointment assisted an orderly transition in several ways. Memmott had an excellent professional relationship with Bangerter, which was solidified by spirited competition on the golf course.[43] Like his boss, Memmott was a governmental insider, whose knowledge about the process could be put to immediate use. In addition, while his legislative position often required an adversarial stance toward the executive branch, the Matheson people respected his competence and envisioned a comfortable working relationship.[44]

After the election the transition plan called for the lines of communication to be modified. In the proper bureaucratic language, "direct interface" was established between the two executive assistants. The role of Robert Huefner became one of advising department heads on how to get information to the Bangerter team, and mediating minor crises when requested by both sides.

The timetable established did allow department heads a day after the election to make any last-minute changes in the transition documents. The documents were ready as Bangerter and key advisers embarked on a working vacation to southern Utah. After their return additional information was disseminated through a formal briefing. Whether affected by the enormity of the task, or disconcerted by the presence of the fourth estate, questions by the governor-elect and his staff were desultory.[45]

Three factors that are likely to place great strain on the logistical transition are interim office space, the transmission of information, and provisions for word processors. Levels of anxiety increased among some lower-level Matheson staffers as they contemplated not only a potential future job loss but an immediate deprivation of office space before the term expired. Bangerter's key staff members were given office space in the lieutenant governor's office in the western wing of the capitol, while those displaced were relocated to space in the capitol basement.

Cooperation was the watchword in the transmission of information between Matheson's staff, the department heads, and the Bangerter team. In the words of one participant, "clear marching orders" were given to act in concert.[46] No hint of problems existed at the top level, while only sporadic difficulties surfaced among some Matheson political appointees at the next layer. The Bangerter transition team did receive calls that some files were being hidden or other information withheld.[47] The reaction from a few members of the Matheson team was predictably hostile. In response, Matheson dispatched a memo stating that all personnel engaged in the transition process would "act as ladies and gentlemen."[48]

As information is useless in the bureaucracy without some means for storage and retrieval, attention turned next to the availability of word processors. Because the machines were hooked to the state's central processing unit, concern was expressed over whether the most sensitive information of the governor-elect would, at the press of a button, become available to Matheson staffers. Only after the operations director of the Central Processing Unit assured Jon Memmott and the staff were the concerns allayed.

By Saturday, January 5, the former governor and his staff had moved out, permitting Bangerter and his staff to leave their temporary quarters. Even as a key legislative leader Bangerter had only been in the governor's private office once before moving in officially. The logistical transition was complete.

In summary, the logistical transition to the Bangerter administration did function relatively smoothly, primarily due to the determination of the two principals to accomplish that purpose. In addition, the prior experience of the governor-elect and Chief of Staff Jon Memmott, combined with the fact that Bangerter did not run against the government in power, minimized the likelihood of ill will emerging between the two administrations.

The Administrative Transition

Perhaps the most sensitive aspect of the administrative phase of the transition involves the selection of personnel, for through this process a new governor communicates both the style and direction of the administration. For example, a careful observer can anticipate the degree of politicization, the policy direction, and the preferred organizational and decision-making styles of the governor by the manner in which personnel are selected, the criteria employed in their selection, and the biases of those selected. Of course, certain institutional and structural, as well as constitutional and legal factors act as important constraints.

The Bangerter team embarked upon the personnel task early during the interim period. A report was requested of the number of positions that had been changed from exempt to merit status, a list that Matheson provided with an assurance that the changes to merit status had been administrative rather than political decisions. Even with these last-minute changes, a Utah governor's patronage powers are not large; nor does appointment power extend to all areas. Out of 13,000 state employees for example, only 260 are nonmerit. This number includes thirteen department directors; but excludes the state school superintendent, who is selected by the State Board of Education. The governor does dominate judicial appointments, but exerts less control over first rank commissions because of legal provisions regarding length of term and political party balance.[49] Finally, no constitutional or legislative provisions exist for a cabinet system. The State Planning Advisory Committee, a statutory group composed of all department heads, has been utilized as a planning mechanism. The committee meets at the discretion of the state planning coordinator.

Immediately following the November 6 election, Bangerter and his aides embarked on a working vacation to plan the administrative transition. The selection of St. George in southern Utah with its temperate climate allowed for morning work sessions with an inevitable round of afternoon golf. The participants at the meeting represented a mix from the political, governmental, and private sectors. Most were trusted members of the governor-elect's "Kitchen Cabinet."[50] However, with one exception, no one could claim practical experience in the executive branch of state government. On the other hand, the influence of the state legislature was pervasive, with Memmott and three savants representing ties to both the pragmatic and ideological conservatives in that branch. Significantly, none of those attending came from powerful families in the state, or from downtown Salt Lake business interests. The participation of the lieutenant governor and Bangerter's campaign director and some of his staff represented ties to the state Republican party, ties that would fray as the transition moved on. Portending future patterns, Bangerter did not play as partisan a role as the Republican party would have liked, and the strong partisanship of Douglas Foxley and Paul Rogers created tensions with executive assistant Jon Memmott. Because parties are not strong institutions in Utah, it is hardly surprising that the role of the state Republican party was not more considerable.

After a period of personal testing and turf disputes, agreement was reached on the role the St. George advisers would play and how the executive branch would be organized. With Memmott setting the agenda and Bangerter acting as manager of the assemblage, it was decided that the group would function as a source of ideas, setting overall policy directions and procedures. To minimize undue influence, however, they would not become involved in the day-to-day operations of executive departments.

In addressing the question of administrative appointments, the group had first to grapple with three dilemmas: the time frame for accomplishing the task, the comprehensiveness of the search, and the criteria used in the selection process. The literature regarding gubernatorial transitions suggests that vast personnel changes made quickly can give the public the impression that the governor is in charge, while incremental changes can aid continuity and the ability to implement policy in the future. Secondly, a highly visible and extensive public search can demonstrate the governor's commitment to quality and an open administration while also creating the impression of policy change. In contrast, a narrow and closed search confined primarily to names known by the governor's intimates might insure a smoother "working administration." Finally, the selection of "professionals" who might on more than one occasion disagree with the executive can work against the attempt to produce coherent policy and may exacerbate internal conflict, whereas "loyalists" may encourage bad or inflexible policy made unilaterally from the top.[51]

Transition director Robert Huefner urged the new administration to move quickly on the department heads they were certain they wished to have removed or retained. The Republican party counseled rapid and widespread change, while executive assistant Jon Memmott argued against mass hirings and firings to avoid governmental disruptions. A decision was first made to break the timetable for administrative decisions into the three categories of immediate action, action within three months, and action within six months. The priority appointments to be filled were that of budget director and members of the new governor's staff (including press secretary and speech writer). In addition, new directors for Administrative Services, Natural Resources, Business Regulation, and the Health Department needed to be found.

The criteria for the selection of department heads were relayed in public and private forums. Publicly the governor-elect stated that political payoffs would not occur, since he was not obligated to individuals or groups.[52] Selecting Republicans for new appointments was an unwritten rule, although the party apparatus played a weak role. Moreover, incumbent department heads would not be automatically terminated, but would be evaluated on three criteria: the competence of the head, the policy direction of the department, and whether the incumbent was a high-profile or "closet" Democrat.[53]

The process of appointing department heads displayed wide variation, ranging from open and thorough searches to executive decisions made without formal searches. For example, the appointment to the Department of Health was the product of an extremely thorough national search, begun by Scott Matheson a year before the election. For most positions the norm was a small, manageable search committee of three. The Natural Resources Committee, for example, consisted of the governor-elect, a state senator, and a law professor from the University of Utah. However, no search committee was formed for the Department of Agriculture. In fact, the appointment of state senate president Miles "Cap" Ferry to the position was widely believed to be a political payoff, although this interpretation was contested by the new administration. In general, the governor heeded the advice of the NGA against the transference of campaign staff to administrative positions. Campaign coordinator Douglas Foxley and kitchen cabinet member Paul Rogers were rumored to be in line for positions, but the appointments did not materialize. In addition, three sitting department heads (Corrections, Social Services, and Transportation) passed the policy and "closet Democrat" political tests and were retained.[54]

The nominees recommended by the search committees were generally pragmatic Republican conservatives, lacking strong ties with the state party organization. Through posts held in state, county, or local government, many were personally acquainted with the governor. Thus in political outlook, political loyalty, and managerial style, compatibility with Bangerter's views could be expected.

Turning to the question of organizing the executive branch, the St. George group recognized that constitutional provisions for a moderately strong executive branch could only be realized though prudent delineation of the chain of command. In regard to the size of the staff, Governor Matheson had operated with a very small personal staff of thirteen; the new administration was determined to operate in just as frugal a manner. Within the top echelon the role of the executive assistant would receive a different focus. Under the Matheson administration Kent Briggs had been closely involved in both policy and political decisions, while Jon Memmott's role would focus on the substance of policy, leaving the governor the responsibility to make the policy judgments politically tenable. The Matheson administration had organized the governor's office by assigning three assistants to handle such major functions as constituent services and development of state policy and three to take responsibility for state agencies (grouped under regulatory, physical development, and human resource agencies). Under the new administration minimal organizational changes were made, reflecting the style of the governor. Responsibilities would be divided according to agencies, with five assistants for Physical Resources (including the Departments of Natural Resources and Transportation), Community and Economic Development (including responsibility for intergovernmental relations), Social Services and Health, Education, and Regulation. In addition, the head of the Criminal and Juvenile Justice Commission, while not an administrative assistant, would assist in the area of criminal justice. Each assistant, in consultation with the governor, the department head, and the appropriate member of the Planning Office, would formulate policy for the area.

While the departments under Matheson had enjoyed a measure of autonomy, the pattern would be enlarged by Bangerter. The governor's staff would not set policy for the departments, but would act as liaisons between the governor and the department heads. Agency heads would be encouraged to develop policy and to formulate legislation when necessary, but in either case the executive assistant would have to be persuaded that all the alternatives had been explored. Further, like many previous chief executives, Bangerter was attracted by the notion of cabinet government. In contrast to the Matheson administration, where the agenda of cabinet meetings tended to concentrate on such matters as finance, personnel, and data processing, the Bangerter cabinet would act as a forum where policy development and resolution could take place.

With the search committees on course, Matheson and Bangerter, along with their executive assistants, attended the New Governors' Conference in South Carolina (December 1 and 2). Matheson's attendance, while officially "academic,"[55] served to further the amicable relationship that already existed between the incoming and outgoing administrations. Kent Briggs used an informal walk on the beach with Jon Memmott to further discuss ideas of the style and demands of the job of executive assistant. Bangerter, who found the NGA conference "the most beneficial experience" of the transition,[56] was particularly impressed by the sessions in which sitting governors related how they had handled the problems and challenges of office. Whether in working sessions, in sport, or at social events, the relatively high levels of cooperation and amiability amongst Utahns of different political persuasions were clear.

The Policy Transition

Just as the logistical transition anticipates and influences the nature and direction of the administrative transition, so the administrative transition anticipates and influences the nature and direction of the policy transition. For example, past gubernatorial studies demonstrate that the administrative transition establishes the limits for the policy transition.[57] Such factors as the extent of departmental housecleaning and the timetable for filling vacancies will weigh heavily on the types of policies that are proposed. In addition the manner in which the decision-making process is institutionalized has an obvious influence on policy outcomes. Finally, the personnel selection process anticipates an administration's general theoretical orientation toward policymaking.

These aspects are important to help foresee the policy direction set during the transition, and beyond; that is, whether policy outcomes will be conservative, innovative, or incremental, or, whether the policy phase will be smooth or rough, long or short, and so on. Moreover, the same factors that explain the nature and direction of the logistical and administrative phases of the transitional period also help to explain the policy phase. Thus, in order to capture the full richness of the policy transition during the Bangerter administration, the impact of behavioral, institutional, political, and cultural factors shall be considered.

The policy phase was relatively smooth and uneventful, that is to say, undramatic, for many of the same reasons the preceding transitional phases were smooth. Among the behavioral factors was the unique and persuasive personality of Scott Matheson. According to one key staffer, "when [Matheson] is around he just pumps you up."[58] During the last year of his administration, Matheson directed his staff to concentrate on the "Eighth Year Plan," that is, the administration's remaining fifteen policy priorities. Despite a lame-duck period, the staff was persuaded to continue to pursue to completion those projects still pending after the election of Norman Bangerter.

This commitment to policy making even under conditions of imminent departure also reflects the strong cultural predisposition to act on behalf of the public good. Matheson operated on the assumption that the two administrations were partners in fulfilling the public trust rather than antagonists who needed to demonstrate the relative virtues of one partisan line over another.

Bangerter, who shares this commitment to the public good, exhibited a leadership style during his legislative and executive tenure characterized by a need to react to rather than innovate new policy. On inauguration day, the governor stated "I came to the legislature and the political process without an agenda. I came with the idea that I would work within the system, and I didn't have anything personal, for myself or for my industry, that I felt I had to get through. I came with the idea of being objective and analyzing what was needed, what was good government, and I am dedicated to that principle. I haven't been one who has come and said we need a new program for everything. I think we've passed that point in time, where a new program is the answer to everything."[59]

A sense of moderation and a lack of dramatic new proposals were also evident in Governor Bangerter's inauguration speech. In a fifteen-minute, workmanlike address Bangerter reiterated his intention to focus on education, economic development, and efficiency rather than on social issues. The pragmatic philosophy espoused failed to support the social agendas of either the ultraconservatives in the Republican party (i.e., school prayer, right-to-life, antipornography) or of liberal advocates of the disadvantaged.

In his relations with the legislature Bangerter would be protected by several factors. First, he would be working with a Republican majority in both houses, with most of the party's members falling in the mainstream of conservatism. However the literature suggests this factor in itself cannot guarantee a smooth policy transition because splinter groups or factionalism may occur if majorities are too large.[60] Ultra-conservatives did, in fact, offer opposition to the governor's program on a select number of issues during the 1985 legislative session, but the instances of factionalism never seriously threatened the administration's programs. A second factor contributing to a smooth transition was the lower rate of turnover among legislators compared to past sessions. After an election usually one-third of the legislators are new, but in 1984 the turnover rate was only 20 percent. Spending less time educating first-term legislators should allow more rapid consideration of the issues. A final factor was Bangerter's status as a legislative insider with strong ties to the leaders of both parties. His willingness to meet with Republicans and Democrats once a week helped to further cement the ties.

The emerging consensus on policy direction stemmed largely from the remarkable fact that legislators of all political persuasions agreed that flooding, education, and economic development should be the priority issues of the session and that increased funding would be necessary to address these issues. Importantly, much of the contentiousness of the first two issues had been resolved during the 1984 legislative session, furthering the prospects for consensus. Moreover, legislators were encouraged by public opinion polls showing citizens supportive of legislative spending for solving education and flooding problems.[61]

In addition to political and behavioral factors, several institutional forces worked to insure that there would be little deviation in policy direction even with Bangerter's assumption of power. The institutional factors are most clearly seen in the preparation of the budget, the major policy document of any administration. Prior to 1985 the Utah legislature met for budgetary purposes one year and policy purposes the next, thus encouraging long-range or multiyear planning. While the legislature's abrogation of this distinction gives the governor greater potential to introduce new policy initiatives in what would normally be a budgetary session, in actuality the time that must be alloted budget preparation tends to preclude the imposition of a radically new direction on government. In Utah the new administration is inaugurated during the first week of January, but the budget must be submitted in mid-December, thirty days before the legislature convenes in mid-January. Cognizant of the importance of the budget, Matheson had provided funds for both gubernatorial candidates to send representatives to the fall budget hearings. Further, Matheson had always indicated a willingness to defer to Bangerter on such items as personnel, education, and capitol facilities. At the NGA conference Bangerter's response was that he would feel more comfortable reacting to a budget that Matheson should draft "as if [he] were the governor" (for the next fiscal year), which Matheson did.[62]

The budget submitted by Norman Bangerter did show evidence of the impact of the personal and institutional factors mentioned above. The governor's proposal was basically similar to Matheson's in terms of the total amounts requested and spending levels within the departments. The budget proposed spending $2.59 billion, an increase of 7.5 percent over the 1984–85 year. In comparison with Matheson's budget, $95.3 million would be pared, representing 3.6 percent less than Matheson desired to spend.[63] The major cuts were proposed in two areas: a $70-million general obligation bond issue for new state buildings was scrapped, and $20 million was cut from the operations budget. What became obvious was that despite differences in temperament and leadership style, the two men were compatible in their philosophies and shared similar fiscal concerns. In three particular areas where incremental policy initiatives were undertaken, the potential for philosophical and fiscal compatibility was clear: education, flooding, and economic development.

Even before the legislative session began, the issues of education and flooding were presumed to represent the greatest potential for conflict. Yet few differences actually materialized among the budget figures proposed by Matheson and Bangerter, or those ultimately appropriated by the legislature. In the area of education, for example, Matheson had recommended a $120-million increase for public and higher education, compared to $100 million for Bangerter. The state surplus in Matheson's proposal would be used for merit base pay, research money, and equity pay for university and college faculty. In contrast, Bangerter's suggestion to use the money for such substantive purchases as equipment and textbooks reflected more of a difference in means rather than ends. Both men exhibited a similar concern for improving the quality of education by designating part of the surplus to finance such improvements.

Within the legislature, ultraconservative Republicans kept the faith by repeatedly voting against exceeding budget figures for education provided by the legislative fiscal analyst. Their annoyance with Republican colleagues is best illustrated by one conservative legislator who responded, "What a bunch of liberals!" when party members voted to increase public employee salaries by 5 percent.[64] Importantly, this does reflect a major shift in the frame of reference of the Republican majority; the analyst's figures represented a substantial increase over those for the previous year. Too, the Republicans, realizing the political benefits that support for an enhanced educational system would produce, granted virtually the exact dollar amount for both public and higher education requested by the governor.

The Republicans' concern with being credited with educational reform also meant support for a controversial teacher career-ladder pay plan. This program would reward teachers for assuming additional responsibilities and for quality performance. The latter policy objective threw educators and legislators into the quagmire of determining what would constitute quality teaching, and how levels of excellence should be monetarily rewarded. In the waning hours of the legislative session pressure from educators retained the $19-million addition to the program, overcoming efforts of dissidents to dilute the concept.

The predicted controversy over the issue of flooding also revolved around the means of finance rather than policy goals. Governor Bangerter proposed spending $100 million to support a two-phase program. In the short term $50 million would be used to build dikes along the shores of the Great Salt Lake. Another $50 million, reluctantly supported, would pay for a controversial long-term attempt to construct facilities to pump excess water to the west desert.[65] Bangerter, who initially declined to specify a funding method, had been an advocate of short-term, low-interest bonding. When the flood proposals reached the legislature, controversy occurred over the *funding* issue rather than either the policy goal or the two-phase recommendation. The senate passed a measure accepting the governor's proposal for short-term bonding, while the house, equating bonding with the mortal sin of deficit spending, demanded that the full amount be appropriated from existing revenues. In this policy area the governor was spared a potentially divisive dispute by higher revenue estimates made at midsession by the legislative fiscal analyst. Therefore both chambers agreed at the end of the session to allocate $20 million to current diking efforts, and to place the bulk of the money in a special reserve account until the June special session, when the results of the spring runoff could be better assessed. At the June session the governor requested that $80 million be left in the flood reserve until next year, as excellent spring weather conditions had resulted in minimal flooding.

In 1985 economic development was a buzzword both for the executive and the legislature. While most of the programs in this policy area can trace their roots to the Matheson administration, a few did represent incremental initiatives proposed by Bangerter. The budgets of both governors recommended a 50 percent increase to support travel promotion and industrial development. The Matheson administration had established the goal of creating 25,000 new jobs each year to absorb the large number of high school and college graduates. The Utah Technology Finance Corporation was established in 1983, and funded in 1984, to support investments in "innovative" or "high-tech" ventures in the private sector. The corporation received an additional $2 million of support from Bangerter, who saw this as a convenient way to reconcile the fine line between government assistance and "giving up the store" to private industry. While the legislature ultimately allocated the funds during the regular session, that decision rankled ultraconservatives in both the legislative and executive branches. To block the corporation from investing public funds in private ventures, Utah attorney general David L. Wilkinson threatened to file a "friendly" lawsuit, citing a state constitutional provision forbidding the state from lending its credit to any individual or corporate undertaking. In response, the corporation filed its own "friendly" lawsuit, naming the attorney general as defendant. A predictable effect of the surfeit of judicial comity is that the majority of the funds sat idle pending resolution of the judicial challenges.

Bangerter's major economic initiative was a proposal to set aside

$5 million of the budget surplus for a program to stimulate business activity. The money was allocated during the regular session, but program details were revealed during a three-day special session at the end of June. The package consisted of creating centers of excellence in academia to spin off jobs ($2.5 million), attracting industry to rural and metropolitan areas, and establishing a state procurement office to help Utah business firms gain government supply contracts (particularly at Hill Air Force Base, the largest employer in the state).[66] Because the lead time from authorizing the program to measuring economic impacts is normally three to five years, policy evaluation must await future events.

Clearly, legislative-executive comity provides significant policymaking advantages. However, one episode in the area of social policy is useful to illustrate some potentially negative consequences of a relationship between a governor and legislature that is decentralized, collegial, and lacks strong input from the minority party. During the regular legislative session the Bangerter administration had been successful in deemphasizing the social agenda of the ultraconservatives. Yet only a few hours before the end of the special session, at the request of Attorney General Wilkinson, the governor placed on the business agenda a bill that would require parental consent for minors requesting birth control measures. Wilkinson saw the bill as necessary in support of his appeal of a U.S. District Court decision reinstating federal Title 10 family-planning funds to Planned Parenthood of Utah. However, the bill's language was so broad that consent would be required when any "health-care provider" (including podiatrists, speech pathologists, and certified social workers) treated a nonadult patient. With the Utah Medical Association and Utah Hospital Association attacking the measure, and conservative citizen groups providing support, the governor vetoed the bill. His veto message indicated surprise at the groundswell of opposition from the medical community and concluded that the broadly drawn nature of the bill would not be in the public interest. While accepting "partial responsibility" for the rushed consideration of the measure, Bangerter, in an effort to mend fences, reiterated his "personal, community and legislative record" in support of parental consent. Because the bill received less than a two-thirds' margin in the house, serious consideration was never given to a veto override session.

In sum, an examination of the policy transition demonstrates that despite differences in personal style, political party affiliation, and degree of party support in the legislature, incremental policy changes were attempted and accomplished during the first legislative session of the Bangerter administration. More impressively, both Matheson and Bangerter registered similar success rates in getting their policy packages through. In general Matheson's style has been described as imperious and distant. Legislators stress that they were rarely consulted on key issues even in an informal manner. Bangerter is described as an insider and a product of the legislature. The new governor admitted to a preference for informal and open relations with his colleagues: "I like to meet and put pressure on people."[67] Despite these differences in style and partisan support, Matheson received almost 80 percent of his policy proposals from the legislature; whereas Bangerter's initial rate was about 90 percent.[68] To explain this irony we can again point to the common philosophical bond of serving the public; the shared conservative approach to fiscal matters; the fact that political parties in Utah are weak, operating more as electoral mechanisms rather than as vehicles for introducing and forging policy platforms; and the importance of having a part-time legislature and a full-time, professional executive office.

On the other hand, the similarities in success rates do not suggest that the policy transition was totally harmonious. On key issues such as flooding or education, splinter groups did appear, particularly in the Republican caucus in the house. Despite an ultra conservative attempt to block bonding as too radical, Bangerter ultimately won approval from the house and the senate, the latter being consistently more sympathetic to the governor. According to one observer, while lawmakers did give Bangerter "generally what he wanted," they also "exhibited an independent streak as well, using different methods to accomplish the same purposes."[69] The observations in this study reinforce the conclusion that the differences that existed were over means rather than ends. Moreover, when pragmatic conservatives were forced to move from the role of gubernatorial critic to active partner in the policy process, Bangerter was able to garner considerable support for his policies.

Conclusion

In many ways, the Utah gubernatorial transition to Norman Bangerter's administration exemplifies a textbook case. In terms of conceptual approaches to the transition, the Utah study further demonstrates the utility of viewing the transition as a four-fold process of electoral, logistical, administrative, and policy phases. Not only is this sequence a useful device for the description of events, but more importantly it allows the analyst to demonstrate how each stage in the process anticipates the next stage and sets the parameters for that subsequent stage. Second, we have found that the nature and direction of the transitional period are explainable by drawing upon cultural, behavioral, structural and institutional, economic, and political factors. Certainly any analysis must begin with Utah's unique cultural factors: the presence of the LDS church and a highly moralistic culture. This cultural factor, in turn, encourages certain behavioral factors, which were most notably present in the style of leadership displayed by both the outgoing and incoming governors. Not only did the two main actors in the drama genuinely respect each other, but they expressed a common obligation to serve the public interest (however imprecisely the term is defined), rather than personal or partisan interests. In fact, more than any other element, the commitment on the part of the key actors in the drama caused the transition to be an amicable one. Further, this personal commitment makes it much easier to overcome the glaring structural deficiency of the absence of legal provisions for the transition. While the makeshift arrangements for appropriations, staff, and office space created substantial logistical inconveniences, the new administration did not face the prospect of having its policy priorities sabotaged by the outgoing administration.

The transition also took place within an auspicious political context. The Reagan landslide, the two-thirds' Republican majority in both houses of the legislature, and a policy agenda in which the framework for the most contentious issues was decided upon in previous legislative sessions provided the governor with useful leverage during the policy transition.

Finally turning to more specific issues, in several instances our findings conform to both the NGA's suggestions for transitions as well as the findings of earlier academic studies on the subject. Under the prodding of key political leaders, the Utah transition process has shown steady movement toward professionalization, as evidenced by the care with which a transition coordinator was chosen and the willingness to call a special session to accomplish business not completed during the forty-five-day general session. Moreover, the Bangerter administration paralleled NGA guidelines in such instances as transferring few members of the campaign staff to administrative positions, delegating many of the functions of the transition, making only those changes in the organization of the governor's office necessary to reflect the governor's style, and limiting the legislative agenda to two or three main issues. The governor departed from the guidelines in such instances as retaining several administrators from the previous administration and not giving absolute priority to the creation of the budget.

The textbook quality of the 1984 Utah transition does not guarantee that this pattern will prevail in the future. While the state enjoyed a professional transition despite the lack of formal provisions, the heavy reliance upon the goodwill of the participants should not lull the state legislature into a false sense of security. Rather, it should spur legislators to enact legal provisions for future transitions. If structural provisions and agreement among the principals are both lacking, future transitions could be unpleasant. Nonetheless, the 1984 transition in Utah presents an example of many of the elements of a clean transition, one which might be profitably used by other states in planning for this crucial political event.

The Gardner Transition:
The Changing of the Guard in
Washington

)))))

Herman D. Lujan

Some say that governors move like kings on a chessboard, boldly changing direction as the situation warrants; but legislators move like knights,
attacking by indirection to minimize conflict. From the beginning of his
ambitious campaign for the governorship, Booth Gardner understood
the distinction.

Born of wealth and stature as an heir to the Weyerhaeuser fortune,
Gardner came to politics by way of a college education and experience
in the business world. He worked his way through the family business
and emerged gradually onto the public scene. After graduating from
the University of Washington in 1958, Gardner went on to the Harvard
Business School, where he completed an M.B.A. He came back to the
Puget Sound area as director of the School of Business and Economics
at the University of Puget Sound in his hometown, Tacoma.

With this background, he successfully ran for the state senate in 1970
and served until 1973. During his short stint, he chaired three committees: Education, Manufacturing and Development, and Commerce
and Regulatory Agencies. In the meantime, he had risen to become the
president of Laird Norton Company, a family enterprise involved in
building materials and related supplies.

That business connection linked Gardner professionally to the Washington business establishment, a linkage supplemented by family relationships with the Weyerhaeuser timber interests and the social status

which that created. But Gardner wandered widely from that narrow base of privilege. He became broadly involved in volunteer activities, culminating in effective mediation between Seattle's central area schools, their resident minority community, and the school district administration over the issue of integration and educational access. He became cofounder of the Central Area Youth Activities, a group working with black youth in Seattle. He was active in working for the developmentally disabled, the Seattle-King County Private Industry Council and its CETA job training activities, and the Washington Commission for the Humanities.

In 1980 he left the presidencies of the Laird Norton Company and the Seattle-King County Private Industry Council to run again for public office, this time for Pierce County executive in his home county south of Seattle. Pierce County has always been the weak sister of the twin cities of the Puget Sound. A port town rimmed by smelters and peopled with blue-collar workers, it had just been riddled by a major scandal involving its sheriff and Mafia-like elements in the tavern and related businesses of Tacoma and the surrounding area. Its budget was $44.7 million in the red, Commencement Bay (its waterfront) was dying of pollution in the otherwise pristine Northwest, its port was struggling, and its downtown was caught between blight and efforts at redevelopment. When Tacoma and Pierce County were ready for new leadership, Gardner was elected and the transformation from knight to chessboard king was under way.

The Making of a Governor

When 1984 came around, Booth Gardner had become known as Tacoma's Mr. Clean, according to the *Weekly*, a magazine for the Seattle intelligentsia. He had moved Pierce County from a deficit to a $2-million surplus, begun water pollution control projects, and moved on affirmative action hiring in Pierce County, a union stronghold where seniority had to be addressed. He had turned management expertise and fiscal conservatism into a launching pad for the run to the executive mansion.

In the Democratic primary he faced a legislative liberal, Senator Jim McDermott of Seattle. McDermott had run for governor most recently in 1980 and lost to incumbent Republican John Spellman. But, as chair of the Ways and Means Committee, McDermott had kept his visibility and his political clout. Groups and individuals owed him in exchange for budgetary largess, his campaign workers were in place for another try, and the mantle of liberalism attached to Mondale also fit the articulate and urbane McDermott.

By contrast, Booth Gardner had ambiguous ideological credentials in the eyes of some observers, was known largely west of the Cascade mountains, possessed no major statewide organization, and was open to the image of a spoiled rich kid riding the family fortune to fame and leadership. But images, like oddsmaking, have room for error.

His campaign struck a maverick theme. His literature proclaimed, "Booth Gardner is different from most officeholders."[1] It went on, "If you are satisfied with the way things are going in state government, then vote for one of the two most powerful men in Olympia [the state capital]—Spellman or McDermott. But if you think things can be better, then vote for me." The theme of being different was emphasized, along with avoiding partisan identification, good management skills, attracting businesses to Washington to bolster a sagging economy, promoting international trade, improving schools, concern for minorities and women, cleaning up the environment, and eliminating corruption in government.

These emphases were fashioned to deal with unemployment in Washington (which was the sixth worst among the fifty states), attract the state teachers and their votes, and entice individuals and business persons to tax-shy Washington (one of the few states without an income tax). Innovation, leadership management, and fiscal responsibility were transformed into everyman virtues in one sleight-of-hand. In his handouts, he transferred the high-brow ambience of an M.B.A. degree into a low-brow M.B.W.A. degree. Translation: change the image of an upper-crust Harvard M.B.A. into that of a boss with sleeves rolled up who "manages by walking around"—pressing the flesh with government workers and dealing with them at their level.

In fact, Gardner was an informal type who did roll up his sleeves and was known for popping in at agencies in Pierce County. This informal style gave credence to the theme and transformed him into a kind of people's candidate. His "regular guy" comportment coupled with a high-pitched voice and a less-than-commanding speaking style separated Gardner from the professional politicians he was out to beat. The combination turned status into sympathy, a lack of polish into sincerity, and an underdog into a breath of fresh air. He became the sensitive but no-nonsense executive who preferred to "skip the show biz and get on with the problems."[2]

The summer of 1984 brought the primary and a poor start for Gardner. Polls showed him trailing Jim McDermott. Facing this and the need to build a statewide reputation, Gardner made changes in his campaign organization. He sharpened his image into that of a politically unknown underdog who had cleaned up Pierce County and began to stalk McDermott, who had already lost once to the incumbent governor in a state badly needing revitalization. The Gardner theme was struck anew: Washington needed not more government, but better government. The urban liberal McDermott was for the former and, therefore, for more of the same.

By September, Gardner had corralled the old liberal and separated himself from the kind of politics already hamstringing Mondale liberals and the national Democratic party. The "better government not more government" theme was working. On primary day, McDermott died at the polls with 32 percent of the party vote and Booth Gardner, with 65 percent of the party vote, was running for governor as the Democratic candidate.

On the day after the primary, Gardner was no longer an enigma. He was the skilled manager, the new face who had proven he could beat a seasoned politico. He had also established himself among the younger, less party-oriented voters, the union membership, the state teachers, and those for whom the pristine environment of the Northwest was an issue—and he did well in the farm country. Even more significantly, however, he had established himself without heavy reliance on or endorsement by business, negating the charge that he was a rich kid buying the governorship.

What followed was a dogfight. Gardner ran to pin the recession of 1980 and the sluggish economy on Spellman, calling for an economic development strategy designed to get people working again. He hammered at such broad issues as improving education, cleaning up the environment, and improving the efficiency of state government. He repeated earlier themes and especially criticized Spellman for promising no new taxes while actually raising ninety-three of them. Spellman countered by taking credit for moving Washington out of a severe recession, promoting trade with Asia, expanding tourism, authorizing industrial development bonds, and keeping Washington from new taxes.

Spellman had won the governorship by stressing his own management style with positive ads. As incumbent, however, he switched from stressing his own record and image to attacking Gardner. In the debates on statewide television, he became the negative candidate. As the polls showed Gardner gaining, Spellman put out hard-hitting ads, particularly one memorable ad in which a cigar-chomping labor boss became the portrayed force behind the lackey Gardner. This label-slinging negativism did not square with the image of the businesslike Spellman who had risen to the governorship. If anything, it fell into the trap of portraying Spellman as responding to Gardner rather than setting the theme. Coupled with a general view that as governor Spellman had not been decisive, this resulted in the residual opinion that Spellman made no bold moves even when the times seemed to warrant some. On election day, the verdict was clear. Gardner received 53 percent of the vote to Spellman's 47 percent and Washington had a new governor.

The results of a poll by the *Seattle Times* are shown in table 1. It can be seen that the most common reasons for backing Gardner involved a desire to replace Spellman and the view that Gardner was a suitable and preferable replacement. According to the *Times*, "it was disapproval of Spellman, for inaction rather than action, that proved to be the most common theme in the poll."[3] Thus, the Gardner strategy of the new face with management skills, an M.B.W.A. style, and a call for better government fit the bill.

The Transition

As things got close to the wire, those around Gardner began to look beyond the fateful Tuesday. Gardner himself came to consider what would be required if he were elected. The name that emerged from these considerations of the transition process was Orin C. Smith, a partner in Touche, Ross Company, a major Seattle accounting firm.

Orin Smith was not new to Democratic politics. He had served as budget director for the last Democratic governor, Dixie Lee Ray. He was a skilled and knowledgeable staffer with political acumen and respect within the business community, in some ways a kind of Northwest Democratic answer to David Stockman. His image and expertise were right for the Gardner approach and the campaign theme. After a private meeting between Gardner and Smith and some persuasiveness on the part of the governor, Smith agreed to head the transition.

Table I Reasons for Backing Gardner over Spellman

	Percent
Voters backed Gardner because	
he was better than Spellman	39
he was a Democrat	17
he did a good job in Pierce County	7
Voters opposed Spellman because	
a change in leadership was needed	18
Spellman has not done much	13
they never liked Spellman	10
they did not like Spellman's policies	9

Source: Seattle Times poll, Nov. 7, 1984.

Outgoing governor Spellman had appointed C. Kenneth Grosse as his designee for the transition process, and on November 15, 1984, Smith and Grosse signed a memorandum of understanding between the two camps. By this memorandum, communication between the new governor and state offices and agencies was set in motion. Specifically, agencies and offices were to create briefing memoranda as background papers for the new administration. These memos were to include the usual organizational charts with pertinent personnel and staffing information as well as a budget synopsis. In this way, the new governor got the bird's-eye view of people and budgets so essential to the changing of the guard.

Washington follows a system of biennial budgeting and the new governor needed to prepare for the upcoming budget proposal to the legislature. It is difficult enough to review and modify annual budgets, but biennial budgets pose a particular challenge. If a new governor is not prepared, the first two years of a term can essentially be spent living by the outgoing governor's budget. That, of course, can constrain innovation and waste considerable time in establishing a record essential for reelection. It can also inhibit the ability to make genuine change take place.

To avoid these pitfalls, the memorandum called for the following specific information:[4]

) the scope of each agency's responsibilities with references to state laws and codes.

) an organizational chart with names and titles of all exempt personnel and those personnel with management positions.

) budget synopses with staffing levels, by program area, for the last two biennia and the request for the coming biennium.

) descriptions of each agency's strengths and weaknesses with emphases on problems that must be addressed in the coming legislative session.

) descriptions of ongoing negotiations with other levels of government.

) descriptions of legislation proposed by each agency for the coming session.

) descriptions of each agency's long-term goals and objectives to improve its operation, management, and service to the public.

) resumes from all agency heads who desired to continue in service.

) descriptions of other pending issues or those requiring immediate attention.

Armed with this information, the governor-elect could assess the situation and begin to develop strategies to prepare for the budget review process necessary for developing recommendations to the legislature via the budget message and sort out policy issues and priorities for the transition year.

The outgoing administration allocated $100,000 from the gubernatorial contingency fund to cover the costs of staffing, office space, supplies, and other essentials related to the transition. Transition staff were placed on personal services contracts to expedite appointments and payroll processing, with a termination date of January 16, 1985—the date of the inauguration of the new governor. None of the contracts were to exceed in cost the annualized amount of compensation for comparable positions in state government. Proper public disclosure of interests was required of the transition staff.

Because Spellman was going ahead as required by law with the submission of a budget recommendation to the legislature, there was obvious concern over the relationship of that process, which was already under way, with the start-up of the process for the governor-elect. As a result, the outgoing budget director was to coordinate budget briefings for the governor, the governor-elect, and the transition staff. An agreement was reached so that the parallel processes would not conflict.

On November 16 the transition staff moved from campaign headquarters in Seattle to Olympia, the state capital. The organization that
was put into place that day had been forming rapidly, with the major
actors being Orin Smith, Greg Barlow (Gardner's staff chief in Pierce
County and a Republican), and Laird Harris (a young staff associate).
Each of these actors had a certain character that blended interestingly
into Gardner's need for a quick and smooth transition. Smith knew
Olympia and the budget process well. His accounting firm connection
fit the governor-elect's business and management image. Barlow had
known the governor since his brief days as a state legislator, and Gardner had brought Barlow into the family business (Laird Norton), where
he handled security for the owners and served as Gardner's trouble-
shooter. A swarthy Vietnam veteran, he was a loyal and tough-minded
aide. Harris was a bright young staff type with a sharp mind to go
along with his Michigan master's degree in public affairs.

The three set about pursuing their specialties. Smith concentrated on
the budget, bringing his political and technical skills to bear on the
mountain of paperwork that characterizes that process. He also went to
work on the talent hunt, along with Gardner and the latter's informal
advisers and confidantes. Barlow turned quartermaster and operations
chief, working with other staff to move operations from Seattle to
Olympia and to be available to the governor-elect as needed. Harris
focused immediately on the issues problem. Throughout his campaign,
Gardner had begun a series of issue forums, designed to broaden the
flow of issues into the campaign as well as to tie a broad group of voters
into the campaign effort. As a management-oriented leader, he wanted
to build the base for a populist candidacy that would cut across party
lines. After the election, he had a ready-made mechanism for casting a
policy net designed to fish out a few key issues, which he could push in
the upcoming session and for which broad support already existed.

In all transitions the basic and most difficult step involves facing
the reality that the team that gets a candidate elected may not possess
the skills necessary to run a government. Gardner had built a team of
old Democrats, business associates, young professionals, and lobbyists
into a winning November coalition. He had been so busy in the close
campaign that he had not had much time to think systematically about
the January coalition that would run the state for four years.

In November Smith, along with the Gardner advisers, had begun to
uncover some of the needed talent. Carol Gregory, a schoolteacher and

past Washington Education Association president who had worked the teacher vote for Gardner, was left to close down the campaign head-quarters. Apart from Smith, Barlow, and Harris, the key actors who emerged in these days were Gregory, Jim Kneeland (Gardner's campaign press secretary), Mary Faulk (overseeing finances), and Rosalie Gittings (a seasoned and trusted assistant handling the important appointment process). This group coordinated the larger transition team.

The larger team handled personnel, issues, operations, finances, and press relations. Of these, the greatest effort was put into identifying and clarifying policy issues, a process that Laird Harris was to coordinate. Gardner wanted the few items he was to bring before the legislature to be substantive ones. He felt that it was essential to start small and successfully because the fiscal condition of the state was still weak, given the 1980 recession and its impact on timber, aircraft manufacturing, and agriculture, the cornerstones of the Washington economy.

With Gardner's concurrence, eighteen policy groups were formed to cull out issues under Harris's guidance: budget, basic education, higher education, energy, ecology, health, human services, transportation, local government, public safety, natural resources, employment and economic development, agriculture, international trade, tourism, minority coordination, and two general activities—boards and commissions and government operations. Each area would involve an advisory group that could retain linkages to campaign supporters and attract people with substantive interest and expertise. The outreach would sift out new ideas and include a talent search that could pay off handsomely. The result was a staff of issue specialists to handle each area:

) transportation: Judy Burns, staff director for the Legislative Transportation Committee—to cover the Transportation Safety Commission, including the Department of Transportation, the Board of Pilotage, and trucking regulation.

) tourism: Larry Coffman, former marketing manager for the Seattle and surrounding King County Public Transportation Authority (Metro)—to handle the Department of Commerce and Industry tourism effort and the state convention and trade center.

) basic education: Martha A. Darling, executive director of the Washington Roundtable, an association of the state's top business executives—to handle the elected superintendent of public instruction and vocational education.

) ecology: Alvin Ewing, from the U.S. Environmental Protection Agency—to review the Department of Ecology, environmental health, conservation, and issues related to the Columbia River Gorge.

) agriculture: Greg Hanon, an agricultural lobbyist—to consider the Department of Agriculture.

) health: Tom L. Hilyard, chair of the Pierce County Facilities Review Committee and Gardner supporter—to assess health insurance, the Department of Licensing, the State Employees Insurance Board, the Department of Health and Human Services (the state's largest agency), and the Department of Labor and Industries (a major union interest).

) human services: Mel Jackson, City of Tacoma director of human development—to study the departments of Social and Health Services, Veteran's Affairs, and Employment Security, as well as the child abuse issue and ethnic minority commissions.

) minorities: Jan Kumusaka, Gardner's constituency coordinator—to relate to broad minority issues.

) international trade: Donald P. Lorentz, vice president of a microcomputer firm—to look at the Department of Commerce and Economic Development, a Gardner priority.

) public safety: Bobbie Budge, attorney—to consider the elected Office of the Attorney General, the Washington State Patrol (a Gardner campaign priority), the Department of Corrections, the Parole Board, and related commissions including the Board of Volunteer Firemen.

) natural resources: David McCraney, a federal employee in natural resources—to review the elected Commissioner of Public Lands, fisheries (a political hot potato involving Indian fishing rights), parks and recreation, and game.

) energy: Joel Merkel, a staff aide to the late Senator Henry M. Jackson and an attorney—to consider the energy office and utilities.

) local government: Wendy Morgan, Bellevue Community College development officer—to provide an overview of the Department of Community Development.

) employment and economic development: Dale A. Vincent, public affairs coordinator for Pacific Northwest Bell—to study the Office of Minority and Women's Business Enterprises, the Departments of Labor and Industries, Employment Security, and Commerce and Economic Development.

) higher education: Sharyn Ward, government relations representative from Metro—the state universities, the Council for Post-Secondary Education, the Community College Board, and the Higher Education Personnel Board.

) government operations: David P. Haworth, partner in the Arthur Young consulting firm—to review general government activities including the Office of the Secretary of State, the Department of General Administration, data processing, retirement programs, and personnel.

) budget: Orin Smith, partner in Touche, Ross Company—to review the Office of Financial Management and the Department of Revenue as well as the Office of the Treasurer.

) miscellaneous boards and commissions: Jay C. Smith, management consultant for Touche, Ross—to handle boards and commissions ranging from fire marshall to gambling and tax appeals.

These individuals led policy teams designed to carry out the following tasks:

) review agency request legislation.
) review pending Washington Administrative Code revisions.
) identify and review state plans.
) interview agency personnel.
) review legislation under development by the legislature and interest groups.
) create an inventory of relevant policy decisions.
) select policy decisions for review by the governor-elect.
) recommend executive request legislation.
) develop summaries of selected policy decisions from human services and write decision packages for each.
) organize materials for and brief incoming appointees.

Through these ten activities, background work for both the governor-elect and the incoming agency heads would be prepared in a decision-oriented approach. This approach would involve identifying the major policy issues to be addressed during the transition and the first sixty days of the new administration. For each issue, the policy team was to prepare a summary analysis, a decision package, and briefings for the governor-elect and his appointees so that priority decisions could be reached in the early days of office. This was essential if the governor was to proceed incrementally and practically with the legislature, given the fiscal constraints that the state faced.

The process involved reviewing request legislation and changes in the administrative code required by recent legislation, interviewing existing agency heads, holding discussions with legislative leaders, committee chairs, and key committee staff, meeting with key lobbyists and interest group leaders, and consulting with knowledgeable individuals. In addition, campaign promises contained in position papers from the campaign, speeches, and newspaper coverage had to be collected, reviewed, and cataloged. It was imperative that Gardner continue the image of a good manager by blending analysis with the requirements of everyday politics to develop a practical and politically feasible legislative and budgetary request.

The staff assigned to the policy teams were by and large on loan from their employers and were assigned full time to the teams. Staff were to carry out the bulk of the analysis, with the teams meeting several times to review and comment on the results. The issue summaries that emerged were to focus on items that had to be effected in the first sixty days of office. Accordingly, these summaries had to include time lines for key actions. The decision packages that would follow were to identify the relevant policy alternatives or decisions, present the principal arguments for and against each decision, recommend consultation prior to making the decision, and suggest appropriate instruments for action, such as executive orders or new legislation.

Because of the sixty-day time frame, the calendar for the policy teams was tight. Staff members were to survey documents and interview knowledgeable agency personnel immediately. This inventory process was to take one week. Policy teams were to review the results immediately thereafter, with issue summaries due by the end of the first week of December, a month after the election. As soon as the move to Olympia was complete and Orin Smith had approved the process, the teams got under way. While things took a little longer than planned, by December 5, 1984, the process was in place and announced by the governor-elect.

The link between business and government evident in the policy teams surfaced again in the group of gubernatorial advisers being dubbed "Booth's Kitchen Cabinet." Throughout the election Gardner received advice from a group of knowledgeable businessmen. They helped raise money, gave advice when the polls showed Gardner lagging, and were there when the time had come to look ahead to actual governance. Because they were attached to Gardner through business rather than party affiliations, they were suspect in some quarters of the Democratic party.

The best-known of the group was Al Rosellini, a former, highly respected Democratic governor and an old neighbor who had known Gardner since he was a youth on Vashon Island. The businessmen included Bill Clapp, Gardner's stepbrother and president of Laird Norton; Gary MacLeod, Gardner's brother-in-law and an officer of Laird Norton; Dave Cohn, owner of a number of Seattle's finer restaurants; Eric Blitz, president of the Tacoma public relations firm of Blitz and Company; Herb Simon, a Tacoma scrap metal dealer; Herb Bridge, chairman of Ben Bridge Jewelers and the Gardner campaign treasurer; and Greg Barlow, head of the Medina Foundation and security director for the Clapp family businesses. The commissioners included Mike Murphy, Grays Harbor County commissioner; Les Eldridge, Thurston County commissioner and a former aide to Senator Dan Evans in his gubernatorial days; and John McKibbin, Clark County commissioner. These were individuals Gardner interacted with in his role as Pierce County executive.

The group was presided over by Herb Simon and met regularly throughout the campaign. They had come together in summer 1984, when the Gardner campaign was floundering and had taken a tough-minded approach in advising the candidate. In the transition they became the screeners and served as a sounding board for general transition activities, cabinet appointments, staffing, and talent searches.

During December, two major elements in the transition came together. The first involved the policy and budget activities, which would culminate in the legislative and budgetary messages. Laird Harris and Orin Smith were shepherding these two activities, with help from A. N. "Bud" Shinpoch, a senator who was dealing with the legislative aspects of the budgetary effort, especially with regard to those agencies with complicated and multisource budgets. A seasoned senator, he knew the budgets of many agencies and had a good feel for legislative temperament in that regard. The second element was the talent search. Gardner had wanted to set a tone in his appointments that would be consistent with a management-oriented and businesslike approach to government. He set up a broad nomination and search process supplemented by knowledgeable screening committees to accomplish this.

The talent search took the limelight. In his campaign Gardner had promised to appoint a new State Patrol chief and the highway patrol strongly backed him. Thus, this appointment took on significance. If it was popular, it would signal a new era and would balance the search for tough management with good political common sense. Besides, many party stalwarts were still skeptical of Gardner's partisanship, especially given the public perception of an influential "Kitchen Cabinet" that was more personal than partisan in its allegiance.

On January 9, 1985, the first appointments were announced. A State Patrol major and western Washington field commander, George Telle-vik, was named State Patrol chief. A twenty-nine-year veteran of the patrol, he was respected as an insider. In one move, Gardner picked a well-liked pro with management experience and political support, letting it be known that brute management was not within the transition strategy.

Other appointments were consistent with this theme. To head the Department of General Administration, Gardner selected the retired commander of McChord Air Force Base, whom he had come to know while serving as the Pierce County executive. Richard Virant had no strong political reputation, a characteristic appropriate to the business management agency in state government. For his director of community development, Gardner reached into city government to find someone to head the agency that works closely with city and local governments. He named Richard Thompson, city manager of Puyallup, a Pierce County municipality. He turned again to city government to find a director of licensing, picking Theresa Aragon, director of human resources for the City of Seattle. A Hispanic woman, she was picked by Gardner for the job that had become the "Hispanic" position in government under the previous governor. Because she had a Ph.D., Aragon would be confirmed without the circus of opposition that had attended the appointment of her predecessor, whose confirmation was dragged out over several legislative sessions.

On January 10 more appointments were made. Retiring Senator A. N. "Bud" Shinpoch was named director of revenue. Knowledgeable about state finances, he was a perfect choice both politically and in management terms, the latter because of his management role in the

Boeing Company. Orin Smith was named to direct the Office of Financial Management, the state budget agency. A former state budget director, he was returning to familiar terrain. Like the Shinpoch appointment, this one was both politically astute and managerially sound.

To the Department of Agriculture, the governor appointed C. Alan Pettibone, an associate dean of the College of Agriculture at Washington State University. Richard A. Davis, assistant vice president for marketing at Pacific Northwest Bell, was named director of the Department of Labor and Industries. Another city manager, Andrea Beatty of the City of Bellevue, a major and competitive Seattle suburb, was selected to head the Department of Ecology, a department with clear intergovernmental responsibilities. Finally, Dean Foster, clerk of the House of Representatives, was named chief of staff to the governor. This last move was popular with the legislature and would give Gardner a resource in dealing with the Pierce County legislative leadership in both houses. It had been some time since Gardner had served in the legislature. His primary election opponent chaired the senate Ways and Means Committee, and Pierce County politicians held the positions of majority leader of the senate, speaker of the house, and chair of the house Ways and Means Committee.

The list of appointees culminated a few days later with the appointment of John Anderson, director of commerce and economic development in Oregon, to the same position in Washington. A former deputy director of the Washington agency, Anderson had been successful in attracting Asian companies to Oregon. With economic development (especially in relation to the Pacific Rim nations) a Gardner priority, Anderson was a natural.

Initially, eleven holdovers from the Spellman administration were retained, most notably Amos Reed of Corrections, Karen Rahm of Social and Health Services—the largest state agency—and Bill Wilkerson, fisheries director. Wilkerson was involved in delicate negotiations with Indian tribes over fishing rights and allocations, a subject of considerable political sensitivity, and was enjoying a level of success that surprised many.

Also surprised were some party regulars who, already suspicious of Gardner's partisanship, were finding their doubts reinforced by the number of holdovers. Gardner, however, was firm in his view that he wished an administration with good professional credentials and the promise of solid management. To that end, he was willing to move

Table 2 Poll of Gardner's Likely Record

Policy dimension	Expected record (in percent)		
	Excellent/good	Fair/poor	Don't know
Managing government	71	17	12
Providing leadership	61	22	17
Initiating programs	56	25	19

Source: *Seattle Times* poll, Jan. 3–5, 1985.

deliberately and to risk criticism of keeping too many Republicans aboard as the transition moved from election to governing.

The Early Days of Governance

On January 15, 1986, Booth Gardner was putting the finishing touches to his inaugural address. While he was touching up the issues he would bring before that citizenry, pollsters were picking at his image. The *Seattle Times* issued a poll taken on January 3–5, asking people how they thought Gardner would do as governor. As table 2 indicates, most respondents saw Gardner as a good manager who would provide leadership and initiate some new programs. According to the *Times*, the 400 voters surveyed "voiced confidence in Gardner's ability to provide leadership to the legislature, initiate new programs and articulate a vision of the state's future."[5] There was a general impression that, while Gardner was still in many ways an unknown quantity statewide, he was expected to be better than his predecessor and was generally viewed as a good administrator.

When these perceptions were viewed by subgroups, those who held managerial jobs felt Gardner would be a good manager (62 percent). Blue collar workers held the same view, though less strongly (51 percent). Women rated Gardner better than men, and the most optimistic about Gardner were those in the 25–34 age group.

The same poll found voters concerned about these key issues: government spending, taxes, the state economy, education, social programs, and the environment, in that order. Spending was to be curbed by budget trimming and the elimination of waste. This popular view, however, was naive, as table 3 and figure 1 illustrate. For example, human resource services (including health and welfare services along with the public schools) accounted for 57 percent of state expenditures from all

Table 3 State Operating Budget: All Funds versus General Funds
(1985–87 biennium) (dollars in millions)

	Amount	Percentage
All funds by category		
Higher education	$ 1,786	11
Community colleges	536	3
Public schools	4,503	28
Natural resources	1,011	6
General government	734	5
Human resources	4,568	29
Transportation	798	5
All other	1,925	12
Total all funds	$15,861	100 (rounded)
General funds by category		
Higher education	$ 931	10
Community colleges	481	5
Public schools	4,241	46
Natural resources	197	2
General government	124	1
Human resources	2,426	27
Transportation	26	1
All other	713	8
Total general funds	$ 9,138	100

funds and 73 percent of expenditures from the state general fund, when
these two areas were combined. Most government agencies fall under
general government, which accounted for 5 percent or less of state expenditures. By emphasizing management, Gardner was setting himself
up for a fall. In reality, there was very little that pure management
could do to affect reductions since most agencies accounted for only
5 percent of state expenditures. This would come to haunt Gardner
near the close of his transition, when the need to deal with health and
human services emerged as federal cuts increased.

With regard to taxes, most citizens wanted a tax reduction of some
sort—in spite of a lowered bond rating and a sluggish economy in a
state in which there was no income tax and where the sales tax was the
big revenue source (see table 4 and figure 2). The Gardner emphasis on
management would clearly raise false hopes. Inflation alone required

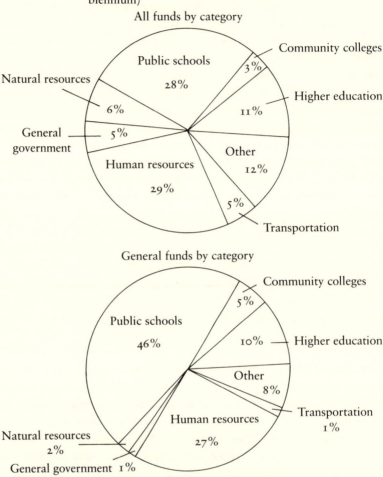

Figure 1 State Operating Budget: All Funds versus General Funds (1985–87 biennium)

All funds by category

Community colleges

Public schools 28%

3%

Natural resources

Higher education

6% 11%

General government

5%

Human resources 29%

Other 12%

5%

Transportation

General funds by category

Community colleges

5%

Public schools 46%

10% Higher education

Other 8%

Human resources 27%

Transportation 1%

Natural resources 2%

General government 1%

increases, and none could come without some new tax or the guts to face the issue of calling for an income tax. In all of Washington's history, no advocate of the income tax had succeeded in bringing it about and most did not remain elected for long.

By contrast, Gardner found compatibility in the issue of the economy. Here his management emphasis, coupled with a bent toward economic development, held some promise for bringing new investment and re-

Table 4 Revenue Sources by Category: State Operating Budget
1983–1985 versus 1985–1987 Revenue Forecast (dollars in millions)

Revenue source	Amount	Percentage
1983–85 biennium		
Retail sales	$3,772	47
Use tax	323	4
Real estate excise	182	2
B & O	1,246	15
Public utility	246	3
Property tax	958	12
Motor vehicle excise	381	5
All other	999	12
1983–85 Total	$8,107	100
1985–87 biennium		
Retail sales	$4,302	46
Use tax	375	4
Real estate excise	234	3
B & O	1,526	16
Public utility	296	3
Property tax	1,127	12
Motor vehicle excise	433	5
All other	979	11
1985–87 Total	$9,272	100

lated jobs into the state. The move to bring Anderson, with his proven record of success, from Oregon to head the Department of Commerce and Economic Development provided Gardner with a needed match between voter expectations and his own approach to governing the state.

However, further conflicts over social programs and the environment stood in the wings. Social program advocates wanted the state to pick up the costs of federal cuts, and environmentalists, politically important in the pristine Northwest, expected new state initiatives. Both expectations meant big dollars and could not be solved by better management or tighter fiscal controls.

The circling of these issues was of no small policy significance, for similar conflicts had plagued the outgoing Spellman administration. During its campaign four years earlier, the Spellman team staunchly

Figure 2 Revenue Sources by Category:
State Operating Budget 1983–85 versus
1985–87 Revenue Forecast

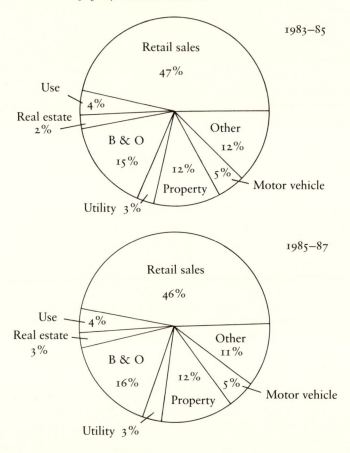

came out against new taxes, knowing that the economy was sputtering. Once in office that line turned into a haunting refrain, forcing the Republican governor to resort to switching capital funds from operations, raiding state contingency funds, and other forms of marginal niggling that were officially labeled "revenue enhancements" and privately called "light bulb snatching." Regardless of terminology, it forced the previous administration into cutting its losses rather than offering leadership. The trap led to Spellman's defeat. It was of some significance, therefore, that as Gardner penned the phrases of his in-

augural address, 600 union and largely Democrat workers in the western lumber center of Shelton, Washington, were preparing to be laid off.
Dealing with that and other elements of economic stagnation would
require more than a few management techniques disguised as revenue
enhancements.

That this was to be the case was already emerging before the ink was
dry. The Temporary Committee on Educational Structure and Management, a joint legislative committee that included private citizens, offered
recommendations costing $250 million, an action which prompted
this headline: "53 Ideas for Education—and No Money."[7] That this
dilemma would persist would be evident one year later. Almost to the
day, the Governor's Task Force on Children's Day Care, one of his
policy mechanisms, was calling for affordable, quality day care in the
state—clearly a high-cost item relevant to many of the women who
had supported Gardner and expected he would do a good job for their
interests.[8] Campaign strategies and issues were coming together, but in
a way that clearly implied a sustained conflict between promise and
pocketbook.

Before the joint session of the legislature, Booth Gardner presented
his inaugural address. In it, he called for:

) four priorities: diversifying the state's economic base, sustaining
   social and health services, making pension funds fiscally sound and
   repairing public works, and creating a larger budget reserve.
) improving education through doubling the preschool enrollment of
   those at risk, rebuilding higher education, and helping the community colleges.
) improving water quality in the Puget Sound.
) developing a strategic plan for economic development.
) providing job training for economically hard-hit areas.
) containing health care costs.
) reorganizing state government to improve efficiency.

The speech won plaudits from legislators on both sides of the aisle.
No wonder, as it contained few specifics, had something in it for everyone, and avoided price tags. There was also a certain similarity in
themes between the agenda of the incoming governor and that of his
predecessor, causing one noted political columnist to quip, "Gardner
grabs wheel and follows rear-view mirror." The same pundit excused
some of it as "freshman innocence," while wondering if Gardner's re-

ferring to the times as the "Age of the Pacific" was any different from Spellman's "Century of the Pacific has dawned."[9] Whatever one felt, however, it was evident that no firm public stance would be taken on dealing with the patchwork-quilt approach to state revenues now in place. Business experience and an M.B.A. notwithstanding, Gardner was not willing to do as governor what he would have done for the family business.

To the public eye, apart from the quality of his appointments, the only eyecatcher was what had become labeled by his own press secretary as Governor Gardner, M.B.W.A., standing for "managing by walking around." Even before the inauguration, the governor-elect began dropping in unannounced on state agencies. He showed up at a staff meeting in the Department of Planning and Community Affairs, causing some consternation in the outgoing administration because the transition agreement had been to notify the Spellman administration of contacts by Gardner's staff. In any event, the informal and open approach to agencies would continue.

Although the public murmurings of a bland beginning conjured up images of Tweedledee and Tweedledum, Gardner was actually busy at work bringing substance to the transition. While Smith and Shinpoch worked on the budget and Harris focused on collating the policy team products, Gardner was busy cementing relationships with the legislature and external interests. Through his appointments he had dealt with most of the interest groups whose support he needed and had responded to most of the major voter groups behind his success. He had brought in professionals, women, some minorities, and had kept the most respected administrators from the previous administration. He had not hurried himself into making bad choices and had clearly created a line-up that could hold up through the early days of the new administration. This had left him time to deal with the central transition issue for his administration: building a working relationship with the legislative leadership.

First of all, three of the four top leaders were from Pierce County, the county in which he had built his political reputation. This did, however, pose some problems. He could not fall into the trap of too close a relationship, one that might imply favoritism on his part or suggest, on the other hand, that he was a pawn of the "Pierce County Mafia," as the legislative leaders were sometimes called. Besides, each leader had his own agenda, especially Dan Grimm, chair of the house Ways and Means Committee. This committee was critical to the governor's budget, and Grimm had the reputation of considering himself a budgetary expert who expected to hand-tool that chamber's budget. He had a maverick tendency to go off on his own to work out details and commitments and then hew to them with a strong pride of ownership.

His counterpart in the senate, Jim McDermott, was not from Pierce County and was a respected budgetary expert who did his homework. Tricks could not be turned in his committee, and, being a liberal, he did not necessarily share the governor's conservatism.

Gardner, however, understood this. He met severally and separately with the leadership, sought their ideas on his legislative message, and made clear his intention to work cooperatively in the upcoming session. Directly and with the counsel of Foster, the ex-legislative staffer, and Becky Bogard, a known lobbyist, he quietly paved the way for initial cooperation. As a result, if conflict were to loom, it would be confined to specific issues. Such conflicts are less likely to scuttle a legislative program and, above all, lend themselves to trade-offs rather more readily than do large issues. He laid no large plans on them, made no heavy demands of them, and went about ferreting out a few issues that he would bring before them in the session. His inaugural speech had laid out a menu of ideas from which he could choose specific items based on the policy task force process and which were deemed feasible by the budgetary analyses of Smith and Shinpoch. It was as if he had read the National Governors' Association handbook on the transition, which reads in part:

> Governors who could be described as "seasoned veterans" caution new governors not only that a consistent focus on a limited number of issues is a prerequisite for success, but also that a sensitivity to timing is crucial for a new administration. . . . During the first six to nine months of his term, a governor generally should minimize "down time" by not undertaking major reorganizations, large-scale personnel changes beyond normal top-level appointments . . . The reason for this caution is that controversial and difficult decisions of this nature can cause the entire attention of the new governor's office and supporters to be focused not on the governor's key issues, but on a change whose timing was not well thought out.[10]

With the exception of the Gardner touch of a broad menu that implied change while holding the specifics for the future, it was a textbook beginning.

The Executive Office

The transition provides the first view of the candidate as chief executive. To the people, that view is one-sided, revealing only the public aspects of governing. Gubernatorial success in an executive sense, however, depends heavily on the organization and talent of the executive staff. While the public search for issues and nominees was underway, the private decisions leading to an executive staff were evolving. The general plan that resulted, outlined in figure 3, reflects Gardner's personal style. A shirt-sleeve governor who manages by walking around will have an idiosyncratic organization. While the traditional elements are present in this case (office management, special assistants, press relations, legal counsel, constituency relations, and patronage services), they are configured in a more open fashion, with the governor dealing directly with individuals as often as through channels. The chief of staff coordinated staff assistance, but the open-door style of the governor meant that staff had access to him without having to go through the chief of staff.

This open system had its advantages. The governor was accessible and people could be put together in a hurry as a crisis or problem management team. The system responded to initiative readily. Staff who took the initiative received attention. Similarly, the governor reached out directly as he saw fit, meaning that problems as well as instructions were delivered without the interpretive warp often present in more traditional models of management.

The system, however, was not without its drawbacks. Because instructions were often given directly and problems presented in the same way, coordination became a problem, as did follow-up. Put colloquially, the left hand did not always know what the right hand was doing. Unless individual staff took the initiative to inform the chief of staff or each other, there would be items slipping through the cracks, commitments undelivered, and a cumulative sense of governing without strong coordination. This would easily be exacerbated by the governor's own serendipity. His impromptu nature meant that he was easily sidelined. He would drop in on anybody if so moved, was known to depart from

Figure 3 The Executive Office

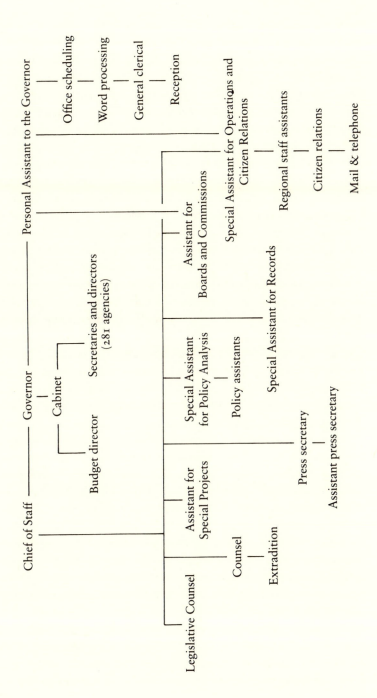

the text, and improvised as he went along—all reflective of his creative instinct, but also fraught with the danger that an unintended course could be set or an essential detail left untended in some abrupt shift of course. Accordingly, the executive need for ordering and structuring both information and problems into a decision queue was not readily appreciated, and at times policy appeared in Parthian fashion, emerging while the staff seemed in some disarray—if not in retreat from the issue at hand. Even an administration of bright "doers" could not govern over the long haul without some structure to the governing process.

This situation was further complicated by the governor's approach to agency heads and the cabinet. Gardner preferred one-on-one inter- actions to formalized group meetings. Moreover, there was no strong tradition of regular cabinet meetings in past administrations. Accord- ingly, no regular cabinet meetings were scheduled. As a consequence, cabinet secretaries and directors were left to the intelligence system of their respective agencies. Because most staff were service protected (i.e., jobs unaffected by a change in administration), they were far senior to their top managers—a common condition in most government agencies. In this case, however, it isolated cabinet officials in external settings, distanced them from the policy center of government, and lent itself too readily to governing at the center by responding to major issues or problems. This reactive posture, in combination with the open system in the executive office, resulted in the overall impression of a Parthian approach to decision-making.

There was, however, some underlying structure to this image of an executive ant hill. Gardner was at the center of the decisions taken and his priorities were emerging and recognizable, even if one was not sure how they had come about. The virtue of adaptability fit the opening days of governance as the executive was sorting things out. Planned or not, it was working all right, saved by the flexibility it allowed and by the creativity it encouraged among a rather young and bright staff. When order was required with line agencies, Smith, the experienced budget director, was there to steady things and to smell danger before a crisis or a catastrophe hit. Perhaps this was enough for the early days of the regime.

On the legislative front, things seemed somewhat more in order. Smith and Shinpoch had used their collective experience in the ex- ecutive and legislative process. Gardner had done his communicating with legislative leadership early, setting the precedent for consultation before action. In so doing, he had acknowledged their critical role in appropriations while retaining for himself policy independence that he could exercise through initiating requests and clarifying the revenue/ spending balance required to avoid new taxes. It was a straightforward managerial strategy, in keeping with the Gardner image.

The strategy emerged early in the session as Gardner consulted with legislators on bill drafts before they were filed. This was a new twist in Olympia and was made possible in part by the fact that both branches were of the same party. In this way, Gardner initially kept differences confined to form rather than substance or priority. It meant that early conflicts were worked out within the Democratic family and kept off the floor and the front page. All of this was helped in part by the fact that Washington uses a biennial budget and the first midbiennium session of the new regime would focus primarily on a modest supplemental budget and those few substantive bills that would result from the policy review process. Gardner, faced with the revenue and spending pictures provided by Smith and Shinpoch, had decided early on that he would select only a few bills for introduction. The vagueness of his legislative message permitted this selectivity.

Learning Some Early Lessons

In early March, just two short months after the inauguration, the new regime came face-to-face with the reality of governing. Gardner, to attract top-flight executive talent, needed top salaries. As a good manager would, he asked for them. In a state capital, of course, one does not ask for raises in the executive branch without acquiescing to raises for legislators as well. Gardner acquiesced, but others did not. Gardner, who had won with the overt support of the Washington schoolteachers and their association, took one look at the price tag for raises in teachers' salaries and proposed none. He also proposed none for state employees, many of whom supported him and who belonged to unions that supported him. He asked for faculty salary increases at the two doctoral universities, but not at the others or the community colleges. All of this hit the news media on March 13, leaving opponents to see this as an ill omen for the future.

Gardner had sought selective raises and turned his back on teachers and unions, two of his major constituencies. The executive team had learned its first lesson. Broken promises have a price and campaign rhetoric usually costs more than one can afford. The move was also rankling because it appeared that the governor gave his executives and his legislative cronies raises, leaving the rank and file to fend for themselves in a sluggish economy marked by inflation.

On other legislative measures, a bill for Puget Sound water quality was introduced with a gubernatorial push, only to be stymied over cost. The proposed selective salary bill floundered as legislators responded to constituency lobbying and as everyone was flustered by the cost of comparable worth.[11] Faced in the midst of this with the need for a budgetary reserve, Gardner asked for a modest tax increase, in spite of public opposition to tax increases and Gardner's own reluctance on the matter. At the same time, revenue forecasts were dismal, suggesting a $500- to $700-million shortfall by the end of the coming biennium. Under all of this pressure, the legislative liaison Gardner had begun to build started to crumble.

In the house, Ways and Means chair Dan Grimm began to hand-fashion his own budget, consulting with hardly anyone, including his legislative colleagues and house leadership. In the senate, McDermott shaped a more collegial budget, but it involved concessions to Republicans and included some of McDermott's pet projects.

Gardner complicated things in several ways. For example, he had called for a constitutional amendment requiring pensions to be fully funded in an effort to avoid putting the cost off to future legislatures at mounting rates. But, when he wanted to hold firm on a budget reserve (to hedge against the plummeting revenue forecasts) he urged that no payment be made on the pension liability. Instead he wanted payments transferred to the reserve. In addition, he did not go to the Democratic house caucus to lobby for his bills or to try to promote a more open and collegial budget bill. Instead, he lobbied representatives individually, leaving them, however, to the vicissitudes and pressures of chamber personalities and conflicts. All of this led one political observer to opine, "The governor never told the Legislature, or the public, just what he expected out of the session. He had a list of bills he wanted passed, but he didn't do the necessary missionary work."

In short, there was no focal point to the session. Blessed with the advantage of a Democratic majority in both chambers and with leadership from his own county, the governor still could not turn advantage into action. The result was obvious and expected. The legislature adjourned without passing a budget bill.

It was only at this point that the governor began to show some leadership. A few short hours after adjournment, Gardner met with the budget director, the speaker, the majority leader of the senate, and several key committee chairs to hammer out a solution to the problem. It began with a plan to call a special session and confine it to the budget, lest other issues that gave rise to personal conflicts and interchamber bickering result in no action.

On June 10, a special session was convened by the governor to deal with the budget issues. In seven hours, the legislature accomplished what it could not do in 105 days. The vote was along party lines and this time the Democrats stuck together in both houses on the vote. Between sessions, the governor had communicated with the leadership. Differences between the house and senate were also ironed out temporarily. Specifically, house Ways and Means chair Dan Grimm gave up his press for a broader tax bill as a part of the budget package. Instead, a carry-forward budget of $9.14 billion was passed to maintain current levels. While it did provide for some increases, including, for example, a raise in faculty salaries at the major universities, it required no major tax increases.

What had Gardner done differently this time to help account for the changed outcome? For one thing, he had convened the leadership at the end of the session to set out his concerns. Second, by settling for what was obtainable and backing away from the need for any broad new taxes, he had provided leadership that shifted the burden for action to the legislature. He had also done it in a way that made the maverick behavior of Grimm, in holding out for a broader tax as part of the budget, appear to be impractical and bordering on a kind of personal power play that was obstructive. So isolated, Grimm had to back down. McDermott, the senate budget pro, could always be dealt with on grounds "for the good of the order," and the senate had been a place where deals could be cut. In effect, Gardner had finally begun to exercise executive leadership; specifically, he had learned to effectively use the power of the "bully pulpit" backed by behind-the-scenes communication. The "bully pulpit" means to cumulatively find and use opportunities to set a theme or two on which the governor exerts leadership by setting the agenda and placing the burden for delivery on others.[12] It involves using the legislative message, the budget message, special sessions, and the like as a means for publicly throwing down the gauntlet of expectations in a way in which noncompliance involves rejection not only of the executive and its priorities, but also of the people and the public interest. By way of the end-of-the-session news conference, his speeches in the interim, and the special session, Gardner had done just that.

This emergence of leadership was to some extent fortuitous and to some extent the result of learning from failures in the regular session. First of all, Gardner had set a theme in the election campaign of needing new leadership. He used generalities about getting the economy moving, setting a direction to state government through better management, and the like. While general in nature, these themes filled the vacuum of the rudderless state that had evolved under Spellman. Given the honeymoon period in the early transition, Gardner was able to use the same general rhetoric in his inaugural speech, but he was wise enough to call for a modest agenda by setting out four priorities. When one-on-one communication with legislators and his early discussion with the Democratic leadership in both houses broke down, he still had the option of what Seattle political pundit Joe Mooney calls the "Gomer Pyle Axiom of High and Low Expectations."[13] The axiom goes something like this. Gomer Pyle was a television country-bumpkin character who joined the Marines and was always bumbling about and crowing with his high squeaky voice. In one show the actor behind the character, Jim Nabors, burst forth in song in a voice of moderate tone and talent but clearly beyond the expectations one would ever have of the squeaky Pyle. In short, even average mouthings exceeded expectations.

Gardner had been speaking in such generalities that any practical result would exceed expectations. Because he failed to use the proactive techniques of leadership that many governors use, such as going to the party caucus and setting forth some priorities in the regular session, any leadership directed to the April stalemate would work. When Gardner used the bully pulpit technique and called for a simple and practical carry-forward budget involving no major new items and no broad taxes, it was the average voice of leadership where none at all had been expected. As Mooney put it, "When much is expected of you, excellence is not enough and simple competence may be a hanging offense; when little or nothing is expected of you, the merest bumbling will be celebrated."[14] Gardner had turned simple competence into executive leadership and his transition was successfully drawing to a close.

Building Executive Leadership

In the twilight of the transition, two matters emerged. First of all, during the first six months of going from candidate to Governor Gardner, the candidate was still the dominant personality. Managing by walking around is not unlike campaigning. It breeds an immediate bond by exhibiting concern and, because it is atypical, it conjures up a good deal of support. Administering by way of an open door is also good politics; it gives the impression of the accessible official. Candidates need to open doors because they need support. Executives, however, need some distance from most people so that they can get the facts that are unlikely to emerge in the limelight. Hard decisions are not easily made in a fishbowl. Yet, the early ambience in the governor's office exhibited open-system attributes.

This was evident in the failure to use the cabinet. Gardner named his cabinet secretaries, held one major meeting with them, and soon disappeared into the whirlwind of openness already described, without systematically communicating via the cabinet. Some of the departments, especially those with holdover leadership, were posing significant problems. Social and Health Services was teetering under the pressure of federal cutbacks and the need for cost cutting, given the state's financial picture. Transportation was in serious public trouble over the cost of the Washington State Ferry System. Governing by responding to individual situations lacked the coherence necessary to set a policy net to contain issues, within which such agencies could operate. One-on-one communications could not accomplish this either, and it left in its wake a clear line of responsibility to the governor anyway. Executives need options and acquire these in part through distancing themselves from overly direct involvement in agency affairs. Policy leadership involves more than problem solving or managing details. It involves setting an aggregate sense of direction for top managers and a context within which they can administer their agencies. When the hard choices come, it helps if top managers concur as to what was expected, isolating the nonachievers into a clearer position of responsibility for the problem at hand.

In the dog days of summer 1985, Gardner's staff came to realize this. To deal with the governor's aversion to government by cabinet, an executive cabinet was created with the director of the Department of Fisheries, Bill Wilkerson, as its coordinator. The executive cabinet would serve as a sounding board for the governor on broad policy and would work on internal management improvements. Several subcabinet groups were created, following a model used in some other states. The subcabinet groups focused on specific policy or issue areas and would allow issues to be addressed by special task forces in an ongoing manner. This approach brought some structure and life into the cabinet, which helped balance the influence of the governor's staff with that of the more dominant cabinet secretaries. Budget director Orin Smith served as the key policy person on the cabinet who could act in case the system sputtered.

This left the matter of the executive staff and its policy role. The policy task forces of the early transition had served their purpose by surfacing several issues. The problem, of course, was that the issues were too complex or their cost was too high. The governor had wisely set his sights lower and chose a few items, nevertheless having a difficult time getting legislative action. The question, therefore, was how better to get effective policy coordination as the administration headed into the next session. The ability to scan issues, identify important ones, and advise the legislature on options was central if the conversion from candidate to executive was to occur. Moreover, coherence within and among the staff was particularly important because of the improvisational style of the governor.

There was also the matter of how better to affect legislative action. Moreover, there was concern over improving the coordination of state agencies. It was not clear who would bear policy news and information to the agencies, a matter exacerbated by the disuse of the cabinet. On occasion, special assistants from the governor's office were carrying directives to agencies. Agencies are bureaucracies that outlive governors, and there is an instinctive reservation about receiving guidance from assistants who are often viewed as neophytes in the policy game. In this regard, there was confusion as to who should monitor events and policy changes, the policy assistants on the executive staff or those persons in agencies designated to perform that function for their agency. Agencies are also territorial and do not take kindly to policy staffs performing functions that agencies carry out anyway. If policy assistance were to occur, therefore, it would have to have some advantage to the agencies or resistance would grow into conflict.

Staff discussions led to action in early autumn. Policy assistance at the executive staff level would be coordinated by Laird Harris, the governor's special assistant for policy analysis. The special assistants would provide the governor with direct staffing on policy matters and special projects. This staffing would include monitoring federal policy for changes, monitoring other states and other agencies within Washington, assisting agencies in communicating with the governor, managing communications between external groups or constituencies and the governor, brokering ideas and complaints (including directing them to the proper office for action), assisting in developing and shepherding the governor's requests for legislation, and representing the governor on request.

These tasks would be assigned by policy issue or area to the several assistants and would include no line authority. Specifically, (1) the governor would not communicate directives to agencies through special assistants; (2) agencies would maintain the primary responsibility for monitoring activities and initiating policy changes in their area of responsibility; (3) special assistants could be assigned roles on issues that might transcend agency jurisdictions; and (4) special assistants would have lead responsibilities for projects requiring a significant commitment from the governor or involving a major public statement.[15]

Special assistants were assigned to one or two substantive policy areas (e.g., human services and corrections) and a number of related agencies (e.g., the Department of Social and Health Services, the Department of Corrections, the parole board, blind and deaf schools, etc.).

Because the policy areas were broad in nature, it meant that some agencies would deal with several policy assistants. It also meant, however, that special assistants would provide the point of contact within the governor's office for specific agency directors: "In this role, special assistants will be available to track down agency communications, determine status, and otherwise assist the agency directors in solving problems involving the Governor's office. It is important to understand that this is purely an assistance role. The special assistant will ordinarily not have the authority to solve the problem on his/her own. The value of this service to the agency director is the presence within the Governor's office of a specific person who is assigned to help on a regular basis."[16] While this clarification helped focus the scope and point of contact between the governor's staff and the agencies, it also served to put some order into the executive staff itself and its open system, which was evidencing a need for coordination.

The issues of staff coordination and the delineation of authority between staff and line agencies are key administrative items in the transition process. While cabinet secretaries and directors may be appointed, they head agencies staffed by knowledgeable individuals with deep roots in the agency. The new heads must rapidly socialize into the existing culture or face difficulty in management and survival. Thus it is critical that at the outset of the transition the new administration "set the tone" of the new regime and identify the policy context for decision making that will prevail.[17] The combination of disuse of the cabinet and an open system in the executive office did not allow the transition to set the tone effectively enough for long-term policy success. With the establishment of the executive cabinet and subcabinet groups and assignment of the policy assistants (with pertinent ground rules), Gardner had completed the move from candidate to governor.

Conclusion

A recent study of the governor as administrator observed that governors are more inclined to be managers than policy leaders. In a study of 778 state department heads, most agreed that governors used line-item budgeting and reorganization to control operations and seemed to focus more on the management aspect of the executive function than on program development or other aspects of policy leadership.[18] Gardner's campaign utterances and his initial focus seemed consistent with this view. The early transition stressed the search for good managers; Gardner spoke of efficient management, and, through communications with legislative leadership, he had tried to use behind-the-scenes management to help shape legislative action. All of these, of course, reflected his knightlike behavior of indirection and led to a legislative stalemate.

When Gardner changed from knight to king in his behavior, he shifted from candidate to governor. Like a chessboard king, when faced with a legislative stalemate he changed direction as the situation warranted. He used the bully pulpit tactic, set forth an obtainable objective in the form of the special session call for a modest carry-forward budget, and placed the burden of proof on legislative leadership to deliver or face the burden of public responsibility for governmental failure. This move turned the transition from one headed for ineptness to one headed for success. It also got Gardner to see that administration differs from policy leadership and that management alone would not bring about the latter.

To bring policy leadership about, something more than an open system of executive organization staffed by talented individuals was required. Individual intelligence and skill did not guarantee organizational talent and skill. The latter required a policy net for administrative agencies, which had to be established in some way through the cabinet mechanism. Via the executive cabinet and cabinet subgroups, discussions could occur that would allow the governor to set a sense of direction for agencies in a way that would encourage accountability. A goal collectively derived cannot easily be ignored by an individual administrator, for it implies the denial of more than just the governor or the governor's program. Group ownership engenders its own incentive for compliance.

Second, only an organized executive office can expect and assure policy consistency elsewhere. Governors who react to issues and problems rarely get beyond reaction to proactively setting goals for others. Moreover, governors whose own houses do not appear to be in order have problems exacting order and accountability from others. This is especially the case for governors who tout management as the centerpiece of their administrations. Furthermore, sending novice policy assistants into line agencies as the harbingers of policy not only ruffles feelings but results in problems that stem from the real differences that exist between neophytes and seasoned bureaucrats. If the lines of communication between the governor and agencies are not clear, the confusion that results will undermine effective policy leadership regardless of who is right or who is wrong in a given case. The move to clarify policy roles complemented the executive cabinet with its working subgroups and put the executive house in order.

The weaknesses of the Gardner transition included an ambitious policy-scanning process (which raised hopes among his electoral followers for the coming of major policy changes); the rhetoric of management (which gave the impression that by cutting the bureaucracy major savings could accrue along with better efficiency); an open executive office organization (which fostered creativity at the price of reacting to those with initiative and failing to coordinate executive responses systematically); and the inability to provide direct leadership to the legislature.

The strengths of the transition included policy scanning through task forces that permitted selecting a few practical priorities for action; a realistic sense of what was financially feasible, given the analysis of the budget undertaken by two old pros; an openness to new and creative ideas; the identification of four priority items for the first session; the eventual use of the "bully pulpit" to bring a recalcitrant legislature to heel; the clarification of policy roles for the governor's staff; and the creation of the executive cabinet with working subgroups.

That Gardner ultimately understood what it took to govern became very clear in the early days of his second year in office. He pursued a bill to clean up Puget Sound and called for the reorganization of the Transportation, Game, and Parks and Recreation Commissions. He moved from short-term to more significant policy issues. He attacked the logging of state parks and the deterioration of a ferry system that suffered diminished service amid rising costs, both issues of growing public concern. He was prepared to twist arms, if necessary, in the legislature. In March 1986 he got his water quality bill and made headway on reorganization. The transition was over and he was exercising policy leadership at last.

1984 Gubernatorial Transition in West Virginia: Rockefeller to Moore

)))))

David J. Webber

The 1984–85 gubernatorial transition in West Virginia from Democrat John D. (Jay) Rockefeller IV to Republican Arch A. Moore, Jr., offered a particularly unusual set of circumstances that held the potential for either an unusually smooth and efficient transition or a potentially explosive one. While not presenting an opportunity for a "textbook transition"—the incoming governor Arch Moore was replacing Jay Rockefeller, who had succeeded him in 1976—this West Virginia transition is most noteworthy because of the experience and personalities of the governors involved. Each man had previously defeated the other in an election: Moore defeated Rockefeller as he won reelection in 1972 and Rockefeller returned the favor by beating Moore to gain reelection in 1980. There were, therefore, previous political and personal factors that might have been expected to color the 1985 transition.

Nevertheless, with the principals being two experienced governors and with the incumbent moving on to the U.S. Senate, there was certainly the foundation for a smooth and professional transfer of power. Further, the political climate in West Virginia was supportive of a smooth transition. There was general agreement on the central importance of economic development as the pressing policy issue facing the newly elected governor and the upcoming legislature. Together with the new, albeit Democratic, legislative leadership, this policy consensus presented Moore with what has been called a "window of opportunity." In a report proposing several economic development programs, a group of prestigious West Virginia business leaders called for increased public-private cooperation, saying:

> The time to prepare this strategic plan, put in place the legislative program, and strengthen the economic development delivery system is during the period November 1984–April 1985. This period will offer a unique window of opportunity in West Virginia. The new governor will have a virtual mandate to breathe new life into state economic development efforts. He will meet a legislature in which many members are eager for an economic action plan. . . . The elected leaders of the state will be in a unique position to harness this momentum and chart a new economic course for the state.[1]

Thus, the 1984 election returning Arch Moore to the capitol after an eight-year absence offered optimism for effective government as well as for a smooth transition. As a *Parkersburg Sentinel* editorial (December 5, 1985) commented on Moore's approach to the transition, "It appears that Moore is taking a fresh look at state government, a benefit of the two-term limit on governors, for the responsibilities of state government are ever changing and what worked in 1968–76 might not be the right approach for 1985."

Prospects for an Interim Transition

Among the difficulties peculiar to this transition was the possibility of the need for an eleven-day interim governor as a result of Rockefeller's election to the Senate. With a gubernatorial inauguration date of January 14, 1985, and the swearing in of U.S. senators set for January 3, and given the state's lack of a lieutenant governor, the resulting eleven-day gubernatorial vacancy would have created legal and practical problems.

Two unsuccessful gubernatorial primary candidates and Governor-elect Moore became involved in the constitutional line of succession: senate president, house speaker, and by virtue of a 1961 law, attorney general, state auditor, and former governors in reverse order of service. Moore was, therefore, fifth in the line of succession. If others disqualified themselves, Moore would quickly have moved up that ordering. The most likely successor, senate president Warren McGraw, had not only been defeated in the Democratic primary but was considered ineligible by Secretary of State A. James Manchin, who maintained that because legislative terms expired November 30, there would be no senate president or house speaker until the next session convened on January 9. Therefore, the secretary of state argued, Attorney General Chauncey Browning should serve as interim governor. Browning had also been defeated in the Democratic gubernatorial primary.

A more desirable scenario would have been for Rockefeller to complete his term or for Moore to assume the governor's office early. If Rockefeller completed his term, he would have become a senator eleven days later than his peers, and would, therefore, be the lowest-ranking member of the Senate. On the other hand, if Moore began his term eleven days early, he would have forfeited his right to seek reelection in 1988. After much media speculation and confusion, Rockefeller elected to complete his term as governor and begin his senate responsibilities eleven days late. According to his former executive assistant, Rockefeller did not seriously consider terminating his term as governor earlier because of the confusing impact it would have on the state.[2]

Aspects of Gubernatorial Transitions

Gubernatorial transitions are amorphous, complex, idiosyncratic processes of administrative change. They tend to be highly uncertain and unorganized for both the incoming and outgoing governors. Previous analyses of gubernatorial transitions in other states suggest that transitions occur on three separate levels: logistical, administrative, and policy. The logistical, or physical, transition refers to events establishing a viable, functioning office for the new governor. The second level, the administrative transition, focuses on gubernatorial appointments and institutionalization of the decision-making process preferred by the new governor. The policy transition level pertains to the goals, principles, and programs that the governor hopes to achieve during his term of office.[3]

While all three levels present a useful way to view the 1985 West Virginia transition, relying on this typology exclusively will result in an incomplete understanding of the Rockefeller–Moore changeover. Moore's return as governor included a fourth level: a historical or symbolic transition that includes much more than individual, specific policy initiatives or new appointments. This level of transition is a critical adjustment, a new frontier, and a pathbreaking transformation involving fundamental changes in a state. In this sense, West Virginia, in 1984–85, was facing more than a "window of opportunity." The state was engaged in nothing less than a struggle to resolve its future. In part, this process was reflected in Moore's campaign slogan, "West Virginia's coming back."

This analysis tries to capture the intensity and immediacy of this struggle and to identify Arch Moore's role and contribution in a historical transition. The heavy reliance on passages from Governor Moore's inaugural and state of the state addresses and quotations from political journalists and newspaper editorials are intended to capture this immediacy and intensity of this critical time for West Virginia's future.

State Politics and Arch Moore's Political Career

West Virginia is a complex and often confusing state: it is difficult to understand and more difficult to govern. While most West Virginians take pleasure in calling themselves "mountaineers," they are probably uncertain of their heritage. Many observers have commented on the state's turbulent history and lack of regional identity. The state's economy depends on what are now declining industries (coal, chemicals, and steel) and West Virginians generally fatalistically accept their depressed economy and other misfortunes (see, for example, Barone and Ujifusa, 1985). In his state of the state address Arch Moore gave credence to this perception of outside observers by referring to this fatalism at some length:

> We can talk about the problems of his or her education, and the status of education generally; we can lament the inadequacies of our highways; the adverse business climate; and the substandard manner in which we address the problems of our economically disadvantaged. We can perceive generally the unfairness of perceptions of our State of West Virginia in the eyes of our sister states. . . . We have been content with the past and sold on the suggestion that West Virginia is economically depressed because of some outside [sic] who have plotted against us and that as a State and a people, we have been dealt with unfairly by business as a whole or by the failures of the national government to grant us that which is rightfully due us.
>
> This is a self-defeating attitude, and we have to understand that we, West Virginians, are going to solve our own problems without

waiting for someone else to do it for us. We have in my lifetime waited for the federal government to respond to our problems, to construct our industries, to build our schools, to construct that road, which is our passport to economic security—none of which has been realized. We have continually blamed others for the existence of this oasis of lost opportunity.

I, for one, do not subscribe to this thinking and resist the suggestion at every opportunity.

Similar to West Virginia's economic dependence on a few industries, the state has depended on just a handful of elected officials for political leadership. Moore previously served as governor between 1969 and 1976, he was the first governor to succeed himself, and he was replaced by Jay Rockefeller, who served from 1977 to 1984. If Moore is successful in seeking reelection to a fourth term in 1988, not an unlikely prospect, these two individuals would have held the governor's chair for nearly a quarter of a century. This dependence on a few individuals is also reflected in the longevity of the state's U.S. senators: Jennings Randolph was first elected to Congress in 1932 and elected to the Senate in 1958, where he served until January 1985. Robert Byrd was also elected senator in 1958.

This paucity of potential political leaders might be explained by a number of structural characteristics. West Virginia, for example, does not have a competitive two-party system. Additionally, its lack of a lieutenant governor might deprive it of a potential source of "leaders-in-waiting" as well as a loyal critic of the sitting governor. Because both Rockefeller and Moore are such formidable personalities, the lack of a strong, visible devil's advocate undoubtedly affected their leadership style.

Moore's long string of political successes is generally considered to represent personal, not Republican Party, success. Moore has been very successful in gaining election in a Democratic state. After serving two years in the West Virginia House of Delegates, he defeated a Democratic incumbent to win a congressional seat in 1956 and was elected governor in 1968 despite a large pro-Humphrey margin in the presidential race. Moore defeated Rockefeller in 1972 to gain reelection and won election in 1984 by a 53 to 47 margin. His only two political defeats came in the 1980 gubernatorial race against Rockefeller, when he lost 54 to 45, and in 1978 when he was not able to unseat Senator Jennings Randolph.

Previous Transitions and Statutory Provisions

Generally, West Virginia does not have a history of orderly and co-operative gubernatorial transitions (see Kidman, 1972) although a major exception is the Smith to Moore transition in 1968–69. While the atmosphere is not usually overtly hostile, incoming governors have typically received little assistance or support from retiring chief executives. Kidman reviewed four transitions (1956–57, 1960–61, 1964–65, and 1968–69) and found little institutional support or policy-advising for the new governor.[4]

The 1956–57 changeover between governors Marland and Underwood was marked by two events that appear, almost as if by tradition, in subsequent transitions: the removal of office furnishings by the outgoing governor and a deluge of last-minute gubernatorial appointments. Kidman reports: "There was one contact between Marland and Underwood during the transition period. Marland telephoned Underwood to advise the Governor-elect that he would do well to order new furniture for the Governor's private statehouse office since custom allowed departing chief executives to take their office furnishings with them when they left office."[5] This transition was also marked by a midnight private swearing-in intended to prevent any more "resignations and lame duck appointments."[6]

The Underwood-Barron transition of 1960–61 avoided the bitterness of its predecessor but still did not see the incoming governor relying on the incumbent to any significant extent. Kidman summarizes this transition as follows:

> The midnight oathtaking was the single interruption in an otherwise orderly transition. There had been little contact between the incumbent Republicans and the incoming Democrats during the period between the election and the inauguration, but this lack of contact was not "caused" by one side or the other. It would seem that the parties to the transition simply felt more comfortable in a rather distant and formal posture. In a significant departure from the precedent of four years earlier, Underwood invited Barron to assume leadership in the drafting of the budget for the upcoming fiscal year and the retiring governor pledged to bow to Barron's judgement on budget questions—Barron, as the incumbent Attorney General, already was sitting as a member of the Board of Public Works—but Barron responded that he had no special suggestions.[7]

The 1964–65 transition involved two Democrats, Barron and Hulett Smith, and was orderly in part due to Smith's service in the Barron administration as commissioner of the Department of Commerce. Smith began his administration by retaining the high-level appointments of the previous administration apparently in the "belief that any unnecessary disruption in the function of the government should be avoided during the transition period."[8]

Because of the direct involvement of Arch Moore, the 1968–69 transition merits in-depth review to identify the procedure in which Moore had participated. It would be expected that this first transition would be an experience that he could duplicate if he was inclined and the present situation was appropriate. The first transition might also be a guide to Moore for pitfalls he wished to avoid the second time around. The incumbent, Hulett Smith, who had not run for reelection, telephoned Moore the afternoon following the election to discuss transition arrangements. The two agreed to appoint a liaison officer to oversee and coordinate the transition. In addition to general cooperation, Smith assured Moore that his department heads would supply any information needed in the preparation of the new administration's program.[9]

Arch Moore and the incumbent Smith met twice during the transition period and had far-reaching discussions about the status of many problems facing the state. The two also reviewed procedures for handling outgoing administration files and arrangements for protecting the security of the governor, his family, and the capitol. Concurrent with the second meeting between the incoming and outgoing governors, their wives met to discuss the operation of the executive mansion.[10]

Moore, perhaps because he was coming back to West Virginia from service in Congress, or perhaps because of the cordial cooperation of the Smith administration, was apparently not in a hurry to appoint his own department heads. Moore did not make his first appointment until nineteen days after the inauguration and did not begin to hire replacements for departed staff until after the first legislative session.[11]

The cordial and cooperative transition that brought Moore into the governor's office was apparently not repeated when he turned the position over to Jay Rockefeller in 1976–77. A week after Rockefeller was elected there still had been no contact between Moore and the new governor. Moore reportedly said that he had no intention of meeting with Rockefeller and would leave the transition to staff members from both sides.[12] The governors' wives apparently also did not cooperate. Sharon Rockefeller expressed interest in receiving an invitation to see the executive mansion but Shelley Moore indicated that she would have to wait until after the first of the year, commenting, "They will have 4 years to settle in." [13]

Additionally, the outgoing Moore administration continued the West Virginia transition tradition of last-minute appointments and furniture removal. After the election Moore extended civil service status to thousands of state employees to protect them from replacement by Rockefeller.[14] Also in keeping with tradition, after his inauguration Rockefeller found that his new office was without furniture, files, secretarial supplies, and properly installed telephones. Moore did reimburse the state $13,606 for his office furniture.[15]

Some of the uncertainty in these transitions would have been reduced had there been formal procedures in place to guide incoming and outgoing administrations. There is currently little guidance for either. *The Book of the States* lists eight provisions and procedures for transition:

) legislation pertaining to gubernatorial transition.
) appropriations available to governor-elect.
) governor-elect participates in preparing state budget for coming year.
) governor-elect hires staff to assist during transition.
) state personnel made available to assist governor elect.
) office space in buildings made available to governor-elect.
) provisions for acquainting governor-elect's staff with office procedures and routine office functions.
) provisions for transfer of records, files, etc.[16]

West Virginia formally has none of these eight provisions, although some informal provision of office space to the governor-elect does take place. In contrast, many other states the size of West Virginia, such as Maine, Vermont, and Wyoming, provide appropriations to the governor-elect to hire staff as well as formally involve him or her in preparing the state's budget for the coming year.

The absence of specific budgetary appropriations for transition presents problems for at least three types of expenditures. First, the incoming governor must compensate his transition staff from private funds, or the outgoing governor (as Rockefeller did in 1984–85) must expend a portion of the governor's contingency fund for the new staff's salaries. This depends on cooperation between the two governors—a condition not always present in a transition. Second, the outgoing governor is expected to prepare his official papers for publication. Without a transition budget, he must find private funding or hope that the legislature will make a specific appropriation to cover the cost of preparation and publication of the official papers. Third, practical matters like accumulated vacation pay for the outgoing governor's staff are problematic. Given the state's general prohibition of lump-sum benefit payments, the new governor must carry the former governor's staff on his payroll for a period of time.[17]

One formal provision in West Virginia pertaining to gubernatorial transition is the Legislative Improvement Amendment to the state constitution, approved in 1970, permitting the legislature to recess for thirty days after its initial organizational meeting to allow the incoming governor time to prepare his program.[18] In effect, this gave Moore from January 14, Inauguration Day, to February 13 as a formal transition period.

Party Nomination and the General Election

Some West Virginia observers contend that the most significant event in 1984 West Virginia politics was Arch Moore's decision not to run for the U.S. Senate seat being vacated by Jennings Randolph. Moore had narrowly lost in his bid to unseat the senator in 1978, and a run for the Senate would have pitted him against his arch-rival, Jay Rockefeller. A year before the election a *Charleston Daily Mail* editorial argued: "In our judgement, for whatever it is worth, Arch Moore cannot be elected to the Senate against Jay Rockefeller. But he can be elected Governor again, and we fervently hope that, before he is pitched into the rocks, he will stop his ears to the sweet Siren song that is luring him toward destruction."[19]

Even a month before that editorial, the state GOP chairman, Kent S. Hall, said it would be a mistake for Moore to run against Rockefeller.[20] Hall believed Moore would pose the greatest threat to Rockefeller and would, therefore, make the best candidate but that "it would be easier to recruit candidates for other statewide offices and raise funds for those races if Moore were running for governor." Hall also noted that the personal animosity between Moore and Rockefeller would play a role in Moore's decision. "He is a fighter and sees the vulnerability of Rockefeller and would like to avenge his defeat."

Another story underscoring the animosity between Moore and

Rockefeller involves a report published by syndicated columnists Rowland Evans and Robert Novak that Rockefeller sent an emissary to Moore saying that "if you run for governor next year, count on my total opposition, including financial support for the Democratic nominee." According to Evans and Novak, Moore responded, "I will be running for the U.S. Senate next year against you, not for governor." Even the denial of this communication by both candidates provides additional insight into their personal relationship. Moore denied the exchange by saying, "I confirm that I had no emissary from him, or any message whatsoever. I haven't heard from the governor for seven years." [21]

Arch Moore announced his candidacy for governor on March 23, 1984, amidst equal speculation that he would run for governor and U.S. senator. Until Moore's official announcement, outgoing governor and Senate candidate Rockefeller maintained that he believed Moore would run for the Senate. [22] There appear to be two rival explanations for Moore's delayed announcement. One explanation focuses on the pressure Moore was under from national Republicans, including President Reagan, to run for the Senate against Rockefeller. Moore, it is argued, was genuinely uncertain about his preference.

The second explanation for Moore's delay, offered in an editorial in the *Charleston Gazette*, focuses more on Moore's advantageous and deliberate use of his options to raise more funds for whichever office he eventually selected. The editorial argued:

> The reasoning behind this Arch antic [the delayed announcement], says one astute Republican observer, is to prepare Republicans, particularly generous big-giver Republicans, for a Moore race for the U.S. Senate against his old enemy, Gov. J.D. Rockefeller IV.
>
> Some big donors to Republican champions and causes have indicated they will turn handsprings and open wide the door to the family fortune once Moore goes for governor. Should he go for senator, however, their generosity and efforts would be far short of strenuous. [23]

Because of his previous service as governor, the 1984 campaign tended to focus on Moore's previous performance as governor and the "integrity issue" as well as new policy issues and proposals. Generally the years 1969 to 1976 are remembered as good years in West Virginia and, as might be expected, Moore takes some credit for that. In response to criticism that those years were "good years when Arch happened to be governor," Moore made an effort to link the 1984 election with the past, saying, "It seems to me that if you had a good governor or a great governor in good times, that is what you require in bad times. You certainly don't want to indulge in a period of time where you give on-the-job training to somebody."

The integrity issue involved three different events: the fact of a Moore aide's conviction for extortion in a proceeding in which the governor himself was charged but acquitted, Moore's decision to release a coal company from liability in the Buffalo Creek mining disaster in 1972, and Moore's refusal to release his income tax returns.

The third set of 1984 campaign issues were policy positions that reflected Moore's vision for the future of the state and were, therefore, suggestive of what a new Moore gubernatorial program would look like. Two specific policy issues were continuous themes of the Moore campaign: energy and economics. In an open-ended newspaper interview with a group of writers from the *Charleston Daily Mail* Moore was asked, "If you are elected what are some of the ways you will reorganize state government? He replied:

> I have suggested that we create an Energy Development Department in West Virginia. That we combine all of our activities in the energy field under one department rather than having a portion of them—surface mining—in the Department of Natural Resources, the other portion in the deep mine section under the Department of Mines.
>
> We've got to view coal as two different products today . . . as a domestic product and as an export product. We are out of the export market today. The difficulty in the southern coalfields is directly attributable to the loss of the export market. Approximately 14 million tons of coal have been lost.[24]

Moore was equally specific when addressing the second major theme —economic development. He proposed the establishment of a Department of Commerce, the retention of the widely criticized business and occupation tax, and "efforts to get 100,000 small businesses in West Virginia back in the production line of producing."[25] These policy issues returned as Moore's major achievements during the 1985 legislative session.

Despite a nominal 2 to 1 Democratic majority among registered voters in West Virginia, Moore's popularity in the spring of 1984 was quite high. A statewide poll in early April found that Moore would easily defeat each of the three potential Democratic candidates for governor. The survey estimated that Moore would get 58 percent of the vote to 37 percent for Clyde See, the current house speaker and his eventual opponent in the general election. Moore received the support of 85 percent of the Republican respondents and 46 percent of the Democrats, compared to See's 12 percent among Republicans and 48 percent among Democrats.[26]

This predicted margin did not stand up in the general election; Moore won by 7 percent, the closest gubernatorial race since 1968. Moore carried thirty-seven of the state's fifty-five counties, losing only four counties (two in the northern panhandle and two on the Virginia border) outside the southern part of the state, which is the traditional Democratic stronghold.

At least three of the significant factors affecting the general election campaign also had implications for the transition. First, normally Democratic labor groups like the United Mine Workers and the West Virginia Labor Federation, AFL-CIO, did not publicly endorse either candidate, thus helping Moore. A third group, the West Virginia Education Association, endorsed Moore. A second factor was Moore's ability to focus the campaign issues around the state's poor business climate and the qualifications of his opponent, thus avoiding the questions raised by Clyde See about Moore's integrity.[27]

A third key factor for both the election and the transition was the passive participation of Rockefeller in the election. It is not clear that the outgoing governor went all out to support his fellow Democrat and gubernatorial nominee, Speaker of the House See. One indication of Rockefeller's indifference was his lack of spending on election day. A columnist for a West Virginia chain of newspapers wrote: "See's only hope of winning from the beginning was to capture a huge number of straight ticket votes. In West Virginia, those straight ticket votes are a result of big bucks being spent on election day. John D. Rockefeller knows this as well as anyone. He spent big bucks—$750,000—on election day in 1980 to prove the point. He put out less than $200,00 on election day in 1984. So, did John D. IV want Clyde See to succeed him as governor? Hardly."[28]

This lack of earnest support for a fellow Democrat is not interpreted as indicating Rockefeller's displeasure with See but rather as a manifestation of a Rockefeller-Moore truce that resulted in Moore's decision to run for governor. This allowed Rockefeller to be more easily elected to the Senate, with the understanding that Jay Rockefeller would keep his influence and money out of the gubernatorial race.

Moore was often harshly critical of his opponent while relatively mild in his criticism of Rockefeller. Moore, aimed his negative comments not at the previous administration but at the legislative leadership of which See was a part. "When asked whether there had been a truce between himself and Rockefeller, Moore said there was 'not a shred of truth to that speculation.' "[29]

Preinauguration

The day after the election Moore and Rockefeller spoke by phone, and Moore reported that the two "agreed on some common interests." "We reached a plateau of cooperation," Moore stated, "Our conversation was varied and not lengthy."[30]

After the election, Moore retained the tough and determined demeanor that has always characterized his leadership style. The first issue Moore chose to make a stand on involved the role of the state courts in ordering state expenditures to rectify inequitable, and therefore unconstitutional, policy situations. The major controversy involved school funding as a result of a 1982 court decision. Speaking to his supporters at his campaign headquarters several days after the election, Moore said he "wasn't about to be pushed around by any court order that might dictate an increase in state taxes." At one point in his speech, Moore reportedly shouted "the A-team is back!"[31]

Moore did not publicly maintain this tough posture in establishing his relationship with the new legislature, choosing instead to project a cooperative, positive image. After the organizational meetings of the legislature, at which a new senate president and a new house speaker were selected, Moore praised the Democratic leadership as "fine and experienced lawmakers" and indicated that he hoped there would be a "spirit of cooperation between the two branches of government despite party differences." He declined to discuss philosophical differences between himself and the new Democratic legislative leaders, saying, "I think we've got to approach these years as West Virginians."[32] This combination of toughness in confronting the courts and cooperativeness in preparing for the legislature preserved Moore's public image as a "down to business," no-nonsense governor yet allowed him, at the same time, to cultivate a positive relationship with those people on whom his legislative successes heavily depended.

In following the state's two major newspapers, the Charleston *Gazette* and the *Daily Mail*, a transition observer is stunned by the absence of news about Arch Moore between the week after the election and the end of December. For a politician of Moore's reputation for attracting the limelight, this conspicuous absence suggests one of two things. First, that Moore was busy preparing for his return to power and devoted to working on policy announcements and appointments that would be worth the wait. Alternatively, as one journalist suggested to me, after seeing how close Rockefeller came to losing the Senate race, Moore was depressed with the knowledge that, as things turned out, he could have been elected to the U.S. Senate!

Rockefeller and Moore each assigned a staff member to take primary responsibility for transitional activity. Moore appointed Tom Craig, a Charleston lawyer who had served as an aide in the first Moore terms and who was a key individual in Moore's campaign effort. Rockefeller assigned Nick Lazaris, his executive assistant, to coordinate the outgoing administration's activities. While Moore and Rockefeller did not meet during the transition, they did speak on the phone several times; Craig and Lazaris along with other staff members had several meetings.[33]

Because of the lack of state-provided office space, the Moore transition staff worked from the Moore campaign headquarters. While there was not a preelection transition team or planning committee, the fact that Moore had previously served as governor provided him considerable preparation to become governor.[34]

During this period, outgoing governor Rockefeller did five things to smooth the transition of power. First, he issued a directive asking all department heads and staff to cooperate fully with Governor-elect Moore's staff and transition teams. Second, Rockefeller's staff prepared a briefing book on current departmental policy issues. Third, George Carenbauer, counsel to Governor Rockefeller, prepared a binder listing the status of the state's numerous boards and commissions in terms of vacancies and current make-up. Fourth, Rockefeller prepared a tentative fiscal year 1986 budget as required by law. He chose not to present a formal budget to the legislature.[35] Fifth, Rockefeller provided funds from the governor's contingency fund to compensate three or four Moore staffers from December 1 to Inauguration Day.[36]

To inform the incoming Moore staff about the status of departmental activities, each of about twenty-five department heads was asked to write a memo reviewing the status of activities in their department. These memos, about two to five pages in length, were collected by Nick Lazaris and delivered as a briefing book to Tom Craig on January 11, three days before Moore took office. Rockefeller's staff made no effort to review or edit these department-head memos.[37]

These briefing memos were requested by Craig with the intention of having the outgoing department heads communicate to their successors, as yet unnamed and not to be appointed for another month, the five or six most important issues of which they should be aware. A similar procedure was employed in the 1976–77 Moore to Rockefeller transition when Moore's outgoing department heads prepared issue memos.[38]

To assist him, Governor-elect Moore organized six task forces to define specific approaches and programs intended to meet his broad goals. These task forces were organized in the following key areas: commerce, energy, tax reform, the state employment security debt, workers' compensation, and the termination of the Alcoholic Beverage Commission.[39] Each task force consisted of people from the private sector who were assigned to examine a specific area of state government in terms of its relative effectiveness and efficiency. The Commerce Task Force, for example, consisted of ten private citizens and three individuals who were to join Moore's staff. Of these ten appointees, two were members of a Charleston law firm, five were from businesses, one was employed by a bank, and one was from the West Virginia University School of Engineering.

The Commerce Task Force was given two main functions: (1) to recommend how state government should be organized to enhance the economic development activities of the State of West Virginia; and (2) to recommend various programs to enhance the retention and expansion of existing West Virginia businesses and the attraction of new businesses into the state. The task force prepared a twenty-three-page report, not including six attachments diagramming alternative organizational structures for conducting economic development activities. The report reviewed the state's existing economic development structure and cited seventeen specific problems and observations about current programs that the task force intended to correct. In addition to commenting on general problems facing economic development activities, the task force proposed twenty specific programs and legislative ideas and identified the necessary action required to make each one of the proposals a reality.

In his farewell address to the legislature, Rockefeller apparently went out of his way to further cooperation with Moore. In addition to listing his own achievements, he mentioned Governor-elect Moore several times. This was well received by the legislators, who commented on the conciliatory nature of the speech. House Minority Leader Larry Swann said it was "very kind to refer to Moore in a positive way" and House Majority Leader William Wooten said he "was pleased to see Rockefeller speak of Governor-Elect Moore well" and thought the governor was well-advised to urge bipartisan cooperation.[40]

Administrative Transition and Appointments

On February 13, the day of his state of the state address, Moore announced his major administrative appointments. These appointments were a mix of familiar faces and new names. Of the twenty-eight appointments announced, only two had served in Moore's previous terms as governor, seven of the appointees had already been working in the departments they were chosen to head, and four were former legislators—two of whom had been defeated in bids for higher office in November. The most surprising of the appointments were three new faces from medical education, the federal government, and the private sector who were selected to head the Department of Health, the Department of Human Services, and the Office of Economic and Community Development, respectively.

Compared to the Smith-Moore transition of 1968–69, Arch Moore appeared more eager and ready to go in 1985. As Herb Little, a veteran state capitol reporter, commented, "Moore took over the Capitol rotunda for the long-awaited announcement of 20 department-head appointments and introduction of the appointees, completing his administration in one stroke." Little called this burst of energy only "a mild warmup" for that evening's state of the state address (discussed below). Little observed that Moore had virtually disappeared since his inauguration January 14 and the "only sign that there was anybody in the governor's office was a freeze order on hiring and new spending, routine when the office changes party hands."[41]

Governor Moore asked for the resignations of all board and commission members. In fact, he was successful in having the legislature refrain from considering several hundred eleventh-hour Rockefeller appointments. Because of the magnitude of the task, the process of appointing the members to the boards and commissions was ongoing, basically on a needs basis[42] and could not be completed until the legislature convened in January 1986, fourteen months following the election.[43] Moore received some criticism from loyal Republicans for both the pace of the board and commission appointments and the governor's appointment of several Democrats to various positions.[44]

The New Governor's Program

Arch Moore was sworn in as governor for the third time on January 14, 1985, amid high hopes for the future. His inaugural address was broadly thematic, as befitted the occasion. Not surprisingly, the new governor returned to the same themes he developed in his campaign: economic development, more efficient regulation of energy, and the role of the courts. In West Virginia recent decisions have mandated fundamental redirection of the state's approach to education, corrections, and mental-health services. In addressing the last concern, Moore came close to criticizing directly outgoing governor Rockefeller, saying:

> We have not assumed the office of governor to abdicate to others the responsibilities of our office . . . In recent years, West Virginia has had government by the courts. . . . With due respect to the court, the judiciary should understand and be aware that this chief executive shall lead and have the vision to address the broad range of human powers that affect us all. Together, with the Legislature, and within the confines of the budget, the creative solutions will originate with this governor and with this government to deal with these human needs.

In terms of specific actions, Moore pledged: (1) to create an economic development program that would retain existing industry and encourage new businesses to come to the state; (2) to examine inequitable laws "that create burdens which our citizens cannot meet and which are driving them from the state"; (3) to streamline government to make West Virginia coal more competitive; and (4) to restructure government to make it "efficient and decisive. We will return the operation of state government to a businesslike basis."

But by far the most dramatic and forceful moments in Moore's inaugural speech were its references to the need for revolutionary ideas, nonpartisan cooperation, and hard work to correct the problems that had plagued West Virginia for decades. Moore pleaded:

These are the times that call for revolutionary ideas, an abundance of idealism and strong resolve to work for a cause greater than ourselves. We must change this state now. Not out of disrespect of our rich heritage and great institutions, but in recognition that we must build a new and vigorous West Virginia of tomorrow. Nothing less is at stake than the very quality of our lives. We must make a new West Virginia. And in doing so, we have to rethink the whole fabric of our life.

The old ways of addressing our problems are no longer sufficient. It has been said: "If most of us are ashamed of shabby clothes and shoddy furniture, let us be more ashamed of shabby ideas, shoddy philosophies, selfish politics, and a self-serving government."

After an evening of traditional inaugural merriment, Arch Moore laid low, except for a few executive orders, until February 13, the day scheduled for the state of the state address and the day he chose to announce his major appointments.

In what was generally regarded to be a bold and forward-looking state of the state speech, Governor Moore outlined, in rather substantial detail for a public address, at least sixteen policy initiatives. Herb Little observed that "it was possibly the most proposal-packed state-of-the-state address veteran lawmakers had heard."[45] The twenty-five page speech, one month into his term, proposed to achieve following:

>) create a Department of Energy to bring together all the current agencies affecting energy.
>) establish a West Virginia Power Generation Authority to construct generating facilities that burn West Virginia coal for export to other states.
>) create a West Virginia Gas Distribution Line Authority intended to reduce natural gas prices, thereby keeping manufacturing jobs in the state.
>) adopt a system of investment tax credits to provide capital for economic development.
>) make a sales pitch to General Motors for the Saturn plant.

> create a Department of Commerce to coordinate parks, recreation, and tourism and to promote West Virginia as a vacationland.
> develop a more responsive Department of Highways that gives top priority to finishing the highway network.
> create a private-public National Institute for Chemical Studies in Charleston.
> take the state out of the retail liquor business.
> call for a referendum on a School Building Amendment that would issue $200-million worth of bonds to build schools.
> put together an Infrastructure Examining Committee with authority to issue bonds to repair the state's infrastructure.
> grant local governments authority to establish hotel-motel taxes.
> reorient county governments, especially in light of their potential windfall revenues due to the tax reappraisal.
> adopt a budget of $1.55 billion ($787,000 less than the current budget) that included a $50-million reduction in individual taxes and $36-million reduction in business taxes.
> adopt a budget with increases of 5 percent for state employees and for education programs.
> increase aid for dependent children and other human services.

In addition to these policy initiatives, Moore used the state of the state address as another occasion to set forth his vision of West Virginia and to comment on recent state policy developments. For example, Governor Moore proclaimed boldly, "West Virginia is going in one direction. The nation is moving in the opposite direction. You and I can change that. You and I must change that attitude."

Moore had continually been critical of the state supreme court's activism.[46] In reference to this concern about the role of the state courts in making policy in West Virginia, Moore stated:

> All of us, citizens of our State, legislators and executives alike over recent years have been treated to an assortment of scare words that have impacted greatly on our abilities to perform. I refer to the Recht Decision, the Hartley Decision, (the) Medley Decision, and I'm sure a host of other pronouncements in which good, perhaps, is hoped for, but for which little else can be said. You and I have the responsibility in our collective wisdom to provide for the common good of our citizens. Our system has always pointed this out. Nevertheless, there seems to be a feeling that you and I are not capable of handling

our responsibilities without the interference of some outside forces. Granted everything is not perfect, but if imperfection exists, it remains our job, yours and mine, legislative and executive, to correct it. I expect to protect, as Governor, our abilities and capabilities to make those decisions.

At that point in his address, Moore reportedly stared down at the justices of the state supreme court seated in the first row of the house chamber. Legislators broke into the loudest applause of the evening.[47]

Two business and labor leaders were also impressed with Moore's policy proposals. Robert Isaacs, chairman of the West Virginia Roundtable, a group that was formed to push for economic development and that saw the "window of opportunity" discussed earlier, said, "He's dreaming big but we're going to have to dream big to turn this state around." Isaacs called Moore's proposal for a state power generating authority "interesting" and praised the governor's plan to help form a National Institute for Chemical Studies.

Joseph Powell, president of the state AFL-CIO, praised Moore's high expectations saying, "It indicates a lot of innovative thinking. I think he realized early on that West Virginians have to do their own thing." Powell said that the proposed power generating authority "ought to be the chief attribute that West Virginia holds out to industry."[48]

An example of how far-reaching some of Moore's sixteen policy initiatives are is the one pertaining to county government. In an editorial two days after Moore's speech, the *Charleston Gazette* agreed with Moore's contention that county governments "are wasteful political nests that should be redirected by the Legislature."[49]

> Far-reaching reform is needed. With seven elected leaders under the roof of each courthouse, county government today consists of little political fiefdoms in ever-changing factional alignments. Lawmakers should revive the county reorganization amendment . . . which would give West Virginia voters the right to choose simpler county governments if they wish.
>
> Further, the Legislature should begin planning to reduce the number of counties in West Virginia. The age of rural isolation, when many local courthouses were necessary for mountain-locked people, has long passed.

As the editorial recognized, such reform is difficult because most legislators owe their elections to the courthouse fiefdoms. Nonetheless, the editorial encouraged them "to risk courthouse disfavor and follow Moore's lead to obtain 'the best value out of county government.' "

While Moore achieved the adoption of many of these proposals the state of the state message was critical in reestablishing Moore's ability to solve problems and to govern the state. The state of the state address was judged a success by most observers. Don Marsh, a Charleston political columnist, argued that to understand Moore's approach it must be viewed as theater.

> My reaction to Arch Moore's State of the State speech was that it was best understood as theater, and very good theater.
>
> I was caught in the drama of the presentation. Because years of newspaper work have caused me to think in cliches . . . words like "sweeping," "boldly imaginative" and "unique" started welling up from my subconscious.
>
> But a few minutes after the speech was over, reality returned. I remembered hearing Moore in his previous life as governor insisting that the $600 million in highway bonds he promoted wouldn't cost the state a penny.[50]

After a further assessment of several of the ideas contained in the speech, Marsh turned to the importance of Moore's address:

> Unlike Moore, I continue to believe that the forces responsible for West Virginia's economic problems are beyond the power of West Virginians to control. However, I fully agree that everybody should try.
>
> I think that's the value of Moore's message, the theater of it. He appeared to be in charge, to have a vast plan. He seemed to be doing something.
>
> I have long held that the people of this state, me included, yearn for strong leadership, for officeholders who are decisive. I think Moore portrayed both qualities very strongly.

Relations with and Successes in the 1985 Legislature

At the same time West Virginia was electing Arch Moore to be governor, it elected seventy-three Democrats and twenty-seven Republicans to the state house of delegates and forty Democrats and four Republicans to the state senate. Both legislative chambers, thought to be more conservative than in previous years, had new leadership. Both the senate president and house speaker were highly regarded legislators but both faced considerable opposition from conservative fragments in their own party. Mere numbers suggested that Moore faced a difficult task in persuading the heavily Democratic legislature of the merits of his policy ideas. However, the more conservative ideology of the members and the perception of a "window of opportunity" made this hurdle potentially surmountable.

Governor Moore had his way with the Democratic legislature. The governor, legislators, and political observers all agree that Moore was very successful in persuading the legislators to adopt his package of policy initiatives and budget proposals. Moore evaluated the 1985 session in such terms as: "It was a West Virginia legislature"; "We now have three of the nine building blocks we need if we are going to turn this state around"; and by saying the legislature was "the most cooperative ever seen." [51] One reporter wrote: "Observers were saying Saturday night (the last day of the session) that Arch Moore got more out of the West Virginia Legislature in one year than Jay Rockefeller got in eight." [52]

The two key bills adopted by the legislature were Moore's proposals creating a Department of Energy and a Department of Commerce. Neither bill was adopted without a legislative fight. Legislative opponents of the energy proposal included Speaker of the House Joseph Albright, who was concerned about the reduction of civil service protection for top-level employees and the elimination of conflict of interest prohibitions for top-level department heads.

Nonetheless, legislators tended to agree that Moore was very successful in getting most of what he asked for. George Farley, House Finance Committee chairman, agreed with Moore's assessment of the legislative session, saying, "The legislature, by and large, has responded to the governor's State of the State address and has provided him with the tools to get the state going again. Now, it's up to the executive branch to provide the leadership of recovery." [53]

Another delegate, Republican William Nicely, said the "recent session was one of the most productive [he] witnessed during the seven terms [he] served in the House." About 75 percent of Governor Moore's requests passed both chambers.[54] Not all Democratic legislators were pleased with their party's support for Moore's proposals. One said that the legislature totally ignored programs to aid the needy and another Democratic delegate said "the leadership merely took the governor's ideas and put their names on them." [55]

A veteran political columnist, Richard Grimes, evaluated Moore's success as overwhelming but used different terms. In a column titled "Democrats succeed in implementing state GOP goals," Grimes reported that he had reread both parties' state platforms and concluded that "the Democrats had done a pretty good job implementing the Republican planks." Grimes suggested that "Republicans may not want to field legislative candidates next year. They might find it hard to improve on their 95 percent success rate at the hands of the Democrats this year." [56]

The governor's legislative success did reduce Democratic harmony. The energy bill, for example, was successfully pushed through the house by a coalition of the Republican minority and conservative Democrats who generally opposed Speaker Joseph Albright. Moore had a much easier time in the senate, where President Dan Tonkovich was quite accommodating to the governor in handling both the energy bill and the economic development bill.[57]

In the final analysis, Governor Moore obtained legislative approval for most of the policy initiatives presented in his state of the state address. Of the sixteen proposals, the only clear disappointment for the governor was the rejection of his proposal to take the state out of liquor retailing.

Several factors contributed to Moore's legislative successes. First, the house was not as unified as the 73–27 partisan breakdown suggests. Albright was elected speaker by a three-vote margin over a conservative, "pro-business" Democrat. Second, the joint effects of a well-organized and well-prepared chief executive and the prevalent "window of opportunity" attitude tipped the benefit of the doubt toward the governor. Apparently, legislators thought Moore should be given a chance to try his programs. Third, Moore was quite successful in exercising gubernatorial influence. Senator Mario Palumbo, a more senior legislator, explained the governor's success: "If you want to get a road paved, who do you go to? If you want to get a constituent into a state hospital, who do you go to? The Legislature is finally realizing that the governor can exercise a hell of a lot of power." [58]

Conclusion

Despite Moore and Rockefeller's being political adversaries for well over fifteen years, the 1984 election and transition appeared remarkably harmonious. From the very beginning of the campaign, with Moore's surprising announcement that he would run for governor instead of the

Senate, the two men seemed to go out of their way to avoid conflict. While Rockefeller's other transition into the U.S. Senate reduced any disappointment or frustration that a defeated or lame-duck governor might experience, Rockefeller apparently did go out of his way to avoid public displays of conflict with Moore and took the affirmative step of allocating a portion of his contingency fund to members of Moore's staff for six weeks.

Moore hit the ground running. With the major department heads appointed and the state of the state address delivered by February 13, 1985, the new governor had the major pieces of his policy transition and administrative transition well in place within a month of taking office. The remainder of the policy transition was completed with the governor's overwhelming legislative successes by April 30. Most of the administrative transition was finished by August 1, when the vast number of administrative appointments were practically complete.[59]

Moore's public support was strong well into his third term as governor. A poll of West Virginia voters in late September 1985 found that 53 percent of the respondents evaluated Moore as doing an excellent or good job while 43 evaluated him as doing a fair or poor job. Moore received an excellent rating from 30 percent of Republicans and 14 percent of Democrats.[60]

In the final analysis the Moore transition must be evaluated as a very positive one: he assembled a full crew of department heads, he identified his policy goals and saw that the legislature adopted them, and he projected an aura of hope through his leadership. A *Parkersburg Sentinel* editorial evaluated the legislative session in terms that apply equally well to the transition: "The session gave impetus to the Moore administration which has four years in which to make its mark, as Arch says, 'to turn this around.' Whether the goodwill continues will be determined in large part on how Moore puts together his other 'six blocks' this year."[61]

The return of Arch Moore as governor in 1985 can best be understood as a symbolic transition back to happier, more prosperous times. Beyond the electorate's apparent desire for a more policy-assertive governor, Moore's election was a result of widespread hope that "West Virginia's Coming Back!" and belief that Arch Moore could lead the way back. The smooth and cooperative administrative transition as well as Moore's political triumphs in the legislature were an extension of this hope.

Two Special Case Studies

))))))

In this section there are two studies of transition with a slightly different focus than the other studies of gubernatorial transition. The first looks at an incumbent governor's transition in the 1984 gubernatorial reelection in Indiana; the second focuses on lieutenant governors and how they relate to the gubernatorial transition.

In the first study, James Owens analyzes how a reelection can provide a governor with more flexibility in office. The reelection can allow a governor to play "fruit-basket upset" and make major changes in approaching a second term rather than staying the course by viewing the reelection as a vote of approval for the status quo.

In the second study, Dean Yarwood reminds us of an all-too-true fact of political and governmental life in the states: there are many separately elected officials, and they can have a significant impact on how a governor operates. Specifically, Yarwood looks at the lieutenant governor's office and those who are a "heartbeat away" from the governorship, the main concern of this book, and presents a Missouri case study on how "office number two" becomes part of the gubernatorial transition.

Gubernatorial Transition: An Incumbent Succession in Indiana

)))))

C. James Owen

The process of gubernatorial transition has been considered to be an important topic of study and debate since at least 1960, when Massachusetts became the first state to pass a transition budget. The 1970s spawned a great deal of activity and academic interest in strengthening the formal authority of the governor and in streamlining the gubernatorial office. The level of debate and inquiry intensified in the 1980s as new federalism initiatives and increased constituent requests intensified programmatic demands on state governments—particularly the governor's office. The challenge of building the gubernatorial program and team through the transition period has increased accordingly. While there is an increasing interest in gubernatorial transitions, the focus has been almost exclusively on the newly elected governor's first succession to office.

Contemporary studies have featured transitions between succeeding teams from opposite political parties as well as intraparty transitions in a number of states.[1] The National Governors' Association (NGA) has for a number of years conducted biennial workshops and publishes a transitional handbook for new governors.[2] Recent reforms, however, that now permit nearly all of the states' governors to succeed themselves at least once (only four states presently forbid successive terms) have made an incumbent's transition a topical and cogent area of study. This chapter undertakes such an inquiry. The case in point is the state of Indiana, where in November 1984 Governor Robert D. Orr became only the second Indiana governor reelected to serve a successive four-year term.[3]

The incumbent's transition in Indiana is both similar to and different from the succession of an entirely new governor to office. Some differences are quite obvious. For example, for an incumbent it is not necessary to hire an immediate office staff or to establish routine office procedures anew. Other distinctions are not so evident; for example, while the 1984 Indiana transition was a marked period of change in policy and administration, incumbent Governor Orr did not seek to break completely with his first-term programs. Thus, as this study will show, it is sometimes difficult to perceive substantive program changes. On the other hand, differences in the procedures followed by a first-term as opposed to a second-term governor are far more evident. These delineations notwithstanding, the three key variables of change identified by Thad Beyle—time, politics, and control—become evident in this study, although with a somewhat different order of significance.[4] The reader will find that in some ways the transition was easier for an experienced governor. Still, in other ways it appeared to be more difficult.

As a subject of study Indiana shares extensive common ground with those other state governments with multiple reporting lines and plural executive arrangements. The governor functions with a part-time state legislature, albeit one that is reasonably well staffed and has extensive oversight capabilities. Studies that rank the formal powers of the fifty state governors place Indiana in the bottom quartile.[5] However, within the state, and for the purposes of this study, the governor is considered to have strong executive authority in terms of establishing his administration. The Indiana governor has extensive appointive powers, the budget is clearly an executive budget, the governor is widely viewed as the key formulator of legislative policy, and the General Assembly generally defers to his or her organizational moves. The informal powers of the Indiana governor provide a strong base to substantiate his formal statute and constitutional authority. The old adage that "Hoosiers are teethed on a basketball hoop and learn to read from a poll book" captures the essence of both "Hoosier hysterias"—basketball and balloting. Politics are a great media event in Indiana and with the major print and electronic media outlets centered in Indianapolis (the state capital), a governor has ready access to statewide news coverage and is generally the most visible political figure in the state after the U.S. president.

In Indiana, where elections are said to be waged instead of conducted, both major political parties are well organized and compete vigorously for most public offices. Although Republican governors have captured the statehouse in all but two elections since 1950, Democrats controlled both U.S. Senate seats during most of the 196qs and 1970s and held a majority of the Congressional seats during that same time. Republican successes in gubernatorial elections notwithstanding, Democrats have established a party organization and voter constituency potent enough to seriously contest for the governor's office in nearly every election. Governors are expected to actively preside over the state party machinery, which they traditionally do.

The job patronage that accompanies electoral victory in Indiana is the sustenance of party organization and constitutes a significant source of gubernatorial administrative authority and responsibility. Former governor Bowen described the process of keeping personnel appointments current as a high priority and a most demanding task: "There are approximately 30,000 state employees in Indiana exclusive of education employees. I think the power of appointment in Indiana is very extensive. There is no legislative sanction over appointments. In fact it was one of my toughest jobs—just keeping offices filled."[6]

Many of these appointments are patronage jobs. Indiana's merit system is not comprehensive. Merit provisions pertain only to employees in designated departments—mostly those administering federal programs—and many employees within these departments are in unclassified jobs and thus are excluded from the State Personnel Act hiring provisions.

Schlessinger and Beyle both rated the Indiana governor's appointive authority as the singularly most formidable element of that administrative office. In comparative ratings, Indiana places very high among the states for its formal powers of gubernatorial appointment. Schlessinger ranked Indiana second only to New Jersey among the states. Beyle also accorded the Indiana governor a "very strong," rating in appointive powers, ranking it behind five states.[7] Thus Orr inherited an extensive patronage tradition and very strong formal appointive authority when he succeeded to the governor's office.

Background: First Term and Reelection

Governor Robert D. Orr, born in 1917, was a successful Evansville industrialist and businessman. He graduated from Yale University in

1940, attended Harvard Business School, and served with distinction in the Pacific Theater during World War II. He was involved in Indiana Republican politics for over thirty years. His first elected office was as a member and a chairman of the Center Township Advisory Board in Vanderburgh County. Elected to the state senate in 1968, he served four years in that office before being elected lieutenant governor in 1972. He served as lieutenant governor for eight years before being elected governor by a record margin in 1980.

Governor Orr's 1980–84 administration can be divided into two segments for study and understanding. During his first two years he faced some of the most difficult problems of state government to arise in the fifty years since the Great Depression. Situated in the center of the Midwest frostbelt region, Indiana was especially hard hit by the 1980–82 economic recession. In just one poignant example nearly 10,000 jobs were lost when International Harvester closed its Fort Wayne plant. As a result of such scenarios as this, many of Orr's early policies were immediate reactive solutions taken to mitigate or reverse emergency situations.

Two key responses, a reduction in the size of the state workforce by nearly 2,000 employees and the convening of a special legislative session to pass a tax increase bill, were difficult and unpopular measures that placed the governor in a position of continually "fighting fires." Neither he nor his staff felt that they were able to develop or pursue their own policy initiatives until the economic crisis subsided.

When Orr was able to set his own agenda, his focus was clearly on improving education and economic development. By early 1983 the recession had eased somewhat and the recently passed tax increase substantially improved the state's revenue situation. The governor's foremost consideration was to invest the newly generated revenue in programs that were intended to advance Indiana's situation in the national economy. He had previously served for eight years as the director of the Department of Commerce and knew the value of a trained and educated workforce in meeting the employment exigencies of the high-tech era. Accordingly he sought to persuade the legislature to pass extensive educational development legislation. His most acclaimed success was in securing passage of Primetime Phase I, his showcase education legislation, designed to reduce the teacher-student ratio to 1:18 in first grade. He was also able to get a number of economic development bills passed to strengthen the lieutenant governor's programs aimed at retaining and attracting industry and commerce in the state. These developments of Orr's first term were key issues during his campaign for reelection in 1984 and influenced his transition policy choices.

The 1984 Election

Despite a large coattail advantage expected for Republican candidates in a presidential election year, Democrat state senator Wayne W. Townsend, a twenty-year veteran of the General Assembly and a successful grain farmer and hog producer, led a vigorous campaign to unseat the incumbent Orr. While President Reagan carried the state with a 518,000-vote margin, Orr defeated Townsend by a closer margin of 105,000 votes.

Republicans also won the three elected state offices of lieutenant governor, attorney general, and superintendent of public instruction in 1984 and again controlled both houses of the General Assembly with a house majority of 61 to 39, and a senate majority of 30 to 20. Despite winning the governor's office for the fifth straight time, Republicans were not complacent about continued programmatic or electoral success. Thus, with the legislature scheduled to convene to debate the next biennium budget in just fifty days, they knew time was essential. Sensing the urgency of making a smooth and rapid transition, Governor Orr eschewed the customary postelection respite in order to proceed with the work of establishing his new administration.

On the day after the election, Orr was quizzed by a statehouse reporter about his decision not to take a vacation:

> "C'mon, governor. Don't you deserve a little break?"
> "Sure I do. But I don't have time to do it. There was a lot of stuff that obviously was put on the back burner until the election was over. We have a future to look at in terms of a legislative session . . . [and] putting a new administration together." [8]

Quite apart from a demanding campaign schedule that forced him to place several things on the back burner, the election debate did not influence Governor Orr to change his policy or administrative programs. Winning the election, of course, meant everything in terms of providing the occasion to implement his programs, but his second term policies were formulated outside the campaign structure.

During the campaign, Townsend's major strategies were to attack

Orr's education and economic development programs for not accomplishing enough and to focus greater attention on increased taxes, rising utility rates, and motor vehicle license-branch reform. The last three issues had a great deal of voter appeal and probably cost Orr some ballots, but they did not result in new policy directions. For Orr's part his strategy was not to let his opponent control the campaign debate agenda, but to accentuate his established record to create jobs and improve education. Accordingly he did not debate the tax, utility, and license-branch issues.

Of the three issues not addressed in the Orr campaign, the utility reform issue was the most likely substantive issue to emerge from the campaign as a high-priority agenda item. But Governor Orr, anticipating this as an issue, appointed a Committee on Indiana's Utility Future in January 1984 to study the problem and make policy recommendations.[9] The committee met throughout the ensuing twelve months before submitting its final report in December 1984. In this manner the governor preempted the opposition's opportunity to make utility reform an exclusive Democratic issue and muted its impact as a campaign item.

A more interesting feature of this situation as it relates to this analysis was the timing of the utility reform issue as a transition topic. The formal transition time frame is generally thought to extend for approximately two months—from the day after the election in November until the legislature convenes in January. At least in the instance of the utility issue, the transition period extended for nearly fourteen months.

The Transition

Substance of Change

While Townsend's supporters described the closeness of his losing margin as a moral victory and a refutation of the incumbent governor's first-term policies, Orr contended that he did the best anyone could do in implementing austerity measures while building new programs simultaneously. Under these circumstances he felt that his victory, whatever the margin, represented a voter endorsement of his first-term policies. He also made it quite evident that he valued the interterm transition as a time of renewal and change when he stated his own assessment of the election and transition process:

Many people ask me wouldn't it be better if I didn't have to run again. Wouldn't it be better to just have one six-year term? I answer no for three reasons. It is good for an incumbent to be forced to test his ideas before the public, to secure their blessing for continuance in office. It is also time for a governor to refine and advance his first term policy priorities. And, lastly, it is an opportunity to recover from first-term mistakes, in personnel or organization.[10]

Thus, according to his own standards Orr had met the electoral challenge of a tough opponent and had prevailed before the electorate. He now welcomed the second term as an opportunity to deliver on the promise of his two first-term program commitments.

Although his two key policy issues were carry-over items from the first term, Orr's decision to pursue them further and to expand on them in the second term was in effect a new policy determination. This policy was new in the sense that his transition decision represented a determined, long-term commitment to economic recovery, while his first-term programs were reactive measures taken in response to the exigencies of the time. As he accentuated in his January 1985 state of the state address, his primary objective was to convince others of the importance of seeking "long-range success, not short-term thinking." [11]

The governor's major concern in seeking support for his policies was that, with some first-term successes already becoming evident and the state revenue situation improved, the legislature might become complacent about economic recovery and revert to previous spending patterns: "Our policy shifts are ones of emphasis rather than new agendas. We are seeking economic growth rather than economic development. The distinction is one of scope and time. I must convince others of the merit of a continued commitment in a number of areas related to the long-term growth of our economy." [12]

Orr's adoption of the term economic "growth" rather than economic development placed an intended emphasis on the magnitude of the change he sought. In terms of the expanded scope of his policies, he viewed educational improvement and new economic development programs as fundamental and related elements of his economic growth strategy. He also sought to convince the public and the legislature to forego politically more glamorous issues in order to invest the state's resources in basic growth programs whose rewards, if attained, would lie in the distant future. He was aware that most of the benefits of his

Primetime program for students in first grade would not materialize until long after he and his contemporaries were out of political office.

Success of Orr's economic growth strategy did not hinge entirely on the will of the legislature. For example, of the two central elements of his economic growth strategy, education was more prominent as a legislative issue while economic programs became a major administrative thrust.

Indiana is in a somewhat unusual and very interesting situation when it comes to the development and implementation of public education policy. Although the state has a separately elected superintendent of public instruction, the General Assembly often looks to the governor for new education policy initiatives, and the superintendent, recognizing the governor's more influential position with the legislature in policy and budgetary affairs, generally defers to him on these matters. The superintendent takes responsibility for implementing established policies.

Governor Orr's 1985 budget requests included additional funding for educational quality improvement at the elementary, secondary, and university levels, with the primary grades targeted for special consideration. Orr's Project Primetime I, a program to reduce class size in early elementary grades, had only been implemented in grade one during the 1983–85 biennium. Primetime II funding for the 1985–87 biennium was increased from the initial one-year expenditure of $17.6 million to $104 million, and the program was expanded to include grades one through three. Education improvement was not the only important program that Orr got through the 1985 General Assembly, but it was the legislation that best reflected his stated transitional policies.

Organizational and Personnel Changes

A number of important transitional activities occurred within the governor's administration, where he made substantial organizational and personnel changes. Ahlberg and Moynihan have noted the delicate balance that needs to be managed during a transition period by a governor-elect seeking to initiate new policies while at the same time maintaining continuity in government: "Concern with political transition has long been directed to the task of providing stability and continuity to the process of government. Clearly the newer task is to provide, as it were, an innovative element that will correspond to the function of government as an instrument of change and adaptation in a society constantly demanding both."[13] Although this assessment applied directly to a first-term governor, it is also applicable to an incumbent governor's transition to a second term, at least in the instance of Governor Orr in Indiana.

Freed from the political trappings of seeking reelection and no longer encumbered with severe economic conditions, Orr, a history major at Yale, viewed his second term as a challenge and opportunity to make a lasting contribution to Indiana state government:

> I believe the second term is critical to the success of any governor. If you look around this room at the pictures of former one-term governors there are too few things that history can remember them for. For me I know that my political life will end when this second term is over. Some might feel the urge to look at a second term as a kind of "lame duck" retirement. I, and I suspect history, will judge it as an opportunity to fulfill the promise of my first term.[14]

To accomplish his goals, Orr had two transitional objectives. He wanted to restructure his administration in order to provide for a more streamlined management process. And he sought to make several key personnel changes to develop his own team.

Organizational Changes

There were two significant transitional reorganizations of the Orr administration. The first were made at the departmental level, while a second set of changes were made within the governor's executive office. The combined effect of these changes was to streamline the governor's office and to improve his own capacity to provide leadership direction for education and economic growth programs.

In a move designed to expand and strengthen Lieutenant Governor John Mutz's administrative control over economic growth, Orr placed two previously separate agencies under the jurisdiction of the lieutenant governor's Department of Commerce. Since 1978, when Orr was lieutenant governor, the Department of Commerce had been the most rapidly growing department of state government. Virtually all of the department's 1978 to 1984 budget and program increases had been directed toward establishing conventional economic development funding mechanisms within its Economic Development Division.

The two agencies that Orr merged to the Department of Commerce in 1985 were the Indiana Employment Security Division, with responsibilities for administration of the state's unemployment service and unemployment compensation program, and the Office of Occupational Development and Employment. The latter office is responsible for the administration of the federal Job Training Partnership Act. The overall plan for merging job development and employment security functions with the Department of Commerce's established programs was to provide a comprehensive and long-term program for improving the business and employment situation in Indiana.

It is interesting to note parenthetically that the Indiana governor and lieutenant governor have served corresponding terms just since 1973, and only recently (1980 and 1984) has the lieutenant governor campaigned as the governor's hand-picked running mate chosen in party convention rather than through the direct primary process. Some critics charged that, because John Mutz was Governor Orr's close political ally and stated heir apparent, the decision to strengthen the lieutenant governor's office may have been influenced by political favoritism. But the fundamental administrative reason was to advance office capabilities and to streamline the governor's far-flung span of control. Besides, according to conventional wisdom, it is the idle lieutenant governor who has free time to campaign, rather than one fully occupied with administrative duties. In balance the expanded office portends to be more valuable as an executive reorganization, rather than a political maneuver.

The reorganization of the governor's executive office was similarly designed to reduce the governor's span of administrative control and to place emphasis on education and economic-growth functions. Orr's two-fold reorganization involved the creation of a chief-of-staff position and the establishment of a special education group.

The chief-of-staff position, entitled senior executive assistant, was filled by Kendall Cochran, Orr's most experienced aide. Cochran, who had been with Orr since 1972, was given the new responsibility of screening agency problems flowing to the governor's office through six other executive assistants. Aides in the governor's office were given responsibility for coordinating the activities of two or three line departments or agencies, usually in related functional areas. During Orr's first term, these aides each reported directly to the governor, placing a demanding administrative burden on his office. The new arrangement would reduce the governor's time spent on day-to-day administrative matters and afford him more time to devote to larger issues—in his own words, "to sort out the consequential from the nonconsequential."[15]

The second staff reorganization was the arrangement of four assistants into a special group assigned to education issues. This group was headed by John R. Hammond, another experienced aide, who reported directly to the governor. Hammond's education group was charged with developing new education programs and policies, maintaining liaison with the superintendent of public instruction's office, and evaluating the established educational programs for efficient and effective implementation.

One additional, almost unnoticed administrative change in the governor's executive office illustrates an important transitional change in managerial mood. This was the reinstitution of the two-tiered arrangement of his office into administrative and executive-assistant levels. This distinction between senior and junior personnel was allowed to fall into disuse during the first term when it was determined that it created some disharmony among the staff. While Orr's two-tiered distinction appeared to be a small detail, it stood as a tacit reminder to staffers that internal discord would be secondary henceforth to productivity as a measure of achievement in the second Orr administration.

Orr's commitment of additional staff time to education and his emphasis on productivity in operational programs were indicative of the direction as well as the depth of change developed during the transition. While he continued to be interested in seeking new legislative policies and funding for education, he wanted to be certain that the policies he sought would be for programs that worked:

> It is much less difficult to measure productivity in the private sector than in the governmental sector. There is no reward for productivity in the public sector, and almost no reliable measure of it.
>
> One of the things I want to try to create during this four year period is a means by which to measure productivity. One of the places I want to try to bring this about is in education. It is ironic to me that we know that Marion High School, current state champion [1985], is the best basketball team in Indiana, but we have no clear idea of how to measure academic success.[16]

Orr's organizational changes were implemented and made public early in January. Thus by the first month of his second term, Orr had established new reporting lines, restructured his administration, and thereby communicated his intent to demand a greater effort of his administration in effectively implementing his priority programs. He was convinced that the time and conditions were ripe to adopt new procedures and objectives:

> The time is such that I am probably better positioned now than I was in my first term to implement my ideas for productivity in government. During the first term we seemed to be continuously caught up in combating the recession that peaked in 1982. Now that we have experienced some economic recovery, I have more time to devote to managerial direction and leadership. The challenge of this period will be to continue the cost saving measures adopted in hard times.[17]

Thus it appears that early in his second term Orr established a management policy designed to place an increased degree of responsibility on his own administration for the sound implementation of his priority programs. And in doing this he made a conscious departure from first-term emphases and administrative procedures.

Personnel

A concern for continuity *and* change was clearly a part of Governor Orr's thinking when he delayed his postelection vacation. As he said at the time, "One of the reasons why I can't go [on vacation] is that there are a lot of people who wonder what the future is for them. I don't think it is fair for me to go gallivanting off to some happy haunt while they are worried about their future."[18] The urgency associated with Orr's postelection duties reflects his desire to move as quickly as possible to prevent delays in ongoing operations while at the same time initiating new programs and making key staff changes. A major factor in this regard derived from the law in Indiana that gubernatorial appointees serve at the pleasure of the governor. Custom has it that the incoming governor officially reappoint those department and agency heads that he plans to retain, in addition to informing those he intends to move or dismiss. This dual action provides both a broad-scale opportunity and a demanding responsibility to review the entire list of gubernatorial appointees and to take action—positive or negative—in each case.

Given the Indiana custom, Orr was correct in asserting that there were a lot of people who were worried about their future. But, in retrospect, most of them had little to be concerned about; changes initiated by the governor were few in number and most of these were done within his own executive staff. Program continuity did not seem to be greatly affected by the transition chånges in personnel.

Staff changes occurred during the 1984–85 transition for a number of reasons—some expected, some not; some welcomed, some not. And, as Orr indicated, the governor does not orchestrate these developments:

> There is a certain amount of natural self selection weeding out of people who sense that they will not be making a contribution to the second term. There are also some loyal, dedicated, and efficient administrators, such as Judith Palmer, who felt that they had dedicated enough of their careers to the public sector and wish to pursue new career possibilities. And there are those who wish to continue on, but have lost their drive or ingenuity in that position. These we have to move elsewhere, or replace entirely.[19]

Where Orr himself determined to initiate personnel changes he was guided by his quest to establish his own management team, one that he was confident would subscribe to his second-term policy directives.

As a close political ally and having served as lieutenant governor in Otis Bowen's two administrations, Orr felt comfortable, and perhaps somewhat obliged, in retaining some of his predecessor's appointees when he succeeded him in 1981. Despite Orr's retention of hand-picked Bowen people, certain natural internecine rivalries began to surface between "Orr's people" and "Bowen's people" during the first term. These staff rivalries were complicated by major differences in the management styles practiced by the two governors. Probably because of his business background, Orr's management style is decidedly one of "tight, tight" management. He gives detailed assignments to his appointees and closely monitors progress on a regular basis. In this he differed from "Doc" Bowen, whose sense of trust, developed during his years as a small town physician, allowed him to place a great deal of individual discretion in the hands of his employees. His style was more of the "loose, loose" kind.

Internal rivalries and staff disharmony stemming from differences in managerial style are not unusual and are generally tolerated in most administrations. What exacerbated these situations during Orr's first term were the cutbacks in management programs necessitated by the economic recession of the first two years. Department heads and their constituent groups who were required to reduce staff and/or programs would sometimes rationalize their dilemmas by blaming the governor or another staffer, especially one who might carry the stigma of being from another administration.

Confronted with this unsettled situation and determined to pursue an astringent second-term policy and management style, Orr decided to make some key personnel changes. In doing this for essentially administrative reasons, Orr's transition differed considerably from previous first-term gubernatorial transitions in the state where political patronage decisions were more in evidence.

Indiana is widely and correctly identified as a political patronage state, and Orr had clearly run as the regular Republican Party organization's candidate. Yet he was given a free hand to form his own administration, primarily for two reasons. Many of his executive staff people doubled up during the election as campaign workers. Thus, when the campaign ended in victory they still held their positions, and no large group of office-seekers emerged as contenders for their jobs.

The second reason is more compelling. Those personnel changes that did develop were nearly all full-time, top-level directorates or executive staff positions. There were not many obvious political plum kinds of patronage jobs to be had. And, in Indiana as elsewhere, the party organization does not try to forcefully place patronage candidates in top-level positions. The party chairman does nominate executive-level candidates, but the actual choice is the governor's to make and to live with. The close personal relationship between Gordon Durnil, the state GOP chairman, and Orr helped to honor this convention.

Too much is probably made of the differences existing between Bowen and Orr appointees. A number of Bowen holdovers still filled key departmental positions in Orr's second term. Besides, some of the appointees removed during the transition were Orr's own first-term appointees who did not meet expectations. The key points to be made are that changes were not politically derived, they were not wholesale, they were generally restricted to high-level appointees, and operational continuity was not broken.

Maintaining continuity did not surface as a major problem during the transition. Governor Orr operated throughout the period more as an heir apparent than a candidate for a second term. He was confident in his record, and his voter polls showed him as the leading candidate throughout the campaign. Staff attitudes were similarly confident, as was evident in the assessment of one of his senior aides: "You do not let major issues go by during the transition period. You may put off small issues that are somewhat controversial, but not a major issue. As far as 'lame duckism' in the Orr transition is concerned, it was never really a problem. The polls continually had us ahead, and there was widespread feeling in the administration that we would be back." [20]

The administration's success in steering forty-two out of forty-five executive-sponsored bills through the 1985 legislative session indicates that a considerable amount of planning and organizing continued throughout the extended transition period. Orr's success in persuading his experienced and respected budget director, Judith Palmer, to stay on until the General Assembly session ended was also a significant factor in maintaining budgetary continuity.

Another factor contributing to a smooth transition was the return of an experienced legislative leadership in both houses. Their involvement in Orr's first-term programs made the transition to his second-term legislative requests much easier than during his first-term getting-acquainted session.

A statehouse reporter for the *Indianapolis Star* actually saw program activities increase during the transition period:

> During the election any relaxation of attention to large issues would immediately become a campaign issue. Most of Orr's top aides were also campaign workers and they were sensitive to this. Even on the small issues, there seemed to be more intense pressure to respond to constituent requests. It makes good political sense.
>
> After the election the thing I saw over there at the statehouse and still do, was a sense of relief and a firm commitment to get on with the work at hand. They operate in a noticeably more confident way now than during the first term. [21]

It makes good sense that, at least until the election results are in, the incumbent candidate for governor must be an efficient administrator, as well as effective campaigner. After the election he needs to move quickly to capture the staff's sense of victory and revived spirits in order to parlay this mood into second-term programs. These things Governor Orr was able to do without major disruptions in state operations.

Process

Two factors are evident as major procedural differences between Governor Orr's 1980 and 1984 transitions to office. First, time and timing became far more critical during his second transition than was previously the case. Second, the organization structured for transition was less formal, more internalized within his staff than in 1980. The combined effect of these factors was that the transition as an incumbent sometimes appeared to be even more difficult than it was for Orr as a first-term governor.

Time was a serious limitation for Governor Orr and his staff. As the incumbent, he was required to continue his executive duties, which were encumbered with a number of back-burner items remaining from the campaign, while he reorganized his administration. Seven months after his 1985 election Orr compared his two successions to office:

> In 1980 I could conveniently sidetrack some of my responsibilities as lieutenant governor and assume the responsibilities of governor elect in getting a new administration off the ground. This time there were things that had to be done in the way of establishing a new beginning, but four years before Governor Bowen was down here in the governor's office dealing with the day-to-day problems of government, and I was upstairs putting an administration together.[22]

Another time demand on an incumbent that Governor Orr experienced was his role as a national political figure. During his first term he developed a larger presence in national affairs than he had attained when he first became governor. And related duties required his continued presence during the transition as well.

Timing his and his staff's activities to correspond to the opening of the General Assembly placed an added urgency on Orr's already crowded schedule. Because of this short time frame some staff members, such as Kendall Cochran, found themselves "tripling up" on functions during the transition: "One of the reasons I say that the transition doesn't end until the legislature goes home, is that after the election most of the staff is busy closing out the campaign, doing their regular job and dealing with the legislature. There isn't always enough time to make all the changes we are contemplating. It was probably the single most difficult time I can remember during my entire time in office."[23] Cochran could have also mentioned a fourth staff function, because some aides were required to cover temporarily vacant posts. Nevertheless his point about the staff's program of work during the transition was well taken, particularly from one who had participated in or observed three other transitions since 1972.

Organization for the transition was an entirely internalized process, conducted by Governor Orr and a few select staff members. No search-and-screen committee was organized; no transition team was formed; no extra staff were hired or office space set aside for the transition. Adopting such measures might have raised unnecessary alarm among staff members, legislators, and constituent groups. This concern for staff morale and continuity of office might be sufficient reason in itself to maintain a low-profile procedure. But the dominant reason Orr chose this course was the confidence he had that he and his staff could do the job best.

Orr and his closest aides were in the best position to know what they wanted to accomplish in the second term. Their confidence, which started to build during the second half of the first term, was reaffirmed by the election victory. Moreover, and perhaps most important, they felt they could now make better choices based on their experiences with what or who performed best in the first term. Accordingly transition decisions were incorporated into regular staff agendas with only a few staff meetings called exclusively for organizational or personnel decisions.

Conclusion

An incumbent's transition to a second term differs from a first-term succession more in procedural matters than in substantive developments. But, in either case, similarities are more apparent than are dissimilarities.

As far as the substance of the transition is concerned, Governor Orr's second-term transition was as much a period of change as was the first. Evidence of change was most notable in organizational adjustments, personnel shifts and replacements, and the establishment of new lines of reporting and control that better suited the governor's preferred management style. Changes in policy were evident but harder to detect because their roots were established in first-term programs. Policy changes made in education and economic development could be described as more of an escalation and long-term entrenchment than entirely new policy initiatives. But the changes were of great enough magnitude in budget and long-term commitments to be considered as new program directions.

In terms of procedure, time and timing were the key variables that seemed to dominate the period and that distinguished it from other interparty or intraparty transitions. The responsibility of managing the governor's office, especially its legislative functions, weighed heavily on the governor while he was trying to put a new administration in place. Maintaining control over departments and programs during the period of change was not perceived as a major problem. The general feeling among the administration was that Orr would win the 1984 election, and the governor and his staff operated on that premise throughout the campaign. Once elected he immediately set out to advance strict management and leadership policies that he felt he could not implement before the election. Thus program continuity was not seriously threatened.

Politics were necessarily a high-priority consideration during the election, when Governor Orr tested his first-term programs before the electorate and felt justified by his victory in pursuing them further during this second term. After the election political influence was not in great evidence in the determination of policy agendas or personnel appointments. Because Governor Orr was a Republican his programs and policies tended to be framed in the Republican mold, and most of his appointees were active Republicans. This was to be expected in the normal course of events and especially so in a patronage-oriented state like Indiana. But partisan politics did not pervade the transitional process in Governor Orr's interterm changes. His legislative programs, organizational realignments, and staff changes were dictated by his personal decision to do things differently in his second term.

Sabato's "Good-Time Charlie"[24] style of governor may choose to follow a different transitional course, whether it be as an incumbent successor in Indiana or elsewhere. But, as this study shows, the "new breed" kind of governor will not likely approach a second term in a business-as-usual mode. The opportunity for change seems to be too obvious and critical for the modern governor not to seize the moment to act. Even if the preferred management style may be a reactive one, time and events most likely will thrust substantial change into an incumbent's transition.

Lieutenant Governors: Gubernatorial Transitions in Missouri

)))))

Dean L. Yarwood

America loves to poke fun at its "seconds in charge." Night-show host Johnny Carson has elicited laughs at the expense of the vice president—any vice president—for almost a quarter century. Larry Sabato opens the section of his book devoted to the lieutenant governor with a Calvin Coolidge joke: When asked by a "solicitous matron" what he did for a living, Coolidge replied, "I'm the lieutenant governor." The excited woman asked him to tell her all about it. He deadpanned, "I just did."[1] And *U.S. News and World Report* in an article about lieutenant governors quoted Nevada lieutenant governor Myron E. Leavitt, who said that his job was to tend to the senate "and check the obituaries to see if I should be in Carson City."[2] In spite of the gags about lieutenant governors, the National Governors' Association in its publication, *Transition and the New Governor*, suggests that on the day after the election the governor-elect "meet with or telephone the lieutenant governor-elect."[3] It is important that the governor-elect get off to a good start by establishing a working relationship with his or her lieutenant governor.

The Office of Lieutenant Governor

The office of lieutenant governor has been undergoing significant changes during the last couple of decades. Though historically the office has been part legislative and part executive, recent trends in some states have moved the office into the executive branch. As Thad Beyle told *U.S. News and World Report*, "States that want to enhance the powers of their governors are making the lieutenant governor part of the executive branch. The lieutenant governor works with the governor and is ready to take his place."[4] Thus, for example, Declercq and Kaminski point out that thirty-one "seconds in command" serve as heads of executive departments.[5] Further, thirty-three states empower the governor constitutionally or on the basis of statutes to assign executive duties to the lieutenant governors[6] while in other states governors do so on their own initiative. Among the chores given lieutenant governors are that they serve on state boards, commissions, and task forces, coordinate administrative activities, serve as liaisons with other levels of government, play some role in state economic development, and act as state ombudsmen.[7] In addition, twenty lieutenant governors are members of their governor's cabinet.[8] Indicative of the movement of the position into the executive branch is the spread of team elections for governor and lieutenant governor. Today twenty-two states have team elections —only one did as recently as 1961.[9]

Still, though there has been movement to the contrary, several lieutenant governors remain significantly involved in the legislative branch. Lieutenant governors, at least formally, preside over the senate in twenty-eight states. In addition, they appoint legislative committees in eight states and assign bills in fourteen.[10]

Traditional powers of lieutenant governors that most still possess also make it advisable that governors go to some lengths to establish good relations with them. In twenty-seven states, the lieutenant governor serves as acting governor when the governor leaves the state,[11] in forty-one the lieutenant governor succeeds to the governorship upon a vacancy, and in forty-five the lieutenant governor becomes the acting governor in the event of the disability of the governor.[12]

From this listing of powers of the "seconds in command," it is evident that the success of the governor-elect as governor may well be significantly affected by the rapport he or she develops with the lieutenant governor at the beginning of the term. Governors are overloaded and they need help; lieutenant governors in many states provide it. Several lieutenant governors possess important powers in their own right and governors need to be able to count on their support and cooperation. Finally, a new governor needs to cultivate good relations with the lieutenant governor to assure continuity in administrative thrust and programs.

The Lieutenant Governor and Gubernatorial Transition in Missouri

Election evening in Missouri in 1976 carried surprising news: incumbent Republican governor Christopher Bond had been defeated in a late surge by "Walkin' Joe" Teasdale. At the same time, incumbent lieutenant governor William C. Phelps, a Republican, had been reelected. To characterize Teasdale and Phelps as a bad match would be an understatement.

Phelps vowed during his first term that he would be a full-time lieutenant governor, and he took for himself the nickname "Full-time Phelps." He had been center stage in state politics for a fleeting moment at the end of the 1973 legislative session. Upon his return from lunch on the final day of that session, he found that the doors to the senate were locked and the sergeant-at-arms had been instructed to bar his entrance. Undaunted, Phelps scurried to find an unsecured door and made his triumphant entry. When he stood at the steps to the rostrum shouting that he was being deprived of his constitutional right to preside over the senate, President Pro Tempore William J. Cason (D, Clinton) had him tossed out of the chamber.[13]

The contentiousness of the Bond-Teasdale transition spilled over to foul transition relationships between Teasdale and Phelps. Finally, when the Teasdale staff was allowed possession of the offices of the governor at noon on inaugural day, they found them barren of supplies, furniture, and equipment. They discovered after a bit of sleuthing that some of the missing merchandise had been given to the lieutenant governor and the rest had been "surplused." Teasdale staffers surreptitiously retrieved the supplies and equipment a few days later while the unsuspecting Phelps was presiding at an official senate function.[14] Astonished to discover that the governor had a key to his storage room, Phelps hired a private locksmith to change the lock, albeit belatedly. Said a Phelps aide: "It won't happen again unless they bribe one of us."[15]

Another Bond-Teasdale dispute affected transition relations between Teasdale and his lieutenant governor. The Teasdale staff was upset to find that Bond had sent all records dealing with ongoing business to the archives. So, when Phelps requested compensation for some days during which he served as acting governor while Bond was out of state (compensation to which he was constitutionally entitled), his request was denied. Cliff Faddis of the governor's staff said he had no records to show when the former governor was out of state and when he wasn't.[16]

The budget was yet another transition irritant between Teasdale and Phelps. The latter cried foul when Teasdale cut his request for the office of the lieutenant governor by $50,000, an amount equal to the cost of operating the volunteer and ombudsman programs. These programs, which had been administered by the lieutenant governor during the previous administration, were funded by the federal government, but this source had run dry.[17] In this case, the two officials worked out their differences when the governor realized he could not leave the state to attend President Carter's inaugural because the lieutenant governor might fill the state auditor post, which had just fallen vacant in early January.[18]

The bad seeds sown during the transition grew into a thistle patch by the end of Teasdale's term. During his last year and a half as governor, Teasdale complained bitterly that he was "a virtual prisoner of Missouri."[19] The problem was Alberta Slavin, chairwoman of the Public Service Commission and controversial consumer advocate who had barely been confirmed for the final year of an unexpired term. Teasdale had made tougher utility regulation a major issue during the campaign, but now it was clear that the senate would not confirm Slavin for a full term. However, under Missouri law she could continue to serve so long as no successor was appointed. Teasdale feared that if he left the state and Phelps assumed the powers of the governorship, he would do just that.[20]

Phelps did little to put Teasdale's mind at ease. He taunted in the press that he might replace Slavin if the governor left, but only maybe, or perhaps he would order an audit of the Revenue Department.[21] In May 1980 Teasdale told the press, "There's nothing new about this. I've remained in Missouri ever since last year when Bill Phelps came into our office demanding legislation and signing it when I was out of the state. Ever since then, I've realized I can't leave. He might do anything—sign bills, veto bills, or make appointments."[22] The only time Teasdale left the state between March 1979 and August 1980, he took the lieutenant governor with him.[23]

The contrast between the relations of the Teasdale-Phelps duo and those of the governor and lieutenant governor in the next two administrations was the contrast of day and night. This was in spite of the fact that in both terms the two positions were filled by persons of opposing political parties. A factor in addition to the change of personal chemistry that eased transitions after 1976 was the passage of the 1977 gubernatorial transition law. Beyond providing transition support for the governor-elect, it provided that up to $5,000 be appropriated for the transition expenses of the lieutenant governor-elect and mandated that the commissioner of administration provide office space, equipment, and furniture for the lieutenant governor-elect during the transition, separate from that provided for the governor-elect.[24]

On election evening of 1980 Republican governor-elect Christopher Bond and Democratic lieutenant governor-elect Kenneth J. Rothman had a "long and cordial discussion." Bond told the press, "He [Rothman] assured me he was willing to work with us, and I will be talking with him about helping with legislative programs."[25] According to Dwight Fine, administrative manager to Rothman, the lieutenant governor stated in his first meeting with Governor Bond that he would not sign any papers without Bond's authorization. "Ken did not want to be viewed as an obstructionist."[26]

The day-to-day work was handled by the governor's staff in Bond's absence. During prolonged leaves Bond's staff would bring papers to the lieutenant governor for his signature. Rothman acted aggressively in dealing with the four or five emergencies (snow storms, floods, etc.) that developed while Bond was out of the state. Here Rothman felt that if things did not go well, he would be blameworthy because he was the only official who could act.[27] (The Bond advisers found some humor in the fact that all the state's emergencies during Bond's second term occurred while the governor was out of the state.)[28] Rothman continued the volunteer and ombudsman programs begun during the first term of Lieutenant Governor Phelps.

The transition from Phelps to Rothman was smooth: contact people were appointed; Phelps did not attempt to "run off with the stamps" or the furniture; and the lieutenant governor's offices were vacated the Friday prior to the inaugural. The Office of Administration acquainted the new lieutenant governor's staff with office forms and so on.[29]

In 1984 outgoing Lieutenant Governor Rothman and Lieutenant Governor-elect Harriett Woods were personal friends. The transition between them was, as one would expect, smooth. Dwight Fine for Rothman and Mary Schantz for Woods met and discussed office matters —the volume of work, the budget, and office procedures. In addition, an orientation to office management was provided by the Office of Administration.[30]

There were no contacts between Governor Ashcroft and Lieutenant Governor Woods until the inaugural. However, relations between the two seemed to be cordial during the transition. Before the governor left the state, he sent a formal letter to the lieutenant governor and there was also much informal contact between them. In addition, early meetings were held between Woods and the adjutant general and the director of public safety that dealt with emergency procedures.[31]

Lieutenant Governor Woods continued to operate the volunteer and ombudsman programs, which seem to have been institutionalized into the office of lieutenant governor. In addition, she opened up a Statewide Volunteers for Efficiency (SAVE) hotline to ferret out waste and abuse in state government. The purpose of SAVE was to encourage workers to report cases of waste and abuse in state government, in exchange for which they were promised anonymity.[32] Though one can imagine that this could cause friction between the lieutenant governor and the governor, it seems not to have done so during the transition. Schantz commented that the department directors had been very cooperative about responding to SAVE reports and that there had been no adverse reaction from the governor's office.[33]

When Governor Ashcroft left the state in February 1985 to pursue the Saturn plant opportunity in Detroit, Harriett Woods made history by becoming the first woman governor in Missouri, albeit an acting one.[34] She also convened a meeting of farm leaders that she called historic. It was attended by members of farm lobbying organizations, bankers and lenders, and agricultural officials, and it focused attention on an issue that heretofore had received scant attention from the Ashcroft administration.[35] During the transition period she also let it be known that as a member of the Board of Public Buildings, she would not "rubber stamp" contracts for public buildings for the Division of Design and Construction.[36] By the end of the first legislative session she was considered a shoo-in for the Democratic nomination for the U.S. Senate seat being vacated by Thomas Eagleton.[37]

Conclusion

It is clear that it is well worth the effort for the governor to attempt to "make an arrangement" with the lieutenant governor early in the transition, even if they are not of the same political party. Lieutenant governors have authority, influence, and power that can be used to help or hurt governors and their administrations. Of course, it is by no means certain that Teasdale and Phelps would have reached an understanding as a result of any such early conference. But then again, it is difficult to imagine how matters could have been made worse by meeting. In the cases of Bond and Rothman and Ashcroft and Woods, early discussions were held between the governor and the lieutenant governor; good rapport developed between these officials even though they were of different political persuasions.

In the larger sense, the problems of lieutenant governors and gubernatorial transitions in Missouri are rooted in the separate elections of the governor and lieutenant governor. This practice needs to be reconsidered in the light of modern circumstances. Prior to 1976 Missouri had had a governor and lieutenant governor of different political parties only once going back as far as 1908; it has happened in three successive elections since 1976. This suggests that perhaps the governor and lieutenant governor should be elected as a team and that the lieutenant governor should be brought more clearly into the executive branch. Senate Joint Resolution No. 1, introduced into the 1985 legislative session, proposed team election for the governor and lieutenant governor, an end to the lieutenant governor's role as ex officio president of the senate, and the governor's appointment of the lieutenant governor as head of an executive department. To be sure, it did not pass that time around. However, informal practices and experience seemed to be leading Missouri to some such solution.

Appendix:
Outline for the State
Analysts

)))))

1 The milieu: The state's politics, government, and policies: At ease, crisis, tax problems, economy, social setting. The backdrop for the transition.

2 Politics of the principals: Outgoing, incoming governors and their chief aides, supporters. The ambience of the situation. Was incumbency a critical variable, and how? Did the winner anticipate governing and detach personnel from the campaign to focus on transition? Was the state bureaucracy part of the campaign as participants or as an issue?

3 The transition provisions, procedures, and support: Timing, state laws and provisions, budgetary considerations. How the state officially prepares for transition. How well do the principals and the staff work within the state's provisions?

4 The politics of the transition: What really happens in the transition—outside the formal provisions and procedures? Where are the squeak points, the places where things work well? What interpersonal, intergroup, or intragroup problems are there?

5 Comings and goings: Personnel turnover, appointments (what they are, who they are). The office staff, major departments, and so forth. How much holdover from previous administration? Shutting down the campaign and campaign organization. The inaugural, a political or governmental event? Who serves the gatekeeper role for the governor-elect, controlling the mob of job seekers?

6 Coping with the processes: Getting an office working—the day-to-day mechanics. Becoming chief budget officer. Putting together the legislative program or package. Establishing a personnel screening process. Meshing the policy advisers and specialists with the more generalist process people. How is turf defined and territory staked out?

7 Reaching out from the governor's office: Constituent relations and the om-

budsman function—chaotic or organized? The political party structures and the personnel. Staff's ability and understanding of the intergovernmental role in regard to:

) the local governments.

) other states and regional entities.

) the national level: Congress, the administration.

) the decision whether to have a Washington representative and what that person(s) should do.

8 Aid and assistance: Where did governor and staff turn for help? Role and impact of the NGA Seminar for New Governors (November). Were the NGA written materials utilized, and did they have an impact? Role and impact of any NGA transition assistance teams. Others who impacted: the universities and their personnel, private industry, consultants, other state personnel. Who was impacted and how? What processes, if any, were impacted?

9 The politics of the new administration: Taking over and creating an image. The state of the state message—from campaign rhetoric to program and policy. The legislative program and its reception. The budget and the new administration's revisions. The team appointed to run state government. How the cabinet works and is perceived. The politics of reaching into the departments to seek loyalty (making the rounds, using the appointive cabinet heads, selecting the governor's person within an agency).

10 Evaluation of the transition: General findings and conclusions. Problems perceived and problems overcome, alleviated, ducked.

Notes

))))))

Gubernatorial Transitions

1 Lamar Alexander, *Steps Along the Way: A Governor's Scrapbook* (Nashville, Tenn.: Thomas Nelson, 1986), 27.
2 Alexander, *Steps Along the Way*, 22, 24.
3 Portions of this section are taken from Thad L. Beyle, "Gubernatorial Transitions: Lessons from 1982–1983," *Publius* 14, no. 3 (Summer 1984): 15–18, and "Gubernatorial Transitions: Lessons from the 1982–1983 Experience," in *Gubernatorial Transitions: The 1982 Election* (Durham, N.C.: Duke University Press, 1985), 4–7.
4 Clark D. Ahlberg and Daniel P. Moynihan, "Changing Governors—and Policies," *Public Administration Review* 20 (1960): 195–205.
5 Norton B. Long, "After the Voting Is Over," *Midwest Journal of Political Science* 6 (1962): 183–200.
6 David J. Allen, *New Governor in Indiana: The Challenge of Executive Power* (Bloomington, Ind.: Institute of Public Administration, Indiana University, 1965).
7 Thad L. Beyle and John Wickman, "Gubernatorial Transition in a One-Party Setting," *Public Administration Review* 30 (1970): 10–17.
8 Dale E. Carter, *When Governors Change: Symbolic Output and Political Support*, Institute of Governmental Affairs Research Report No. 5, (Davis: University of California, Davis, 1968).
9 Peter N. Kidman, "Gubernatorial Transition in West Virginia" (Ph.D. diss., University of West Virginia, 1972). Also presented as a paper at the West Virginia Political Science Association Annual Meeting, Morganton, Oct. 1972.
10 Leonard K. Bradley, Jr., "Gubernatorial Transition in Tennessee: The

1970–1971 Experience," (M.A. thesis, University of Tennessee, Knoxville, 1973).

11 Bernard Caton, "Gubernatorial Transitions in Virginia," *Newsletter* (Institute of Government, University of Virginia, Charlottesville, 1978).

12 Diane Blair and Robert Savage, "The Rhetorical Challenge of a Gubernatorial Transition: Constructing the Image of Statecraft" (Paper presented at the 1980 Conference of the International Communications Association, Acapulco, Mexico, May 1980).

13 Stuart R. Ringham, "The Governor-Elect to Governor: Transition in the American States," (Ph.D. diss., University of Iowa, 1972).

14 Kenneth Warner, "Planning for Transition," *State Government* 34 (1961): 102–103.

15 Charles Gibbons, "Transition of Government in Massachusetts," *State Government* 34 (1961): 100–101; and Wayne F. McGown, "Gubernatorial Transition in Wisconsin," *State Government* 44 (1971): 103–106.

16 Arkansas Legislative Council, *Pre-Inaugural Staff, Office and Other Allowances for the Governors of Arkansas and Various States* (Little Rock: 1971); Ohio Legislative Service Commission, *Problems in the Transition of Government*, Staff Report No. 57 (Columbus, 1963); and Wisconsin Department of Administration, *The Executive Office Transition* (Madison, 1970).

17 Gibbons, "Transition of Government in Massachusetts," 100 and McGown, "Gubernatorial Transition in Wisconsin," 106.

18 Ahlberg and Moynihan, "Changing Governors," 197; Beyle and Wickman, "Gubernatorial Transition in a One-Party Setting," 11, 15.

19 Ahlberg and Moynihan, "Changing Governors," 195; Long, "After the Voting Is Over," 196.

20 Beyle and Wickman, "Gubernatorial Transition in a One-Party Setting," 14; Long "After the Voting Is Over," 188.

21 Beyle and Wickman, "Gubernatorial Transition in a One-Party Setting," 14–15; Blair and Savage "The Rhetorical Challenge of a Gubernatorial Transition"; Long, "After the Voting Is Over," 190.

22 Beyle, "Gubernatorial Transitions: Lessons from the 1982–1983 Experience," 29.

23 Scott M. Matheson, *Out of Balance* (Salt Lake City, Utah: Peregrine Smith, 1986), 189.

24 Matheson, *Out of Balance*, 185.

25 Lauren L. Henry, *Presidential Transitions* (Washington, D.C.: The Brookings Institution, 1960); Paul T. David, *The Presidential Election and Transition, 1960–1961* (Washington, D.C.: The Brookings Institution, 1961); and most recently, Frederick C. Mosher, W. David Clinton, and Daniel G. Lang, *Presidential Transitions and Foreign Affairs* (Baton Rouge, La.: Louisiana State University Press, 1987).

26 Mosher, Clinton, and Lang, *Presidential Transitions*, xiii.

27 Ibid, 252–53.

28 Ibid.

29 Ibid., 256.

30 Ibid., 257.

31 National Governors' Conference (now NGA), *The Critical Hundred Days: A Handbook for New Governors* (Washington, D.C.: NGC, 1975); *The Governors' Office* (Washington, D.C.: NGA, 1976); *Governing the American States: A Handbook for New Governors* (Washington, D.C.: NGA, 1978); *Transition and the New Governor: A Critical Overview* (Washington, D.C.: NGA, 1982).

32 Public Affairs Research Council of Louisiana (PARC), *The Great Louisiana Campaign Spendathon* (Baton Rouge: PARC, 1980).

33 Beyle, *Gubernatorial Transitions: The 1982 Election*; and *Re-Electing the Governor: The 1982 Elections* (Lanham, Md.: University Press of America, 1986).

34 There was one state analysis that failed to materialize because of the perception of the participants around the newly elected governor that the analysts involved were biased against them, i.e., they were members of the opposition party and considerably more conservative than the new administration. Lack of access shut down the ability of the analysts to fully observe and report on the transition process.

35 Portions of this section were developed under a contract with the Office of State Services of the NGA. These were published by the NGA in the Office of State Services' *State Services Management Notes* series, "The Transition: A View from Academe," in November 1986, to be part of the materials made available to the newly elected governors of that year.

36 George Weeks, "Gubernatorial Transition: Leaving There," *State Government* 57, no. 3 (1984): 74.

Protecting Options

1 When new governors defeat an incumbent, they may owe their victory to a public call for more action: see Herman Lujan on Washington (unless otherwise indicated, the references in these footnotes are to essays in this volume). Even a governor going into a second term also feels pressure for quick action, to parlay the sense of victory into second-term programs: see James Owen on Indiana. The pressure is evident in most of the reports: e.g., Elmer Cornwell on Rhode Island (concern that the new governor "hit the ground running") and Joel A. Thompson on North Carolina (where Governor Martin lost the initiative).

2 Lujan's Washington essay suggests that Governor Gardner drew wisdom and commitment from a disastrous first legislative session to lead a remarkable recovery in a special session. Note the frequency with which the essays in this volume and in Thad L. Beyle, ed., *Gubernatorial Transitions: The 1982 Election* (Durham, N.C.: Duke University Press, 1985) praise the seminar for new governors sponsored by the National Governors' Association (NGA).

3 Thompson's North Carolina essay points out that we don't know much

about whether or how, a governor can recover from a poor start. Malcolm E. Jewell and Philip Roeder raise the possibility that Governor Collins's failure with her first Kentucky legislature could be a step toward ultimate success. Such speculations point out the need for more studies of governors' full tenure, relating problems and successes to the foundations established by the transitions or other events and circumstances. See also Richard W. Gable, Mark Sektnan, and Joel King on the 1982 California transition in Beyle, *Gubernatorial Transitions*, 151. Louis C. Gawthrop argues that political executives, more than most administrators, must learn, or "relearn," on the job to sharpen their subjective judgments: see *Bureaucratic Behavior in the Executive Branch* (Glencoe, Ill.: Free Press, 1969), particularly chapter 5.

4 Lujan's Washington essay suggests that governors learn to change directions easily, like the king on a chess board.

5 NGA, *Transition and the New Governor: A Critical Overview* (Washington, D.C.: NGA, 1982), 56. Jose Z. Garcia indicated that New Mexico found problems in "keeping options open" in regard to personal staff in Beyle, *Gubernatorial Transitions*, 324–25.

6 See Theodore S. Pedeliski on North Dakota (for success) and Thompson on North Carolina and Jewell and Roeder on Kentucky (for problems).

7 Diane D. Blair in Beyle, *Gubernatorial Transitions*, 96.

8 Of course other considerations are important in choosing staff—e.g., technical skills and ability to relate to the particular management style of the administration: see Lujan on Washington. If formal powers are limited and patronage is extensive and a major source of gubernatorial influence, the game changes: see Owen on Indiana and Thompson on North Carolina.

9 Thompson on North Carolina.

10 See essays on Kentucky, North Carolina, North Dakota, Rhode Island, and Utah and Don Sprengel's statistics cited by Beyle in *Gubernatorial Transitions*, 21. Even in the "transition" between first and second terms, the governor's confidence that a person will subscribe to the governor's second-term policy directives is cited as a major criterion in staff selection and reorganization: see Owen on Indiana.

11 From a discussion of presidents in John D. Steinbruner, *The Cybernetic Theory of Decision* (Princeton, N.J.: Princeton University Press, 1974), 332. A simple mutual trust has the great danger of not seeing analytic or factual flaws, a problem well described by Irving L. Janis in *Groupthink*, 2d ed. (Boston: Houghton Mifflin, 1983).

12 The NGA calls this "strategic recruiting" in their handbook for new governors, *Transition and the New Governor*, 56–57. See discussion of the director of agriculture in Nebraska by Keith J. Mueller and Margery M. Ambrosius in Beyle, *Gubernatorial Transitions*, 269–70. The greater import of technical skills may be one reason that new governors frequently rely upon recruitment and selection committees for agency directors: see Cornwell on Rhode Island and Robert Benedict and Lauren Holland on

Utah. Gary G. Hamilton and Nicole Woolsey Biggart offer an insight-
ful and useful analysis of the roles played by personal staff, nontenured
agency directors, and civil service personnel whom the governor appoints
to administrative responsibilities. They carefully consider the "loyalty"
associated with these various roles, finding that personal staff have a loyalty to the governor as a person while nontenured agency administrators
have a loyalty or allegiance to the philosophy of the governor: see *Governor Reagan, Governor Brown* (New York: Columbia University Press,
1984).

13 See Benedict and Holland on Utah in regard to how Governor Bangerter
brought a nonpolitical, professional chief of staff from the legislative staff
rather than from the campaign. But Michigan governor Blanchard sought
political commitment above skills, according to Charles Press and Kenneth
VerBurg in Beyle, *Gubernatorial Transitions*, 229.

14 See Cornwell on Rhode Island; Robert Huefner and Michael Nash in
Beyle, *Gubernatorial Transitions*, 435–37, 444–49.

15 See Martha Wagner Weinberg's discussion of the 1982 Massachusetts
experience for an example of the problem in Beyle, *Gubernatorial Transitions*, 210.

16 Lujan on Washington.

17 Thompson on North Carolina and Pedeliski on North Dakota. The opportunity for "political" balance includes diverse wings within a party, interest groups, and persons skilled in and dedicated to the policies expressed
by the statute involved.

18 See essays on North Carolina, North Dakota, Rhode Island, and Washington; David Webber's essay on West Virginia. See also the discussion
by William T. Gormley, Jr., of the 1982 Wisconsin transition ("A cabinet
secretary who is capable of taking the heat can deflect criticism from the
chief executive") and the report by Delmer D. Dunn that Governor Harris
in Georgia asked all agency heads to stay on through the first legislative
session and that he moved slowly even after that. Beyle, *Gubernatorial
Transitions*, 428–29, 165–66, and 174, respectively.

19 NGA, *Transition and the New Governor*, 57.

20 Gerald A. McBeath's study of the 1982 Alaska transition showed a problem that occurred not because professional perspectives overpowered
political sensitivity but because business backgrounds did not provide
appreciation of the political context of public policy; see Beyle, *Gubernatorial Transitions*, 78–91.

21 For a useful exploration of the difficulties and limits of such learning, see
Steinbruner, *The Cybernetic Theory of Decision*.

22 See NGA, *Transition and the New Governor*, 30; and Beyle, *Gubernatorial
Transitions*, 30–31.

23 See Lujan on Washington: "Campaign rhetoric usually costs more than
you can afford"; and Pedeliski on North Dakota.

24 Blair in Beyle, *Gubernatorial Transitions*, 95.

25 See Thompson on North Carolina.

26 See Lujan on Washington; and Richard F. Winters on New Hampshire in Beyle, *Gubernatorial Transitions*, 22–24. For success see Cornwell on Rhode Island in regard to Governor DiPrete's first budget.

27 The Pedeliski essay on North Dakota and the Benedict and Holland essay on Utah report three-item agendas with considerable flexibility in implementation. Laurence J. O'Toole, Jr., reports the problems Alabama governor James created by having too many priorities and in being rigid in pursuing them in Beyle, *Gubernatorial Transitions*, 38.

28 McBeath on Alaska in Beyle, *Gubernatorial Transitions*, 75–76.

29 Stopping action can symbolize action, as McBeath reports Governor Sheffield did in Alaska by freezing all personnel and large financial transactions; see Beyle, *Gubernatorial Transitions*, 78–79.

30 California chapter by Gable, Sektnan, and King in Beyle, *Gubernatorial Transitions*, 132.

31 Another way in which Governor Ashcroft may have bought time and future flexibility was to use his first budget to finance a reserve fund and a "rainy day" fund, thereby enlarging future financial options; see Dean L. Yarwood and Richard J. Hardy on Missouri.

32 Gormley comments upon the burden governors assume in becoming tied to all action in Beyle, *Gubernatorial Transitions*, 429–30.

33 See Pedeliski on North Dakota.

34 See Pedeliski on North Dakota. Also, Blair offers related counsel—that the burdens of appointment decisions can be usefully transferred to a later time *and* to other people. Governor Dukakis, in his second Massachusetts transition, similarly argued that quality is more important than quickness. But Weinberg, in evaluating this transition, warns that being too slow in appointments will "slow down the process of taking control of the government"; see Beyle, *Gubernatorial Transitions*, 112, 197, 209.

35 McBeath opines "a 'successful' formal transition might handicap a governor if not accompanied by effective political learning" in Beyle, *Gubernatorial Transitions*, 91.

Kentucky

1 Information on the administration transition and relations with the legislature came from several officials involved in the transition and from a number of legislators, as well as from the Louisville *Courier-Journal* and the Lexington *Herald-Leader*.

2 *Louisville Courier-Journal*, Dec. 3, 1983, p. 1.

3 *Louisville Courier-Journal*, Dec. 3, 1983, p. A8.

4 The main points of the supreme court's decision were: (1) the legislature cannot delegate its legislative power to the LRC during the period between regular sessions; (2) the LRC cannot suspend administrative regulations because doing so would constitute a legislative veto; (3) the LRC has no authority to modify or reject block grant applications; (4) the LRC cannot delay implementation of administrative reorganization plans; and

(5) in implementation of its budgetary powers, the legislature may require agencies to specify how they would deal with budgetary shortfalls and incorporate such plans in the budget, and the LRC may monitor compliance with such plans. Legislative Research Commission v. John Y. Brown, Ky., 664 S.W. 2d 907 (Jan. 19, 1984).

5 This account of the governor's decision to seek a tax increase is based on the account in the *Louisville Courier-Journal*, Jan. 30, 1984, pp. 1, A8.

6 *Louisville Courier-Journal*, Jan. 6, 1984, p. 1.

7 *Lexington Herald-Leader*, Jan. 6, 1984, pp. 1, A12.

Missouri

1 The material on areas of party strength is taken from Timothy R. Coughlin and Richard J. Hardy, "The Political Parties in Missouri," in Richard J. Hardy and Richard R. Dohm, *Missouri Government and Politics* (Columbia: University of Missouri Press, 1985), 48.

2 *Official Manual, State of Missouri, 1983–1984*, 31.

3 Karen Ball and Mike Reilly, "Rothman Predicts Rout to Repeat in November," *Columbia Daily Tribune*, Aug. 8, 1984, p. 8.

4 Terry Ganey, "Spending Hit Record in '84 State Elections," *St. Louis Post-Dispatch*, Sept. 19, 1985, p. 3A.

5 Ball and Reilly, "Rothman Predicts Rout."

6 Much of the material on Ashcroft's career can be found in the *Official Manual, State of Missouri, 1983–1984*, 61.

7 Ganey, "Spending Hit Record."

8 Jeff Truesdell, "Ashcroft Stuns McNary in Third Statewide Loss," *Columbia Daily Tribune*, Aug. 8, 1984, p. 1.

9 "New Poll Widens Ashcroft Lead," *Columbia Missourian*, Oct. 28, 1984, p. 12A.

10 These characterizations of candidates' stands on the issues are based on "Head to Head," a series of four interviews by Karen Ball and Jeff Truesdell with candidates Rothman and Ashcroft that appeared in the *Columbia Daily Tribune* from Oct. 31, 1984, through Nov. 3, 1984. The quotation is from Nov. 3, 1984, p. 10.

11 Ibid., Oct. 31, 1984, p. 8.

12 John Ashcroft, "Excellence in Education," Position paper no. 4, June 20, 1984.

13 Interview with Shannon Cave, executive director of the Missouri Republican party, Aug. 13, 1986. His observation is based on tracking polls taken by the party during the election and substantially parallels an analysis done at the time by David Leuthold of the University of Missouri-Columbia Political Science Department.

14 Ibid.

15 Jeff Truesdell, "Candidates' Alley Fight," *Columbia Daily Tribune*, Oct. 30, 1984, p. 1.

16 Ibid.

17 Ibid.

18 Ibid.

19 Ibid.

20 Ibid.

21 "Ashcroft Predicts Victory," *Columbia Missourian*, Oct. 31, 1984, p. 7A.

22 Robert L. Koenig, "Ashcroft Spends His Halloween Scrambling from 'Ghost of 76,' " *St. Louis Post-Dispatch*, Nov. 1, 1984, p. 6A.

23 "Ashcroft Predicts Victory," *Columbia Missourian*.

24 Jeff Truesdell, "Republican Push for Power," *Columbia Daily Tribune*, Nov. 1, 1984, p. 1.

25 Ganey, "Spending Hit Record." However, if we normalize the campaign costs to 1985 dollars, then the 1984 governor's race represented a 74-percent increase in spending compared to 1976 and a 6.3-percent *decrease* relative to 1980 costs. For the consumer price indexes on which these adjustments are based, see *Economic Report of the President* (Washington, D.C.: U.S. Government Printing Office, February 1986), 315.

26 Helene Feger, "Ashcroft's Ads Sour Relations, Say Legislators," *Columbia Missourian*, Nov. 11, 1984, pp. 1A, 10A.

27 Ibid.

28 Much of the material in this paragraph is based on a personal interview with Gary O. Passmore, Mar. 27, 1986. Passmore was brought into the Teasdale administration as director of the Division of Budget and Planning and later served as executive assistant in the office of the governor.

It is not clear whether Nielsen could have stayed on through the transition of the Teasdale administration. One newspaper article speculated that Teasdale planned to replace the commissioner of administration and the director of the Division of Budget and Planning. The report does not indicate when they would have been replaced. See Robert E. Boczkiewicz, "Top-level Bond Officials May Be Retained," *St. Louis Globe-Democrat*, Nov. 25, 1976, p. 2D.

29 Passmore interview.

30 William C. Lhotka, "Teasdale Aide Finds Moving into His Office a Shocking Experience in Both Senses of Word," *St. Louis Post-Dispatch*, Jan. 16, 1977, p. 7D.

31 "Teasdale Staff Raids Phelps for Supplies," *St. Louis Globe-Democrat*, Jan. 22–23, 1977, p. 3A; and Passmore interview. The *Globe* article of Jan. 22–23 quotes capitol employees who recalled that former governor Warren Hearnes had removed personal furniture from the governor's office, leaving a bare office for incoming governor Bond to occupy.

32 "State Mansion Getting Big Bed for Teasdale," *St. Louis Post-Dispatch*, Mar. 2, 1977, p. 3A; Passmore interview.

33 Lhotka, "Teasdale Aide."

34 Bob Fick, "Bond Destroyed Correspondence; Kirkpatrick Objects," *St. Louis Post-Dispatch*, Aug. 28, 1977, p. 11B.

35 "Kirkpatrick Ponders Court on Bond Letters," *Jefferson City Post-Tribune*, Aug. 30, 1977, p. 1.

36 "Kirkpatrick Charges Ludicrous Bond Says," *Jefferson City Post-Tribune*, Aug. 31, 1977, p. 1; and "Bond Cleared of Destroying Papers," *St. Louis Post-Dispatch*, Sept. 1, 1977, p. 3A (final). This paragraph is also enlightened by a personal interview with Gary W. Beahan, director, Records and Archives Center, Mar. 27, 1986. It is of significance that though the 1969 records retention schedule allowed for the destruction of general correspondence, Governor Hearnes, operating under that schedule, sent 602 boxes of records to the state archives after his two terms as governor. (See "Kirkpatrick Ponders Court.")

An important question at the time was when the correspondence was destroyed. Was it shredded in a tiff during the waning days of the Bond administration? Bond's legal adviser, Charles Valier, said that the Bond administration took the position "from day one" that correspondence was not an official record because it involved no legal action by the governor. He further stated that it was the policy of the administration from the beginning to dispose of correspondence after three months. To that Kirkpatrick retorted, "He [Valier] comes up with that explanation awfully late, especially in view of the number of times we [Office of Secretary of State] tried to work with them to set up a records schedule for that office." He said his office had contacted the office of the governor on at least four different occasions beginning in 1973 to try to work out a records management program. (See sources cited in footnotes 34 through 36.) The State and Local Records Law is found in Sec. 109.200, RSMo 1978.

37 "Teasdale Will Review Bond's Appointments," *St. Louis Globe-Democrat*, Jan. 18, 1977, p. 4A.

38 Lhotka, "Teasdale Aide."

39 *Elrod v. Burns*, 427 U.S. 347 (1976).

40 Passmore interview.

41 Sec. 26.215, RSMo 1978.

42 Personal interview with C. K. "Chip" Casteel, Jr., Jan. 7, 1985. Casteel was the coordinator for the first publicly funded gubernatorial transition in Missouri. He also served as the legal and legislative counsel during Governor Bond's second term.

43 Ibid. See also Howard S. Goller and Terry Ganey, "Familiarity Breeding Smooth Transition for Bond," *St. Louis Post-Dispatch*, Nov. 6, 1980, p. 3A.

44 Kevin Horrigan, "Bond Turns '76 Lesson into Teasdale Loss," *St. Louis Post-Dispatch*, Nov. 5, 1980, p. 1A (final).

45 Passmore interview.

46 Ibid.

47 Casteel interview.

48 Passmore interview.

49 Ibid.

50 Personal interview with Anthony D. "Tony" Moulton, assistant director for state planning, Division of Budget and Planning, Mar. 18, 1985.

51 Terry Ganey, "Missouri Officials Keeping Eye on How Other States Are Handling Fiscal Woes," *St. Louis Post-Dispatch*, Dec. 21, 1980, p. 16D.
52 Moulton interview.
53 Casteel interview.
54 Ibid.
55 For a discussion of the transition out process, see Thad L. Beyle, "Transition Out of the Governor's Chair: The 1982 Experience"; and George Weeks, "Gubernatorial Transition: Leaving There." These articles are to be found in *State Government* 57, no. 3 (1984): 73–84.
56 Casteel interview.
57 Ibid; also Moulton interview.
58 Personal interview with Carl M. Koupal, Jr., May 16, 1985. Koupal was Ashcroft's campaign manager, coordinator of the transition, and then director of the Department of Economic Development.
59 Casteel interview.
60 Ibid.
61 Passmore interview.; Casteel interview.
62 Casteel interview.
63 Ibid.
64 "Teasdale Will Review Bond's Appointments."
65 Moulton interview.
66 Ibid.
67 Casteel interview.
68 Ibid.
69 Moulton interview.
70 Sec. 109.200, RSMo 1978.
71 Interview with Gary W. Beahan, July 14, 1986. George Weeks, chief of staff to former Michigan governor William Milliken, has written, "A strong word of advice: soon after taking office, a governor should work with the state archivist in setting up filing systems and procedures for eventual disposition of the papers." See Weeks, "Gubernatorial Transition," 77. Help in setting up a filing system for records is available from the Division of Archives in Missouri, if the office of the governor wants it. Interview with Beahan, Aug. 25, 1986.
72 This organization of the transition into a series of transitions is based on the work of William T. Gormley, Jr., "Wisconsin's Gubernatorial Transition," in *Gubernatorial Transitions: The 1982 Election*, ed. Thad L. Beyle (Durham, N.C.: Duke University Press, 1985), esp. pp. 425–32. However, to the three transitions Gormley discusses, we add the budgetary transition. Our logic for this is that the budget process is important in its own right, and that in American government the budgetary process is both executive and legislative.
73 Sec. 26.220, RSMo 1978.
74 Koupal interview.
75 "Staff Members Named to Coordinate Transition," *Jefferson City Post-Tribune*, Nov. 15, 1984. p. 5.
    Contrary to the counsel of the National Governors' Association (NGA),

Ashcroft appointed his campaign manager to coordinate the transition. The NGA might want to reconsider its recommendation on this point. It advises the governor-elect to take a family vacation soon after the election, leaving the transition team to make many critical decisions. Considering this, along with the time constraints of gubernatorial transitions, who better than the campaign manager knows the governor-elect's mind, and who is better able to act in his absence without specific supervision?

76 Koupal interview.

77 Personal interview with Randy Sissel, special assistant for public and press operations, May 16, 1985.

78 See, for example, John A. Dvorak, "Ashcroft Will Make Major Decisions Soon," *Kansas City Times*, Nov. 15, 1984, pp. 1B, 10B.

79 Sissel interview. Along with the planning and staging of the inaugural, the media presentation of it is an important concern during the logistical transition. To facilitate and channel media coverage, packets were prepared by Sissel. These packets contained times and places of inaugural events, times of press conferences, and biographical sketches of the governor and other officials being sworn in. Even some of the governor's favorite recipes were included.

80 Personal interview with Edward "Chip" Robertson, budget coordinator during the transition, later appointed chief of staff to Governor Ashcroft. The interview was conducted April 11, 1985.

81 This insight was first offered by Casteel (interview).

82 Ibid.

83 Interview with Robertson. Missouri has had a law for over half a century that specifies that in any year in which a new governor takes office, the new budget shall be the governor-elect's. It further mandates that the Division of the Budget shall give to the governor-elect "all possible assistance" in the preparation of the budget and that the governor and the departments and agencies shall furnish him with estimates and other budget information. Sec. 33.260 RSMo 1978.

This law would seem to be supportive of the norm of standing aside. However, by itself, it does not assure that the norm will guide the transition. Recall, the norm provides that the departing governor will reduce his demands on the Office of Administration. If the transition is a bitter one, or if the outgoing governor wants to establish a defense of his record in office to support his future political aspirations, he may not reduce his demands on the Office of Administration. In this case the operant rule would seem to be that the state can have only one governor at a time; "all possible assistance" might not leave the governor-elect with much aid from the Office of Administration in getting control of the budget process.

84 The Office of Administration is described in the state manual as "the state's service and administrative control agency." It is composed of eight different divisions including Accounting, Budget and Planning, Design and Construction, Data Processing and Telecommunications, Flight Operations, General Services, Personnel, and Purchasing.

85 Sec. 26.215.2 RSMo 1978.

86 *Laws of Missouri* (1971), 122. Another provision of this law that James did not meet when he was originally appointed in 1973 to be commissioner of administration was a five-year residency requirement.

87 Robert E. Boczkiewicz, "Confirmation of Bond's Appointees Is in Doubt," *St. Louis Globe-Democrat*, Nov. 27, 1974, p. 6A; and idem, "Bond Aide Quits, Accuses Senators of Political Abuse," *St. Louis Globe-Democrat*, Nov. 30/Dec. 1, 1974, pp. 1A, 4A.

88 *Laws of Missouri* (1977) 145–46.

89 Personal interview with Duncan Kincheloe, director of policy development in the Ashcroft administration, Mar. 29, 1985.

90 The material in this paragraph is based on Terry Ganey, "Education Tops Ashcroft's Fiscal Plans," *St. Louis Post-Dispatch*, Jan. 24, 1985, pp. 1A, 5A; John Ashcroft, "Legislative and Budget Address Before the 83rd General Assembly," Jan. 23, 1985.

91 Karen L. Loman, "Ashcroft Cuts $50.2 Million," *St. Louis Post-Dispatch*, June 28, 1985, pp. 1A, 6A.

92 Terry Ganey, "Auditor Says Missouri May Owe $30.5 Million in Tax Refunds," *St. Louis Post-Dispatch*, Mar. 6, 1985, p. 4A.

93 Robertson interview.

94 Ibid.

95 See, for example, Richard P. Nathan, *The Administrative Presidency* (New York: Wiley, 1983), for an account of the administrative strategies of the Nixon and Reagan administrations.

96 Robertson interview.

97 Personal interview with Jo Frappier, director of governmental operations and legislation, Mar. 29, 1985.

98 Charles Phillips, "Well-run Staff Contributes to Ashcroft Success," *Columbia Missourian*, May 6, 1985, p. 1A.

99 Ibid.

100 Personal interview with Tom Deuschle, director of appointments and personnel, Apr. 11, 1985.

101 Ibid.

102 Kincheloe interview.

103 Deuschle interview.

104 Frappier interview.

105 The weakest "Missouri link" of the new Ashcroft director appointees was that of Robert G. Harmon, appointed to be director of the newly created Department of Health. A native of Springfield, Ill., his link is that he received his bachelor's degree and a medical degree from Washington University in St. Louis.

106 Governor Bond was criticized in 1972 for importing too much of his administrative talent. It is possible that this sort of criticism encouraged Governor Ashcroft to seek persons from Missouri or with Missouri connections. See Dvorak, "Ashcroft Will Make Major Decisions," 10B.

107 Ibid.

108 Ken Cook, "New Revenue Director Must Mend Fences," *Columbia Missourian*, Apr. 14, 1985, p. 6B.

109 However, it should be pointed out that King's reappointment was opposed by a number of Republican senators, among them Richard Webster, the powerful minority floor leader. See Cook, "New Revenue Director."

110 Kincheloe interview.

111 "Gov. Ashcroft's Mistake," *St. Louis Post-Dispatch*, Mar. 21, 1985, p. 2B.

112 Moulton interview.

113 Robertson interview.

114 Kincheloe interview.

115 Moulton interview.

116 Ibid.

117 Frappier interview.

118 Terry Ganey, "Ashcroft, Legislators Call Session One of State's Most Productive," *St. Louis Post-Dispatch*, June 17, 1985, p. 1A.

119 Andy Scott, "Governor Ashcroft Sees Solid Successes," *Columbia Missourian*, June 17, 1985, p. 1A.

120 Ganey, "Ashcroft, Legislators Call Session One of State's Most Productive."

121 Ibid.

122 Ibid., pp. 1A, 5A.

123 "Productive Session for Missouri," *St. Louis Post-Dispatch*, June 18, 1985, p. 2B.

124 Frappier interview.

125 Ibid.

126 Jerry Stroud, "Vacant Farms Haunt Countryside," *St. Louis Post-Dispatch*, Mar. 10, 1985, p. 1A.

127 "States Step in with Farm Aid," *Columbia Daily Tribune*, June 6, 1985, p. 3.

128 "South Dakota's Legislature Going to Washington," *St. Louis Post-Dispatch*, Feb. 20, 1985, p. 7A.

129 Deborah Simon, "Ashcroft Enjoys Honeymoon Despite Two Legislative Defeats," *Columbia Missourian*, Apr. 5, 1985.

130 Rich Hood, "Bond–Teasdale Transition Is Criticized," *Kansas City Star*, Apr. 20, 1986, p. 1A, 7A.

131 Frappier interview.

132 Moulton interview.

133 For a similar argument made in relation to the Office of Management and Budget, see Hugh Heclo, "OMB and the Presidency—The Problem of Neutral Competence," *The Public Interest*, no. 38 (Winter 1975), 80–98, as reprinted in *Bureaucratic Power in National Policy Making*, ed. Francis E. Rourke (Boston: Little, Brown, 1986, 4th ed.), 106-19.

We plead guilty to presenting a worst-case scenario in this last paragraph. Even here, the governor-elect could hope to improve his lot by seeking political solutions. He could, for example, go to the media and hope for a public outcry on behalf of fair play, or he could hope for cooperation from some officials of the outgoing administration because they hope to keep their jobs or are moved by civic conscience. Still, time is short and the task is difficult under the best of circumstances. The governor-elect in contemporary Missouri foregoes much if he does not avail himself of the resources of the Office of Administration during the transition.

North Carolina

The information used to develop this paper was obtained from interviews with members of the Martin transition team and administration (Jack Hawke, special assistant for policy; James Loftin, executive assistant and staff director; Phillip Kirk, secretary of human resources; and Ruby Hooper, deputy secretary of human resources), legislative leaders (House Speaker Liston Ramsey and Lieutenant Governor Robert Jordan), two staff members of Governor James B. Hunt, Jr., who were involved in the transition process (Doug Champion, director of executive and organizational development, and Paul Essex, special assistant to the governor), and various news accounts from the *Charlotte Observer*, *Greensboro Daily News*, *Raleigh News and Observer*, and the *Winston-Salem Journal*.

Funding for this research was provided by the School of Graduate Studies and Research and the Office of the Dean, College of Arts and Sciences, Appalachian State University. I would also like to acknowledge the assistance of the Department of Political Science, University of Arizona, where I was visiting associate professor during 1985–86.

1 See Thad L. Beyle, "Governors," in *Politics in the American States*, ed. Virginia Gray, Herbert Jacob, and Kenneth Vines (Boston: Little, Brown, 1983), 202.
2 Joe Doster, "As I See It," *Winston-Salem Journal*, July 8, 1985, p. D2.
3 See Tim Funk, "Minding Martin's Office," *Charlotte Observer*, May 6, 1985, p. A1.
4 "Disputes Mark Session," *Watauga Democrat*, July 15, 1985, p. 20A.
5 Funk, "Minding Martin's Office," p. A1.

North Dakota

The source for the vast majority of statements made in this chapter is personal interviews conducted by the author in May and August 1985. Interviewed were: Governor George Sinner; Lieutenant Governor Ruth Meiers; Chief of Staff Charles Fleming; Governor's Counsel Richard Gross; Administrative Assistant to the Governor Carole Siegert; Director of Office of Management and Budget Dick Rayl; Director of Institutions Herb Geigle; Director of Human Services John Graham; Highway Commissioner Walter Hjelle; confidant to the governor Joseph Lamb; chairman, Judicial Nominating Committee, Owen Anderson; attorney Harlan Fuglestan; congressional aide Lucy Caulutti; Minority Leader in the House Charles Mertens; Minority Leader in the Senate Bill Heigaard; Majority Leader in the House Earl Strinden; Representative Judy DeMers; and, through a questionnaire interview, former governor Allen Olson.

1 Bureau of Governmental Affairs, University of North Dakota, Grand Forks, poll conducted May 14–17, 1984.

2 James Lauer and Associates, Alexandria, Va. Poll conducted Oct. 1983.

3 Mike Jacobs, "Matters at Hand," *Grand Forks Herald*, Sept. 15, 1986, p. 6.

4 Bureau of Governmental Affairs, University of North Dakota, Grand Forks. Poll conducted Sept. 30–Oct. 3, 1984.

5 Bureau of Governmental Affairs, University of North Dakota, Grand Forks, poll conducted Oct. 29–Nov. 1, 1984; James Lauer and Associates, Alexandria, Va., poll conducted Oct. 25–26, 1984.

6 An area in the south-central portion of North Dakota settled predominantly by Germans from Russia at the turn of the century. Studies have identified this area, first as having strong isolationist orientation and later as one of the strongest Republican voting areas in the nation.

7 Daniel Elazar, *Federalism: A View From the States* (New York: Thomas Crowell, 1972), 96–99, esp. 97.

8 Mike Jacobs, "Matters at Hand," p. 6.

9 The legislature would provide additional reimbursement both to the Olson and Sinner staffs for the cost of the transition with supplemental appropriations (governor's transition, $10,500; governor-elect, $10,000) in the 1985 session. Chapter 50, *Laws of North Dakota: 49th Session of the Legislative Assembly* (1985), 1:93.

10 Interview with George Sinner, May 1985.

11 Interview with Joe Lamb, May 1985.

12 Garrison Diversion is a massive federal water project to transmit waters from Lake Sakakawea in western North Dakota to municipalities and irrigation districts in the eastern part of the state. The state has struggled with Congress for twenty-five years to get authorization and adequate funding for this project.

13 Attorney General's Opinion 85-1, Jan. 2, 1985.

14 Letter from Governor Olson to Governor-elect Sinner, Jan. 2, 1985.

15 Brief of realtor George Sinner in State of North Dakota ex rel Nicholas Spaeth v. Allen I. Olson ex rel George Sinner, no. 10,878.

16 See editorials of Chuck Haga, *Grand Forks Herald*, Jan. 1–4, 1985.

17 Interview with Owen Anderson, May 1985.

18 North Dakota ex rel Spaeth v. Olson ex rel Sinner, 359 N.W.2d.876 (1985).

19 Stuart Ringham, "The Governor-Elect to Governor: Transition in the American States" (Ph.D. diss., University of Iowa, 1972), 191–93.

20 Presentation of Earl Strinden, majority floor leader, to House Republican Caucus, Jan. 17, 1985.

21 Philip Brasher, "Sinner-Streibel: Heck of a Pair," *Grand Forks Herald*, Feb. 18, 1985, p. 7.

22 In 1979 the legislature instituted a program of state aid to taxing districts (county, municipal, school) that demonstrated actual or anticipated extraordinary expenditures caused by coal or gas development.

23 Earl Strinden, "Majority Party Response to Governor's Budget," Feb. 15, 1985.

24 Greg Turosak, "A Topsy Turvy Legislature," *Grand Forks Herald*, Feb. 17, 1985, p. 1.

25 Daniel Elazar, *Federalism*, p. 97.

Rhode Island

1 *Providence Journal*, Sept. 16, 1984.

2 *Providence Journal*, Nov. 8, 1984.

3 Much of the discussion of the Garrahy administration's role in the transition is based on an interview with Maureen Massiwer, Aug. 6, 1985.

4 National Governors' Association (NGA), *Transition and the New Governor: A Critical Overview* (Washington, D.C.: NGA, 1982).

5 Robert Murray was a principal source of information on the transition from the point of view of the incoming governor. Information is taken from interviews conducted July 17, 1985, and Aug. 22, 1985.

6 NGA, *Transition and the New Governor*, 41ff.

7 *Providence Journal*, June 5, 1985.

8 *Providence Journal*, Jan. 30/31, 1985.

9 *Providence Journal*, Feb. 2, 1985.

10 *Providence Journal*, Mar. 13, 1985.

11 *Providence Journal*, Mar. 16, 1985.

12 *Providence Journal*, June 15, 1985.

13 *Providence Journal*, June 22, 1985.

14 *Providence Journal*, June 23, 1985.

Utah

Much of the information for this chapter is based on interviews with the following people: Governor Norman Bangerter; former governor Scott Matheson; Robert Huefner (transition coordinator); Jon Memmott (executive assistant to Norman Bangerter); Douglas Foxley (campaign manager for Norman Bangerter); Robert Garff (speaker of the house); Nolan Karras (chair, House Appropriations Committee); Arnold Christensen (president of the senate); Fred Finlinson (R, Salt Lake, a water attorney and recognized expert on flooding problems and water development); Kent Briggs (former executive assistant to Scott Matheson); Mike Zuhl (former budget director under Scott Matheson); Jed Kee (former director of the Department of Administrative Services under Matheson); and Karen Hashimoto (former director of the Personnel Department in the Department of Administrative Services under Matheson).

1 "Bangerter Quietly Settling In," *Salt Lake Tribune*, Dec. 23, 1984.

2 The last time the Republicans controlled both the governorship and the legislature was in 1963 when Governor Clyde faced a legislature where the Republican Party maintained a four-seat majority in the house and

single-seat edge in the senate. The last case of overwhelming one-party dominance was in the administration of Democratic governor Herbert Maw, who controlled the executive branch in 1945 while his party captured two-thirds' majorities in both the state senate and the house of representatives.

3 Authors' interview with Scott Matheson, Feb. 28, 1985.

4 William Gormley, "Wisconsin's Gubernatorial Transition," in *Gubernatorial Transitions: The 1982 Election*, ed. Thad L. Beyle (Durham, N.C.: Duke University Press, 1985), 426.

5 Thad L. Beyle, "Lessons From 1982–83," in Beyle, *Gubernatorial Transitions*, 19–26.

6 Leonard Arrington, *From Wilderness to Empire: The Role of Utah in Western Economic History* (Salt Lake City: Institute of American Studies, University of Utah, Monograph No. 1, 1961).

7 Frank Jonas, "Utah," in *Politics in the American West*, ed. Frank Jonas (Salt Lake City: University of Utah Press, 1969), 375.

8 "U.S. Grant Disbursements for Fiscal '84 Exceeded Utah's Contribution in Taxes," *Salt Lake Tribune*, May 31, 1985.

9 Seventy-two percent of the land in Utah is owned by the federal government. This percentage is the second highest among the fifty states. Of the 52.5 million acres in the state, only 12.5 million are privately owned. Data from Bureau of Land Management reports, 1984.

10 Anthony Downs has described Utah's birth rate as one "which resembles that of China before the institution of population control measures." See also *Deseret News*, Dec. 23, 1984.

11 Daniel Elazar, *American Federalism, A View From the States*, 2d ed. (New York: Thomas Crowell, 1972), 96–99.

12 Ibid., 98–99.

13 Ibid., 96.

14 "Percentage of Voting Age Population Casting Votes," Statistical Abstract of the United States, 1985. (Washington, D.C.: U.S. Chamber of Commerce, 1985), 254.

15 For example, in 1984 the length of the legislative session was changed to forty-five days, contrasting with the previous sixty-day general session followed by a thirty-day budget session in alternate years. In addition the 1985 special session determined that in future years legislators would be allowed to prefile bills in April rather than the previous mid-November date, to allow interim committees meeting once a month greater time for evaluation.

16 Jonas, "Utah," 328–29.

17 *New York Times*, Jan. 8, 1985.

18 The most accurate prediction of the results of state races was found in a poll directed by Dr. David Magleby of the Political Science Department of Brigham Young University. When respondents were asked whether it was true that "a person cannot be a good Mormon and a Democrat," only 10 percent agreed with the statement. The figures were: strongly agree 4

percent; agree 2 percent; somewhat agree 4 percent; somewhat disagree 7 percent; disagree 31 percent; strongly disagree 39 percent; don't know 14 percent.

19 *Deseret News*/KSL-TV poll, *Deseret News*, Oct. 4, 1984.

20 Authors' interviews.

21 Because Matheson was a relatively young man (forty-seven years old when he became governor), many expected him to become Utah's second consecutive three-term Democratic governor. However, during his second term, Matheson suffered a mild heart attack from which he recovered with no apparent ill effects. Politicos speculated this factor was one of several that led to the decision not to run.

22 Authors' interviews.

23 Interview with Douglas Foxley, Apr. 8, 1985.

24 *Deseret News*/KSL-TV poll.

25 "Right Words Sometimes Can Be Hard to Come By," *Deseret News*, Nov. 7, 1984.

26 Beyle, "Lessons from 1982–83," 8–9.

27 LaVarr Webb, *Deseret News*, Nov. 27, 1984.

28 Beyle, "Lessons from 1982–83," 30–31.

29 Brigham Young University poll.

30 Foxley interview.

31 Authors' interview.

32 Interestingly, the Brigham Young University poll demonstrated that each of the issues selected by the Owens campaign was a priority for 12–13% of the electorate.

33 Gormley, "Wisconsin's Gubernatorial Transition," 428.

34 *Book of the States: 1984–85* (Lexington, Ky.: Council of State Governments, 1984), 54.

35 Matheson interview.

36 Ibid.

37 Ibid.

38 Interview with Jed Kee, Feb. 12, 1985.

39 Authors' interview.

40 Robert Huefner and Michael Nash, "What Guides Governors in Transition?" in Beyle, *Gubernatorial Transitions*, 433–53; Thad L. Beyle and Robert Huefner, "Quips and Quotes from Old Governors to New," *Public Administration Review* 43 (1983): 268–70.

41 Matheson interview.

42 "Governor Matheson Selects U. Professor to Head State Transition Team," *Deseret News*, May 15, 1984.

43 In college Memmott was a member of the golf team. When faced with a decision about future directions, he chose law school. He has been able to consistently best Bangerter on the links, yet the results have not appeared to be a drubbing.

44 Authors' interview.

45 Bangerter's staff trooped in only to discover the press encamped as well—

the result of Matheson's previously established rule that the media could attend any executive meeting unless specifically excluded. The budget director outlined the latest revenue projections while the planning director concentrated upon what Robert Huefner called the Utah "time bombs": the soaring school-age population, rising levels of the Great Salt Lake, retraining of heavy industry workers for high-tech jobs, and other issues where large-scale change could be anticipated. Emergency issues were discussed by the public safety director, although information of a more sensitive nature already had been passed on in private. The discussions concerned emergency measures to handle prison riots during the first few months of the new administration, should prisoners decide to take advantage of the situation.

46 Interview with Mike Zuhl, Feb. 12, 1985.

47 Authors' interview.

48 Matheson interview.

49 The chief executive appoints lawyers to vacancies on the juvenile, circuit, district, and state Supreme Court benches. In addition ten members are appointed to three first-rank commissions (public service, tax, and industrial), but commissioners serve a set term unless they resign. Moreover, by law the Tax Commission can have no more than two of the four commissioners from the same political party. State advisory boards and commissions also abound; some 2,000 people receive gubernatorial appointment to such boards.

50 The kitchen cabinet included Douglas Foxley, his campaign manager and a man with good political instincts; Senator Fred Finlinson, a good friend who is known as a problem solver in the senate; Representative Franklin Knowlton, a low-key expert on taxes and the budget; Senator Paul Rogers, a top campaign strategist with ties to the most conservative legislators; Mike Levitt, a Utah insurance executive and consultant to the campaign; and Dan Jones, a Salt Lake pollster long associated with Republican politics.

51 Gormley, "Wisconsin's Gubernatorial Transition," 428–29.

52 "Bangerter Transition Team Keeps an Eye Out for Bumps in the Road," *Deseret News*, Nov. 24, 1984.

53 Authors' interview.

54 State corrections director William C. Vickery subsequently resigned in mid-April and was named state court administrator.

55 Matheson attended to cochair a panel with Montana governor Ted Schwinden on the subject of organizing the executive branch.

56 "Bangerter Quietly Settling In," *Salt Lake Tribune*.

57 Gormley, "Wisconsin's Gubernatorial Transition," 432.

58 Zuhl interview.

59 *Salt Lake Tribune*, Jan. 6, 1985.

60 Sarah McCalley,"The Governor and His Legislative Party," *American Political Science Review* 60 (Dec. 1966): 935.

61 "Utahns Think Taxes Are High, But Don't Mind Raising Them," *De-*

seret News, Jan. 24, 1985; "Most Utahns Willing to Dig into Pockets for Education," *Deseret News,* Jan. 25, 1985.

62 Matheson interview.

63 However, Bangerter did propose a $60-million supplemental budget for 1985–86, compared to $43 million for the former governor, lowering the figure to $77 million.

64 Senator Wayne Sandberg, quoted in the *Deseret News,* Feb. 28, 1985.

65 The long-term plan was expected to be controversial because it called for pumping the water twenty miles to the west, and then ten to twenty feet up to clear a saddle separating the lake and the west desert bowl.

66 Speaker of the House Robert Garff has indicated that from 1980 to 1984 over $1.4 billion in contracts have been awarded out of Hill Air Force Base, while only 3–8 percent of the money was spent in the state of Utah.

67 Interview with Norman Bangerter, Apr. 15, 1985.

68 Authors' interviews.

69 "Legislature Puts Own Stamp on Session Agenda," *Deseret News,* June 29, 1985.

Washington

1 Booth Gardner for governor brochure.

2 Shelby Scates, *Seattle Post-Intelligencer,* May 8, 1983.

3 Jack Broom, *Times* poll, *Seattle Times,* Nov. 7, 1984, p. B7.

4 Memorandum of Understanding, Nov. 15, 1984.

5 Jack Broom, *Times* poll, *Seattle Times,* Jan. 15, 1985, pp. A1, A8.

6 Jack Broom, *Times* poll, *Seattle Times,* Jan. 16, 1985, p. A1.

7 Laura Parker, "53 Ideas for Education—and No Money," *Seattle Post-Intelligencer,* Jan. 17, 1985, p. A5.

8 Pete McConnell, "Day Care Reformers Hope for Some '86 Action," *Seattle Post-Intelligencer,* Jan. 15, 1986, p. A9.

9 Mike Layton, "Gardner Grabs Wheel and Follows Rear-View Mirror," *Seattle Post-Intelligencer,* Jan. 17, 1986, p. A4.

10 National Governors' Association (NGA), *Transition and the New Governor: A Critical Overview* (Washington, D.C.: NGA, 1982), 33.

11 That issue centered on the need to pay workers according to the task performed and the skills required, rather than to structure compensation so that jobs performed primarily by a given gender would be paid less, regardless of the skills or tasks involved. Historically, such tasks had involved women in clerical and paraprofessional occupations. A Washington court case pioneered efforts to deal with this issue and resulted in the court ordering the state to compensate employees so victimized for damages. The cost was significant.

12 NGA, *Transition and the New Governor,* 31.

13 Joe Mooney, " 'Small Laws' and the Legislature: A Morality Tale," *Seattle Post-Intelligencer,* Jan. 17, 1985, p. A7.

14 Ibid.

15 Laird Harris, "Assignments for Governor's Special Assistants" (memorandum to agency directors, Oct. 23, 1985).

16 Ibid., 2.

17 Charles T. Goodsell, "Collegial State Administration: Design for Today?" *Western Political Quarterly* 33 (Sept. 1981): 452.

18 Glenn Abney and Thomas P. Lauth, "The Governor as Chief Administrator," *Public Administration Review* 43 (Jan./Feb. 1983): 40–49.

West Virginia

Three sources supplied the necessary background for an understanding of West Virginia politics and the roles of Moore and Rockefeller in particular: Peter Kidman's excellent report on previous transitions, the views and opinions of colleagues and friends—especially Jay Stern, David Williams, Allan Hammock, Max Stephenson, and Barbara Webber—and, whenever possible, citizens' opinions of the governors.

My major sources of factual information were West Virginia newspapers, particularly the *Charleston Gazette* and the *Charleston Daily Mail*. Tom Hildago of the Morgantown *Dominion-Post* was helpful in providing additional ideas and information. Members of both Governor Moore's and Senator Rockefeller's staffs also supplied information requested.

1 West Virginia Roundtable, *Economic Development Action Plan*, 3.

2 Nick Lazaris (executive assistant to Governor Rockefeller), interview with author, Oct. 2, 1985.

3 Thad L. Beyle, "Lessons from the 1982–83 Transitions," in *Gubernatorial Transitions: The 1982 Election*, ed. Thad L. Beyle (Durham, N.C.: Duke University Press, 1985), 31–33.

4 Peter Neal Kidman, "Gubernatorial Transition in West Virginia" (Ph.D. diss., West Virginia University, 1972).

5 Ibid., 5.

6 Ibid., 8.

7 Ibid., 11.

8 Ibid., 13.

9 Ibid., 19.

10 Ibid., 22–23.

11 Ibid., 24–25.

12 *Charleston Gazette*, Nov. 12, 1976.

13 *Charleston Daily Mail*, Dec. 3, 1976.

14 Ibid., Dec. 26, 1976.

15 *Charleston Gazette*, Jan. 19, 1977.

16 *The Book of the States, 1986–87* (Lexington, Ky.: Council of State Governments, 1986), 42.

17 Lazaris interview.

18 Kidman, "Gubernatorial Transition."

19 *Charleston Daily Mail*, Sept. 19, 1983.

20 Ibid., Aug. 13, 1983.

21 *Charleston Gazette*, July 20, 1983.

22 Ibid., Mar. 23, 1984.

23 Ibid., Feb. 16, 1984.

24 *Charleston Daily Mail*, Oct. 16, 1984.

25 Ibid., Oct. 16, 1984.

26 Ibid., Apr. 16, 1984.

27 Ibid., Oct. 24, 1984.

28 *Times West Virginian*, Dec. 27, 1984.

29 *Charleston Daily Mail*, Oct. 24, 1984.

30 Ibid., Nov. 9, 1984.

31 Ibid., Nov. 9, 1984.

32 Ibid.

33 Lazaris interview.

34 Thomas Craig (transition coordinator for Governor Arch Moore), interview with author, Oct. 8, 1985.

35 Dan Green (former special assistant to Governor Jay Rockefeller), interview with author, Oct. 2, 1985.

36 Lazaris interview.

37 Ibid.

38 Craig interview.

39 Ibid.

40 *Charleston Gazette*, Jan. 10, 1985.

41 *Dominion-Post*, Feb. 17, 1985.

42 John Price (press secretary to Governor Arch Moore), interview with author, Oct. 2, 1985.

43 Craig interview.

44 Price interview.

45 *Dominion-Post*, Feb. 17, 1985.

46 For a historical analysis of this topic see Patrick Hagan, "Policy Activism in the West Virginia Supreme Court of Appeals: 1930–1980," *West Virginia Law Review* 89, no. 1 (1985): 149–65.

47 *Charleston Daily Mail*, Feb. 14, 1985.

48 Ibid.

49 *Charleston Gazette*, Feb. 15, 1985.

50 Ibid.

51 *Parkersburg Sentinel*, Apr. 23, 1985.

52 *Charleston Gazette*, Apr. 14, 1985.

53 *Parkersburg Sentinel*, Apr. 15, 1985.

54 Ibid.

55 *Dominion-Post*, May 3, 1985.

56 Ibid.

57 *Charleston Gazette*, Apr. 14, 1985.

58 Ibid.

59 Craig interview.

60 *Charleston Daily Mail*, Sept. 25, 1985.

61 *Parkersburg Sentinel*, Apr. 23, 1985.

Gubernatorial Transition:
An Incumbent Succession in Indiana

1 See especially chapters 4 and 5 in Thad L. Beyle and J. Oliver Williams, *The American Governor in Behavioral Perspective* (New York: Harper and Row, 1972); also Thad L. Beyle, ed., *Gubernatorial Transitions: The 1982 Election* (Durham, N.C.: Duke University Press, 1985); National Governors' Association (NGA), *Reflections on Being Governor* (Washington, D.C.: NGA, 1981); Council of State Governments, "Gubernatorial Transitions in the States," *State Government Administration*, vol. 3 (1968) and vol. 9 (1974); George Weeks, "Gubernatorial Transition: Leaving There," in *State Government*, ed. Thad L. Beyle (Washington, D.C.: Congressional Quarterly, 1985).

2 NGA, *Governing the American States: A Handbook for New Governors* (Washington, D.C.: NGA, 1978); idem, *Transition and the New Governor: A Critical Overview* (Washington, D.C.: NGA, 1982); National Governors' Conference, *The Critical Hundred Days* (Washington, D.C.: NGC, 1975).

3 A 1972 amendment to the Indiana State Constitution now allows a governor to serve two four-year terms in a twelve-year period.

4 Thad L. Beyle and John Wickham, "Gubernatorial Transition in a One-Party Setting," in *The American Governor in Behavioral Perspective*, 91.

5 Joseph A. Schlessinger, "The Politics of the Executive," in *Politics in the American States*, ed. Herbert Jacob and Kenneth N. Vines, 2d ed. (Boston: Little, Brown, 1971); and Thad L. Beyle, "Governors," in *Politics in the American States*, ed. Virginia Gray, Hubert Jacob, and Kenneth N. Vines, 4th ed. (Boston: Little, Brown, 1981).

6 Otis R. Bowen, interview with author, Indianapolis, Ind., Dec. 21, 1984.

7 Schlessinger, "Politics of the Executive"; Beyle, "Governors."

8 Patrick J. Traub, "Orr Too Busy to Celebrate Election Victory Just Now," *Indianapolis Star*, Nov. 8, 1984, p. 1.

9 *Indiana's Utility Future* (Indianapolis, Ind., Governor's Office, Dec. 1984).

10 Robert D. Orr, interview with author, Indianapolis, Ind., Mar. 27, 1985.

11 Jim Mellowitz, "Long-Range Success Sought for Indiana," *Fort Wayne News-Sentinel*, Jan. 18, 1985, p. 23.

12 Orr interview.

13 Clark D. Ahlberg and Daniel P. Moynihan, "Changing Governors and Policies" in *The American Governor in Behavioral Perspective*.

14 Orr interview.

15 Ibid.

16 Ibid.

17 Ibid.

18 Traub, "Orr Too Busy."

19 Orr interview.

20 Kendall Cochran, interview with author, Indianapolis, Ind., June 3, 1985.

21 Patrick J. Traub, interview with author, Indianapolis, Ind., June 3, 1985.

22 Orr interview.

23 Cochran interview.

24 Larry Sabato, *Goodbye to Good-Time Charlie* (Washington, D.C.: Congressional Quarterly, 1983).

Lieutenant Governors:
Gubernatorial Transitions in Missouri

1 Larry Sabato, *Goodbye to Good-Time Charlie: The American Governorship Transformed*, 2d ed. (Washington, D.C.: Congressional Quarterly, 1983), 69–70.
2 "They're No. 2—and Trying Harder," *U.S. News and World Report*, Nov. 5, 1979, 54.
3 National Governors' Association (NGA), *Transition and the New Governor: A Critical View* (Washington, D.C.: NGA, 1982), 17.
4 "They're No. 2," *U.S. News and World Report.*
5 Eugene Declercq and John Kaminski, "A New Look at the Office of Lieutenant Governor," *Public Administration Review* 38 (May/June, 1978): 256.
6 Council of State Governments, *The Book of the States 1986–1987* (Lexington, Ky.: Council of State Governments, 1986), 65, table 2.13.
7 Deborah A. Gona, *The Lieutenant Governor: The Office and Its Powers*, rev. ed. (Lexington, Ky.: Council of State Governments, 1983), 11–13; Council of State Governments, *Book of the States.*
8 Council of State Governments, *Book of the States.*
9 Declercq and Kaminski, "A New Look," 258; and Sabato, *Goodbye to Good-Time Charlie*, 72.
10 Council of State Governments, *Book of the States.* The count of those who preside over the senate includes Nebraska, which has a unicameral legislature.
11 Ibid.
12 Gona, *The Lieutenant Governor*, 10, table 3. Gona's count includes the states of Arizona, Oregon, and Wyoming, where the secretaries of state are next in line of succession. Her definition and its rationale are found on page 1 of her study.
13 For accounts of the events of 1973, see Jack Flach, "Phelps Is Tossed Out by Senate Democrats," *St. Louis Globe-Democrat*, June 16–17, 1973, pp. 1A, 20A; and Fred W. Lindecke, "Assembly Ends in Party Row," *St. Louis Post-Dispatch*, June 16, 1973, pp. 1A, 8A.
14 "Teasdale Staff Raids Phelps for Supplies," *St. Louis Globe-Democrat*, Jan. 22–23, 1977, p. 3A; and Gary O. Passmore, interview with author, March 27, 1986. Passmore was brought into the Teasdale administration as director of the Division of Budget and Planning and later served as executive assistant in the office of the governor.
15 "Teasdale Staff Raids Phelps," p. 3A.
16 William C. Lhotka, "Teasdale Aide Finds Moving into His Office a Shocking Experience in Both Senses of Word," *St. Louis Post-Dispatch*, Jan. 16, 1977, p. 7D.

17 William C. Lhotka, "Phelps Angry at Teasdale's Cut in Lieutenant Governor's Budget," *St. Louis Post-Dispatch*, Jan. 19, 1977. Teasdale rejoined that there were no statutory provisions for the lieutenant governor to operate either of these programs.

18 "Phelps Accepts Teasdale Deal," *St. Louis Post-Dispatch*, Jan. 20, 1977, p. 13A.

19 " 'Virtual Prisoner,' Teasdale Laments," *St. Louis Post-Dispatch*, Feb. 26, 1980, p. 4A.

20 Phill Brooks, "Missouri's Captive Governor," *Comparative State Politics Newsletter* 1, no. 6 (Oct., 1980): 12–13.

21 Kevin Horrigan, "Phelps: Teasdale Should Be Worried," *St. Louis Post-Dispatch*, Mar. 7, 1980, p. 8A; and Fred W. Lindecke, "Teasdale Sees Great Peril in Leaving Reins to Phelps," *St. Louis Post-Dispatch*, May 22, 1980, p. 11A.

22 "Rift with Phelps May Keep Teasdale from Convention," *St. Louis Post-Dispatch*, May 20, 1980. For Phelps's version of what took place, see Lindecke, "Teasdale Sees Great Peril."

23 "Teasdale Going to Conference and Leaving Phelps in Charge," *St. Louis Post-Dispatch*, Aug. 2, 1980.

24 Sec. 26.215, RSMo 1978.

25 Kevin Horrigan and Howard S. Goller, "Bond Declares Open Season for Hiring," *St. Louis Post-Dispatch*, Nov. 5, 1980, p. 1A, final.

26 Dwight L. Fine (administrative manager to Lieutenant Governor Rothman), interview with author, Mar. 27, 1986.

27 Ibid.

28 Personal interview with C. K. "Chip" Casteel, Jr., Jan. 7, 1985. Casteel served as coordinator of Governor Bond's 1980 transition and also as Bond's legal and legislative coordinator during his second term.

29 Fine interview.

30 Mary Schantz (government affairs director to Lieutenant Governor Woods), interview with author, Mar. 27, 1986.

31 Ibid.

32 News release from the office of the lieutenant governor, Apr. 15, 1985.

33 Schantz interview.

34 Tracey Plymell, "State Sees First Woman Governor," *Columbia Missourian*, Feb. 21, 1985, p. 1A.

35 Fred W. Lindecke, "Missourians Join Push for More Farm Credit," *St. Louis Post-Dispatch*, Feb. 23, 1985, p. 6A.

36 "Webster, Mrs. Woods Demand Changes in Contract System," *St. Louis Post-Dispatch*, Apr. 6, 1985, p. 4A.

37 Fred W. Lindecke, "Mrs. Woods Is Seen as Shoo-In Nominee," *St. Louis Post-Dispatch*, Apr. 19, 1985, p. 5A.

Index

Contributors

)))))

Thad L. Beyle, Department of Political Science, University of North Carolina at Chapel Hill, North Carolina.

Robert Benedict, Department of Political Science, University of Utah, Salt Lake City, Utah.

Elmer E. Cornwell, Jr., Department of Political Science, Brown University, Providence, Rhode Island.

Richard J. Hardy, Department of Political Science, University of Missouri-Columbia, Missouri.

Lauren Holland, Department of Political Science, University of Utah, Salt Lake City, Utah.

Robert Huefner, Department of Political Science, University of Utah, Salt Lake City, Utah.

Malcolm E. Jewell, Department of Political Science, University of Kentucky, Lexington, Kentucky.

Herman D. Lujan, Office of Minority Affairs, University of Washington, Seattle, Washington.

C. James Owen, School of Public and Environmental Affairs, Indiana University-Purdue University, Fort Wayne, Indiana.

Theodore B. Pedeliski, Department of Political Science, University of North Dakota, Grand Forks, North Dakota.

Philip Roeder, Department of Political Science, University of Kentucky, Lexington, Kentucky.

Joel A. Thompson, Department of Political Science and Criminal Justice, Appalachian State University, Boone, North Carolina.

Barry Van Lare, Office of State Services, National Governors' Association, Washington, D.C.

David J. Webber, Department of Political Science, University of Missouri-Columbia, Missouri.

Dean L. Yarwood, Department of Political Science, University of Missouri-Columbia, Missouri.